Byzan
and Islam

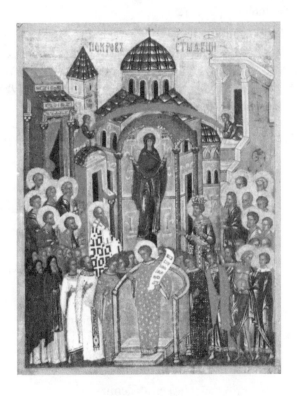

Historical and Pastoral Reflections

Jack Figel, Editor

Eastern Christian Publications

December 2001

Library of Congress Cataloging-in-Publication Data

Byzantine Christianity and Islam: Historical and Pastoral Reflections
Jack Figel, editor
        p. cm.
Includes bibliographical references.
        ISBN 1-892278-18-9 (alk. paper)
1. Islam - Relations - Orthodox Eastern Church. 2. Orthodox Eastern
Church - Relations - Islam. 3. Islam - Relations - Christianity.
4. Christianity and other religions - Islam. I. Figel, Jack, 1954 -
        BP172.5.O77 B99 2002
        261.2'7 - dc21

                                        2002002497

Eastern Christian Publications
PO Box 146
Fairfax, VA 22030

www.ecpubs.com

ISBN: 1-892278-18-9

Table of Contents

Pastoral Reflections

Preface

With the events of September 11th, and the need for Christians to better understand the history and relations between Christianity and Islam, Eastern Christian Publications is pleased to present this collection of essays by various authors entitled *Byzantine Christianity and Islam.*

The issues covered by the authors chosen include one or more of the following questions:

- How did the Crusades impact the ability of the Byzantine Empire to defend against invasion by the Turks?

- How did the Byzantine Empire deflect Turkish aggression away from the Christian West?

- How do Christian Arabs, both Catholic and Orthodox, relate to Islamic people in the US? in the Middle East?

- How did Eastern Orthodox and Eastern Catholic Churches function within Islamic countries in the past? How do they function today?

- How do Byzantine Christian moral values compare with those of Islam?

- How has Islam influenced either Byzantine or Latin Christianity?

- How has Latin or Byzantine Christianity influenced Islam?

- What were the relations of the Holy Roman Empire, the Byzantine Empire and various Muslim empires at different points of history?

- How did the Patristic Fathers view the Islamic religion?

The purpose of this book is to help people better understand the background of Eastern Christianity as it relates to Islam, and perhaps provide some pastoral guidance or helpful information for Catholic and Orthodox priests and lay persons in dealing with the ongoing conflict that is unfolding day by day!

Feast of the Protection of the Mother of God
October 1, 2001

Jack Figel
Editor and Publisher

Publisher's Note: Eastern Christian Publications may produce additional volumes of essays concerning the questions raised above, or other topics dealing with the relationship of Byzantine Christianity and Islam. We welcome submissions from readers, scholars, theologians, Church officials, or anyone who would like to contribute to help develop an understanding of Islam and Byzantine Christianity. Please send electronic form and hardcopy to:

Eastern Christian Publications
PO Box 146
Fairfax, VA 22030
Email: jackfigel@compuserve.com

Introduction

The Beginning of the War

Before September 11, 2001, several terrorist attacks were inflicted against Americans in various parts of the world. These included military bases in Saudi Arabia, Somalia, Lebanon and two embassies in Africa. One of these attacks also occurred on U.S. soil in the 1993 bombing of the World Trade Center in New York.

These events may have been the beginning of the "war on terrorism" even though not recognized at the time. The tragic incidents of September 11th have given the U.S. a "wake up call" that this war is underway and that it can effect our entire culture and way of life. In addition, these events have been identified as attacks on Western Civilization in general, in that they were aimed at financial institutions and people from over 80 countries of the civilized world.

Many have speculated that the date of September 11th was simply chosen as the date matching the emergency phone number in the U.S. – 911. Terrorist organizations are known to plan their attacks around dates of significant historical or religious importance. A quick look at history points out that a significant event occurred on the following day, namely September 12 of the year 1683 when the Ottoman Turks were repelled and defeated at the Battle of Vienna. This is considered by many to be the "high water mark" of the Turkish Empire which declined over the following centuries. This may well have been the linkage to history intended by the attacks in New York and Washington and may illuminate the justification behind them.

Byzantine Empire Responses

This war against Islamic terrorism is the latest conflict that the Allies and their belief in religious and economic freedom have faced. Over the centuries, the Byzantine Empire faced many similar challenges from the Islamic world.

First, territories in the Holy Land were lost to Muslim armies up through the seventh century. Next the Byzantine Empire was confronted with Islamic prohibitions against depicting the deity which influenced the rise of Iconoclasm. This internal conflict over holy images further weakened the empire until icons were officially restored in the ninth century. Further losses of territory and permanent loss of the Holy Land caused the Papal declaration for the Crusades. Although these were intended to assist the Byzantine Empire and free the Holy Land from occupation by the Muslims, they in fact weakened the Empire, solidified the division between the Roman Catholic and Orthodox Churches, and culminated in the sacking of Constantinople in 1204. The Empire continued in a diminished state until the final collapse and fall of Constantinople in 1453 at the hands of the Ottoman Turks.

Division of the Roman Empire by Diocletian

The source of many east/west conflicts can actually be traced to the division of the Roman Empire by Diocletian in the early fourth century. He divided the single empire into two halves to improve administration and security. This division manifested the cultural and political rift between East and West, Greek and Latin, Orthodox and Catholic Christianity that can still be seen today. (map) Clashes between East and West have come and gone, and are more or less significant in today's world order. The most recent was the "cold war" between the U.S. and Western Europe and the Soviet Union and Eastern Europe. Now that this conflict has been resolved, the world now faces a new challenge as proven by the attacks of September 11th and subsequent actions and reactions of Muslims in countries around the world.

Over the past century, the population of those who follow Christianity and those who follow Islam has changed dramatically. For the first time in history, Christians are not the most populous religion of the world – those who follow Islam are.

This conflict is not only between Christianity and Islam. At a macro level it is also a conflict between first and third world countries, prosperity and poverty, secular and religious lifestyles, supernatural and natural views of a deity. As those in the West and already developed countries expand their ability and practice to limit and kill offspring through contraception and abortion, those in the East and developing countries are in the midst of a "baby boom" with many offspring per family. Baby booms have caused societal upheavals in the past as recognized in post WWII America and the Chinese Cultural Revolution.

These should be warning signs for how we understand and deal with the current worldwide situation.

The latest statistics indicate that although a majority of the world's population still identifies themselves as Christian (2 billion or 33% as of August 2001), those identified with Islam (1.3 billion or 25%) are growing much more rapidly and may in fact have a larger number who are "actively practicing" their religious beliefs rather than simply being "identified" with their religion.[1]

Parallels with the Fall of the Byzantine Empire

There are several parallels between the fall of the Byzantine Empire and current events. The Byzantine Empire was severely weakened through its ongoing wars and final defeat of the Persian Empire. In this weakened state, Muslim attacks in lifestyle, ideas and military conquest were successful and eventually caused its collapse. Similarly, western civilization and capitalism have won the "cold war" and defeated communism.

Map showing the dividing line of the Roman Empire by Diocletian and present-day national boundaries of East Central Europe

---

[1]   Cf. www.adherents.com.

However, through secularism, reduced fervor for the ideals of the American Revolution, and reduction in religious commitment, western civilization is also in a weakened state that could easily fall to further Islamic incursions.

Contents of this Book

This collection is divided into the following categories.

The first section provides a general background on the Byzantine Empire, Eastern Christianity and the Orthodox Christian Church, for those who are not familiar with this part of world history.

The second section includes an overview of Christianity and Islam, including the origins of Islam by Mohammed, a comparison of the respective holy books – the Bible and Qu'ran, the moral values of each religion, and how they have functioned since their founding. These views are based on a series of lectures written by W. R. W. Stephens in the late 19th century. Although dated in style, they provide an insight into how Christianity and Islam were viewed 100 years ago, and the terminology used in describing each at that time. Samuel P. Huntington shows a reversal of this attitude in his recent book when he says:

> "... the Resurgence was stimulated and fueled by the oil boom of the 1970s, which greatly increased the wealth and power of many Muslim nations and enabled them to reverse the relations of domination and subordination that thad existed with the West. ... The Saudi, Libyan and other governments used their oil riches to stimulate and finance the Muslim revival, and Muslim wealth led Muslims to swing from fascination with Western culture to deep involvement in their own and willingness to assert the place and importance of Islam in non-Islamic societies. Just as Western wealth had previously been seen as the evidence of the superiority of Western culture, oil wealth was seen as evidence of the superiority of Islam."[2]

---

[2] Samuel P. Huntington, *The Clash of Civilizations and the Remaking of Wolrd Order*, Simon & Schuster, New York, NY: 1996, p. 116.

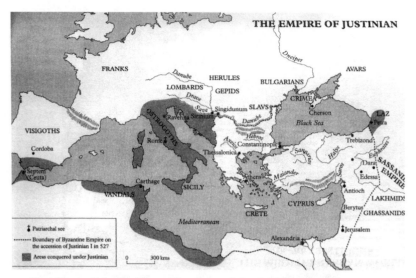

The Byzantine Empire at the time of Justinian in the 6th century

The Byzantine Empire in the 7th to 9th centuries

The majority of essays are a variety of theological and pastoral reflections on how Byzantine Christianity and Islam have interacted, how they coexist in certain countries of the world, and how their religious tenants may or may not be similar.

We hope to offer further volumes of this series in the future, with additional information especially in the area of historical and geopolitical considerations by current-day scholars.

In order to deal with the current worldwide crises and what an uncertain future may bring, we hope that this collection of essays will help all to better understand each other, and provide a background that may alleviate conflict in the future.

However, as Christ has instructed us, "be clever as snakes and innocent as doves" (Matt. 10:16). We should not ignore or simply "turn the other cheek" when confronted with attacks on Christianity, but should not respond in the same way that our enemies attack us. We must be truly Christian in our outlook and dialogue with others who hold different beliefs.

Contributors

Eastern Christian Publications wishes to thank the following contributors to this volume.

- Brother David Carroll, FSC, PhD, Assistant to the Secretary General, Catholic Near East Welfare Association, New York, New York, USA.

- Father Raymond F. Collins, SSD, Professor of New Testament, Department of Theology, The Catholic University of America, Washington, District of Columbia, USA.

- Patriarch Gregory III of Antioch, Melkite Greek-Catholic Church, Damascus, Syria.

- Richard Hooker, Professor of History, Washington State University, Pullman, Washington, USA.

- J. M. Hussey, Professor of History, University of London, London, England.

- Bishop Basil H. Losten, Ukrainian Greek-Catholic Eparchy of Stamford, Connecticut, USA.

- Rev. Bassam M. Madany, Retired Minister of the Christian Reformed Church of North America, Chicago, Illinois, USA.

- Stavrophore Maximos, Holy Resurrection Byzantine Catholic Monastery , Newberry Springs, California, USA.

- Father Jonathan Morse, PhD, Director of Religious Education, Eparchy of Stamford, Connecticut, USA.

- Patriarch Petros VII of Alexandria, Greek Orthodox Church, Egypt.

- Metropolitan Seraphim of Glastonbury, Coptic Orthodox Church, England.

- W. R. W. Stephens, Prebendary of Chichester, England.

- Father Alexander Webster, PhD, Orthodox Church of America, Falls Church, Virginia, USA.

Interior of Hagia Sophia, the Great Church of Constantinople, in the 19th century

Acknowledgments

In addition to the contributors, Eastern Christian Publications acknowledges the following sources for some essays appearing in this volume:

- The essay entitled "The Orthodox Church in the Byzantine Empire" is a chapter from the book named *The Byzantine World* by J. M. Hussey, Harper & Row, New York, 1961.

- The essay entitled *The Byzantines* by Richard Hooker is from the World Cultures website of Washington State University, Pullman, Washington, USA.

- The four lectures on *Christianity and Islam* by W. R. W. Stephens were first published in 1877 by Scribner, Armstrong & Co., New York, and made available from the website of the Active Bible Church of God, Chicago, Illinois, USA.

- The general essay on *Eastern Christianity* is from the website on World Religions by the Religion and Ethics Department of St. Martin's College, Lancaster, England.

The Byzantines

Richard Hooker

It is not possible to effectually distinguish between the later empire in Rome and the Byzantine empire centered around Constantinople. For the Byzantines were the Roman Empire, not simply a continuation of it in the East. The capital city, Constantinople, had been founded as the capital of Rome by the Emperor Constantine, but a uniquely Greek or Byzantine character to the Roman Empire can be distinguished as early as Diocletian. When Rome was seized by Goths, this was a great blow to the Roman Empire, but it didn't effectively end it. Although Rome was under the control of foreigners who themselves claimed to be continuing the empire, the Byzantine empire continued as before, believing themselves to be the Roman Empire.

Over the centuries, however, Byzantium evolved into a very different civilization. The eastern Empire had always had a predominately Greek character, but the Byzantines through the course of the first millenium AD had to deal with cultural influences and political threats from European cultures, Asian cultures and, primarily, Islam after the seventh century.

Through the later Middle Ages, however, Byzantium both gradually declined politically and became more isolated from the rest of Europe. While the last centuries of the European Middle Ages saw the consolidation of the idea of Europe and the incorporation of European cultures into a larger, overarching European monoculture, Byzantium was left out of this new European concept. By the beginning of the modern period, when "Europe" had become a solid, cultural idea, the Byzantine Empire had come to an end with the Ottoman conquest of Constantinople.

Byzantine history, then, stretches in a continuous line from the latter centuries of Rome to the very beginning of the modern period. It transmitted the classical culture of Greece and Rome but it also developed a unique historical and cultural character based on a synthesis of Greek, Roman, European, and Islamic elements.

Justinian

Most historians consider the reign of Justinian (527-565) as marking a significant break with the Roman past. This is difficult to support – Justinian not only considered himself the emperor of all of Rome, including the territories occupied by the Goths, but also spoke Latin as his primary language.

After the fall of Rome, the Byzantine emperors never gave over the idea of reconquering Rome. They did, however, take a lesson from the fall of Rome and all throughout the fifth century, the Byzantine emperors wrought a series of administrative and financial reforms. They produced the single most extensive corpus of Roman law in 425 and reformed taxation dramatically. Most importantly, however, they did not entrust their military to German generals; this had been the downfall of the Latin portion of the empire. They could not, however, maintain a powerful military; the loss of territory in the west had dramatically shrunk their financial resources.

Justinian was perhaps the last emperor that seriously entertained notions of reconquering the west; the institution of the western emperor fell permanently vacant in 476 and the Byzantine emperors claimed it as theirs. His expeditions against Italy, however, failed. Although he conquered North Africa and retook Italy from the Ostrogoths, this Gothic War drained the Byzantine Empire of much-needed resources. Most importantly, the Gothic War devestated Italy economically. The economic destruction of Italy was so total that it destroyed Italian urban culture for centuries. The great cities of Rome and her allies would be abandoned as Italy would fall into a long period of backwardness. The impoverishment of Italy and the drain on Byzantium made it impossible for the Byzantines to hold Italy. Only three years after the death of Justinian, the Italian territories fell into the hands of another Germanic tribe, the "Long Beards," or Langobardi (Lombards).

Justinian, however, is most famous for the body of laws that he promulgated, the *Corpus iuris civilis*. This was not only a great legal achievement in codifying Roman law, it was also the first systematic attempt to synthesize Roman law and jurisprudence with Christianity. Although Byzantium would eventually fade in influence, from the eleventh century onwards, Justinian's Corpus iuris civilis became the foundation of all European law and legal practice (except for England).

Justinian is also credited for founding Byzantine architecture with his building of the Santa Sophia in Constantinople and the church of San Vitale in Ravenna, Italy. The Santa Sophia continued the Roman tradition of building domes, the architecture of the Roman basilica, but it was carried out on a scale unheard of in earlier centuries. In fact, it would remain the largest dome ever built until Sinan built the Selimye Mosque in the sixteenth century. Both Santa Sophia and San Vitale are decorated inside with a uniquely Byzantine mosaic style, a style that was to characterize Byzantine architecture for nearly another millenium. It is a style that fuses both Roman mosaic realism and an otherworldly, almost abstract use of simple forms and dramatic colors.

The most serious and lasting mistake of Justinian's reign was the persecution of heretical Christians. The eastern empire had always been distinguished from the western empire by the proliferation of religions and metaphysical speculation as a characteristic of religions. This did not substantially change with the advent of Christianity. Although non-Christians were stamped, the eastern Christians engaged in high intellectual speculation on theological and Christological questions with a fervor unmatched in the West. You might say that the model of Christian belief in the east was more mystical and philosophical while the Christian belief in the west was more practical and obedience-centered. This meant that a number of competing doctrines circulated in the Greek-centered areas of the Byzantine world. One of these doctrines, the Monophysite doctrine, was so serious a challenge to the western church that it was declared heretical.

The Monophysite doctrine arose from Christological speculation. What was the nature of Christ? This was one of the dominant speculative questions in the eastern empire from the fifth century onwards. The Monophysites argued that Christ had one and only nature (mono=one, physis=nature) and that nature was divine – the Orthodox Christian church held that Christ had a double nature, that of divinity and humanity. In the latter decades of the fifth century, the Byzantine Emperor declared himself to be a Monophysite – this estranged the Byzantines from the Roman Pope.

But Justinian – and his father before him, Justin I – needed the support of the Pope in order to retake Italy. So both Justin and Justinian renounced Monophysite belief and were reincorporated into the Latin church. But Justinian went even further – to demonstrate his commitment to Latin Christianity, he began a series of oppressive persecutions of Monophysites in Syria and Egypt. This would have a profound effect on later history – the Monophysite Christians, horribly persecuted by the Byzantines, welcomed Muslim conquerors with open arms based on their promise to tolerate their religion.

Heraclius I

It fell to Justinian's successors to rescue Byzantium from the financial ruin caused by Justinian's ill-fated attempt to retake Italy. The emperor most responsible for saving this empire was Heraclius I (610-641). When he assumed the throne, things looked pretty hopeless. From the east, the Persian Empire threatened to overwhelm Asia Minor while from the west, a mix of German, Slavic, and Mongolian peoples were pressing into Greece and the Balkans. Heraclius decided to allow a group of Huns to settle the Balkans and protect the western border while the Byzantine empire focussed on Persia, which Heraclius finally defeated and permanently ended the long history of that great empire.

A new cultural force, however, emerged during his reign – in fact, the very year that Heraclius assumed the throne, a forty-year old Arab named Muhammad in the city of Mecca first heard the message that would sweep across the face of the world: Islam. By the end of his reign, Muslim armies were making raids into Byzantine territory in Syria and were beginning to conquer the Persian territories. From this period onwards, Byzantine energies focussed almost entirely to the east and to the south. The western countries, the Europe that Byzantium at one time looked to for their identity and history, began to steadily fade from their horizon.

Islam

Almost all of Byzantine energy over the next centuries would be focussed on Islam. The Muslims very quickly conquered Byzantine territory in Syria and Egypt largely because of disaffected populations of Christians and Jews who had been persecuted since the time of Justinian. The patriarchal caliphs and later the Umayyad caliphs, however, really had their sights on Byzantine territory – in fact, the conquest of Byzantium itself. They easily conquered all the Persian territories, but they could never quite conquer the heart of Byzantium itself. In 670, they attempted this conquest with a large fleet; in 717, they tried again with a land and sea operation against the city.

This operation, however, turned the tide away from the Muslims. Under the emperor Leo the Isaurian (717-741), the Muslim invasion was turned back and the Byzantines began to hold their own against Islamic incursions.

As the centralized Islamic government under the caliph began to disintegrate in the ninth century, the Byzantines began to reassert their dominance over Asia Minor. By the middle of the tenth century, they reconquered most of Syria and were once again a powerful and influential empire stretching from Greece to Arabia.

In 1071, however, the Seljuk Turks conquered the Byzantine army at Manzikert in Asia Minor – after this victory, the Seljuks quickly overran all of Byzantine territory in the east.

The Crusaders

The Byzantines, however, turned to Europe for help against the Muslims – the Byzantine emperor, Alexius Comnenius, called upon the European states to push back the Muslim conquerors. While Byzantium and the Europeans had drifted apart culturally, they still shared a common religion, and the European states complied. They had, however, designs of their own on Byzantine territories. While they successfully pushed back the Seljuks and returned territory to the Byzantines, the western Europeans also carved out kingdoms of their own in Syria and Palestine. This wasn't quite enough for them – in 1204, the Crusaders attacked, conquered, and pillaged the city of Constantinople, a goal that the Muslims had been trying for for centuries.

The amazing thing about this event is that it did not spell the end of the Byzantines. For a few decades, the Byzantine imperial government continued to function in Greece – in 1261, they returned to

Constantinople and retook the city! The Byzantine Empire was no longer an empire after 1261, but rather a small kingdom centered around Constantinople. In 1453, the city was finally and permanently conquered by the Ottoman Turks and renamed Istanbul. Byzantine culture, law, and administration came to its final end.

Byzantine Christianity

Byzantine Christianity was a substantially different religion and cultural practice than Latin Christianity. One of its predominant characteristics was the role of the emperor in matters of faith. The Latin church had battled emperors for control of the church and with the disintegration of centralized authority in Europe and the proliferation of European kingdoms, the primacy of the Pope in matters of faith was relatively solidified.

The Byzantines, however, inherited the Roman idea that the emperor was near divinity and practiced a form of Christianity where enormous ecclesiastical and theological authority was vested in the emperor. This would eventually create a permanent breach in the world of Christianity between west and east and the event that would produce this breach was the Iconoclastic controversy.

The Iconoclastic theologians believed that the worship of images, or icons, was a fundamentally pagan belief. Products of human hands should not be worshipped, they argued, but only Christ and God should be the proper objects of veneration. The movement was inaugurated by Leo the Isaurian. It was Leo, remember, that turned the tide against the Muslim in 717. Islam is itself opposed to the worship of images, icons, and idols – one of the founding acts of Islam is Muhammad's destruction of all the idols and images in the sacred Ka'aba in Mecca. There is no doubt that the Iconoclasts were in part inspired by the religious purity of the Islamic faith. There is also little doubt that Iconoclasm would help the Byzantines regain territory conquered by the Muslims since it made Christianity more in line with the Islamic faith.

Iconoclasm, however, was fiercely opposed by the papacy which saw it as a threat not only to Latin ecclesiastical practices, but to the authority of the pope himself. When Leo's son, Constantine V, even more zealously carried out the Iconoclastic program during his reign (740-775), the breach between the Latin and Byzantine church became permanent. Eventually, Iconoclasm would be abandoned in the ninth century – the breach, however, would never be healed.

The most significant result of the Iconoclastic controversy was the adoption of a strict traditionalism in the Byzantine church. The eastern church had long been characterized by speculation and innovation, but the Iconoclastic controversy was too disorienting. Almost overnight, the Byzantine church became averse to innovation and speculation. This created a more or less static religious culture and it also permanently ended the intellectual dynamism of Byzantine life.

Byzantine Philosophy

Perhaps the single most salient aspect of Byzantine culture was the transmission of classical culture. While classical studies, science, and philosophy largely dissipated in the Latin west, Byzantine education and philosophy still zealously pursued these intellectual traditions. It was in Byzantium that Plato and Aristotle continued to be studied and were eventually transmitted first into the Islamic world and then back into western Europe. A basic education in Byzantium consisted first of the mastery of classical Greek literature, such as Homer (largely unknown in the West during this period) – almost all of the Greek literature we have today was only preserved by the Byzantines.

Unlike Greece and Rome during the classical period or the Latin West during the Middle Ages, women actively participated in the intellectual life of the culture. While they could not attend schools, aristocratic women were often well-educated at home by tutors in literature, history, composition, and philosophy. The greatest of Byzantine writers, in fact, was the historian Anna Comnena, the daughter of the emperor Alexius. Her biography of her father is one of the greatest works of medieval historiography in existence, including the histories written in Europe.

The Slavs

Byzantine culture is important because of two lines of transmission. One line of transmission involved exporting classical Greek and Roman culture into Islam and, to a lesser extent, the transmission of Byzantine theological speculation into Islamic theology. The second is the transmission of Byzantine culture and religion to Slavic peoples, especially to the Russians.

We know very little about the Slavs before the Middle Ages – what we do know we only know through archaeology. As Byzantium, however, turned less of its attention towards Europe and the west, they became increasingly interested in the peoples to the north. We don't know how cultural contact was initiated between these two peoples, but sometime around 988 a Russian ruler named Vladimir converted to Byzantine Christianity. From that point onwards, the Slavs in Russia became a kind of cultural inheritor of Byzantine culture, adopting the religion, theology, some social structures, and writing from the Byzantines to the south. In many ways Russian and Slavic culture is the continuance of Byzantine culture and many Byzantine cultural practices and beliefs are still practiced among Slavs today. Russian religion, art, philosophy, and even literature, such as the writings of Chekhov and Dostoevsky, show profound influences from Byzantine culture. The Byzantine inheritance also included the sense that Byzantine culture and practice was fundamentally different from European culture and practice. This sense of Byzantine distinctiveness would also impress itself on Slavic cultures up until the present.

So close was this cultural connection, that Russians believed that they were the inheritors of the Byzantine Empire when it finally collapsed in 1453. The Russian rulers assumed the title of "Caesar," the title bestowed on Byzantine emperors – in Russian, the word is "Tsar." With the government centered in Moscow, the Russian Tsars declared Moscow to be the "third Rome," after Rome and Byzantium, and so located themselves in a cultural and historical trajectory that began with the Roman empire.

Eastern Christianity

During the early history of Christianity five cities became particularly important for the church: Antioch, Alexandria, Constantinople, Jerusalem and Rome. Antioch was one of the first cities to be evangelised by Christian missionaries and it was there that the followers of Christ acquired the name Christian (Acts 11:26). The church in Alexandria was, according to tradition, founded by Mark the Evangelist. Constantinople, founded on the ancient city of Byzantium, became the capital of the new pro-Christian empire under Constantine. Jerusalem was at the heart of Christ's ministry and the place of his crucifixion, burial, resurrection and ascension. And it was in Rome that St Paul was martyred under Nero and where, tradition claims, the apostle Peter was martyred.

The stature of these cities, combined with their cultural and political importance for the empire, made them obvious candidates as administrative centres for the church following the edict of toleration of 313. In 325 the Christian emperor, Constantine, called the Council of Nicaea with the purpose of resolving the dispute between the Arian and Orthodox Christians on the divine status of the Son. It was at Nicaea that Antioch, Alexandria and Rome were singled out as the three great centres of the Christian world. The second ecumenical council, held in Constantinople in 381, made Constantinople a patriarchate and assigned to it second place in importance after Rome. The third ecumenical council, held at Ephesus, made the island of Cyprus autocephalous (that is, self-governing). The fourth ecumenical council, held at Chalcedon, made Jerusalem a patriarchate. The order of the patriarchates in terms of importance were Rome, Constantinople, Alexandria, Antioch, Jerusalem, each of which had jurisdiction over large parts of the empire.

With the exception of Rome, which became separated from the eastern church in 1054, all of these areas fell under the dominion of Islam as it spread rapidly westwards. Within fifteen years after the death of Muhammad (632), Muslim armies had taken Syria, Palestine, and Egypt, thus placing the patriarchates of Antioch, Alexandria and Jerusalem under Muslim control.

In all these regions the strength of the church declined under the impact of the presence of Islam. The patriarchate of Antioch – which had already been considerably weakened as a result of the separation of the monophysite Syrian Orthodox Church and the Nestorian Church from the Catholic Church in the 5th century – was further weakened when the Arab Islamic rulers moved the capital of Syria from Antioch to Damascus, a decision which forced the patriarch to transfer his residence to Damascus, where he continues to reside today.

In 637 Jerusalem fell to the invading Arab armies. Relations between Muslims and Christians were relatively good until the crusades of the 11th to 13th centuries. In 1099 the crusaders from western Europe captured Jerusalem and massacred the Muslim and Jewish population of the city. A Latin kingdom was established in Palestine and the Greek patriarch was expelled from Jerusalem and forced to reside in Cyprus. In 1187 the crusaders were expelled from Palestine, and Jerusalem came once again under Muslim control. The renewed Muslim presence enabled the return of the Greek patriarch to Jerusalem. Since then the city has been overseen by rival Latin and Greek patriarchs.

The patriarchate of Alexandria, like that of Antioch, had been considerably weakened by the separation of the Egyptian copts from the mainstream church in the 4th century. When the Arab armies arrived at the gates of Alexandria, the city surrendered to them without a fight. The patriarchate went into severe decline from the 16th century when the Ottoman Turks invaded Egypt and placed the Alexandrian patriarchate under the jurisdiction of the Patriarch of Constantinople. Between the 16th and 19th centuries Alexandria and, with it, the Christian church in Egypt was allowed to decline. Evangelism in Africa has strengthened the position of the Alexandrian patriarch in the 19th and 20th centuries.

The history of the patriarchate of Constantinople has been one of great spiritual prestige as well as oppression at the hands of its political rivals. Between the 8th and 11th centuries the patriarchate saw its jurisdiction spread westwards into southern Italy and northwards into Russia. The patriarchate was, however, greatly weakened by the events of the fourth crusade when, in 1204, Constantinople was conquered, sacked and a Latin patriarch temporarily placed over the city. The sacking of Constantinople made the city more vulnerable to the advancing Muslim Ottoman empire. In 1453 Constantinople fell to the Ottoman armies. With the fall of Constantinople came the end of the imperial lineage as the last Byzantine emperor died in battle defending the city walls.

The fall of the city signalled the end of the independence of the patriarchate of Constantinople. Henceforth Islam was to be the protector of Christian Orthodoxy rather than the Byzantine emperor. The power of the Constantinopolitan patriarch was enhanced as he was made both the political and spiritual ruler of the Christian peoples within the Ottoman empire. Such rule, however, was effected over a people that, while offered official protection, were also regarded and treated as second class citizens. Christians were required to pay heavier taxes than the Muslims, to wear a distinctive dress, were disallowed from undertaking missionary work, from establishing new churches, from marrying Muslim women or serving in the army.

This situation prevailed for four hundred and fifty years until the Ottoman empire was pushed out of south-eastern Europe in the 19th century and defeated at the end of the first world war. As regions such as Greece, Bulgaria, Serbia and Romania were liberated, they were able to establish their own churches which were independent of Constantinople. To these was added the Orthodox Church of Albania, which became autocephalous in 1937.

An important consequence of the fall of Constantinople in 1453 was that the centre of Eastern Orthodoxy shifted from Constantinople to Russia. A mission had been sent to Russia as early as the 860s, but it was not until the baptism of Vladimir, the ruler of Kiev, in 988, that Christianity became firmly established in the region. In 1448 the Russian church became independent of Constantinople, and became a patriarchate in 1589.

The Russian church was weakened by a schismatic dispute in the 17th century. Patriarch Nikon of Moscow wanted to reform the Russian service books, which contained a number of errors, so that the errors were corrected and the service books conformed more closely to those of the Greek church. A large number of Russians rejected these reforms. They came to be known as the Old Believers on account of their commitment to the former rituals of the church. Although brutally persecuted by both church and state, the Old Believers have survived and remain active to the present day.

A number of other churches have emerged from within Russian Orthodoxy, usually due to missionary activities or the establishment of new states in areas formally under the control of Russia. Following the Russian revolution in 1917, the Orthodox church in Finland placed itself within the jurisdiction of the Patriarch of Constantinople. The Orthodox church in Georgia, which had been annexed by Russia in 1811, regained its independence after the revolution of 1917. The Orthodox Chuch of Poland came into existence in 1924 when the state of Poland was established following the end of the first world war. Missionary activities at the beginning of the 18th century brought Eastern Orthodoxy to China. The small numbers of believers in China were greatly enlarged following the Russian revolution which caused hundreds of thousands of Russians to flee to China. The church in China became independent of its Russian mother church in 1957. Eastern Orthodoxy was brought to North America in the 18th century when Alaska was owned by Russia. Ties between the Orthodox community in America and Russia were broken after the 1917 revolution; in 1970 the Orthodox Church in America was granted autocephalous status. Eastern Orthodoxy was transplanted onto Japanese soil when the first Russian diplomatic mission was established there in 1853. In 1970 the church became independent of the church in Moscow.

With the collapse of the Soviet Union and its influence over Eastern Europe, new autonomous churches came into existence. Ukraine's declaration of independence in 1991 from the Soviet Union enabled the Orthodox church there to become independent of Moscow. Similarly, following the withdrawal of Soviet forces from Eastern Europe, the church in Czecholsovakia, which had officially been autocephalous since 1951, was able to establish itself as fully independent. The separation of Czechoslovakia into two distinct states in 1993 meant that the church had to rename itself the Orthodox Church of Czech and Slovak Lands.

Finally, something should be said about the Uniate churches. The majority of these churches are former Eastern Orthodox churches that have entered into union with the Church of Rome. They are churches which, while using the same rites as the Eastern Orthodox churches, are in fact in communion with Rome and consider themselves to be within the jurisdiction of Rome. Among the largest and most important of these are the Maronites of Lebanon; the Melkites, who exist mainly in Syria; and the Ukrainian Catholic Church.

The history and theology of the Melkites is rather complex. Following the Council of Chalcedon in 451, which led to a split in the eastern church over the question of how the person of Christ should be defined, those Christians in Syria who remained loyal to the Byzantine Church came to be called Melkites. (Those who broke away from the mainstream church in Syria formed the Syrian Orthodox Church of Antioch.) In the 18th century a split took place within the Melkite Church between those who wanted to remain under the authority of the Patriarch of Constantinople and those who wished to place themselves within the jurisdiction of the Roman Catholic Church. This latter group is known as the Melkite Catholic Church. This church, while identifying itself as Catholic, continues to use the Byzantine rite.

No less complicated is the history of the Maronite Church. The Maronites trace their origins to a group of Christians who gathered around the fourth century monk, St Maron. Following the Muslim invasions of Syria and the surrounding regions, the Maronites took refuge in the remote mountains of Lebanon, where they began to develop their own distinct identity. Contact with the Latin crusaders in the 11th and 12th centuries led the Maronites to affirm their union with Rome. The Maronites remain a strong group within Lebanon and play a major role in Lebanese politics.

Finally, the Ukrainian Catholic Church was established in 1596 by the Union of Brest Litovsk, which brought the Orthodox metropolitan province of Kiev into full communion with the Roman Catholic Church. The church was suppressed by the Russian government in 1945, leaving Ukrainian Catholics with the option of either joining the Russian Orthodox Church or going underground. In 1989 Ukrainian Catholics were given legal protection by the Soviet government. Allowed to recover the churches that had been confiscated and handed over to the Russian Orthodox Church, the Ukrainian Catholics enjoyed a rapid resurgence so that by 1991 there were 5 million faithful worshipping in over 2000 churches.

Bibliography

Baker, Derek (ed.) *The Orthodox Churches in the West*. Blackwell, 1976.

Bourdeaux, Michael. *Patriarch and Prophets: Persecution of the Russian Orthodox Church Today*. Macmillan, 1969.

Constantinides, Michael. *The Orthodox Church*. Williams and Norgate, 1931.

Doak, Margaret. *The Orthodox Church*. Pergamon, 1978.

Hackel, Sergei. *The Orthodox Church*. Ward Lock, 1971.

Hussey, J.M. *The Orthodox Churches in the Byzantine Empire*. Oxford University Press, 1986.

Limouris, Gennadios and Nomikos Michael Vaporis. *Orthodox Perspectives on Baptism, Eucharist and Ministry*. Holy Cross Orthodox Press, 1985.

Runciman, Steven. *The Orthodox Churches and the Secular State*. Oxford University Press, 1971.

Waddams, Hervbert. *Meeting the Orthodox Churches*. London: SCM, 1964.

Walter, Christopher. *Art and Ritual of the Byzantine Church*. Birmingham Byzantine Services, 1982.

Ware, Kallistos. *The Orthodox Church*. Penguin, 1963.

Ware, Kallistos. *The Orthodox Way*. St Vladimir's Seminary Press, 1995.

Ware, Timothy. *The Orthodox Church*. Penguin, 1993.

The Orthodox Church in the Byzantine Empire

J. M. Hussey

The recognition of the Christian religion by Constantine the Great in the early fourth century could not affect the essentials of Christianity nor alter the nature of the divinely constituted Church. It did however initiate certain changes. The old Roman Empire with its many different religions was replaced by a Christian *imperium romanum*. In the early middle ages imperial unity was disrupted in the West, but in spite of political and linguistic differences there emerged a society retaining a measure of unity based on its common Christian faith.

This was medieval Christendom, consisting at first of the young states of the Latin West and the Byzantine Empire of the Greek and oriental East Mediterranean, to which were later added the converted Slav peoples. There were also certain other Christian countries, as Armenia or Ethiopia, as well as communities living in non-Christian polities, for instance in the Persian Empire, and later in the Muslim principalities.

Even before it was allowed to worship openly and in peace the Christian Church was widespread and had its strongholds, notably Rome, Antioch and Alexandria. In the course of the fourth and fifth centuries it was organized apace, following the pattern of the secular government. It was split into provinces under metropolitans. The chief or 'arch' metropolitans were those of Rome, Antioch and Alexandria, the old sees of apostolic foundation, of which Rome had always had primacy of honour.

During this period Jerusalem and Constantinople took their place amongst these bishops of first rank. Thus there came into being the five at patriarchates, the pentarchy, into which medieval Christendom was divided. Jerusalem had special claims to veneration and to this high rank. The importance of Constantinople was derived not from apostolic foundation or special association with the struggles of the early Church but from its position as the imperial residence and the new capital. This was recognized by the General Council of Constantinople in 381 when it stated that the bishop of Constantinople was second only to the bishop of Old Rome and had the same prerogatives of honour because Constantinople was New Rome.

In 451 at the end of the Council of Chalcedon, when the Roman legates were absent, this was reaffirmed at a special sitting in the so-called twenty-eighth canon of Chalcedon. Though at the time not accepted by the Papacy, this canon was regarded by the Orthodox Church as a valid statement of its rights. It was also bitterly resented by Alexandria and Antioch, but in any case Muslim conquests from the seventh century onwards were to deprive these two cities of much of their influence and Constantinople was destined to become the most important ecclesiastical centre in the Christian East, also exercising considerable influence over northern Slav territories.

From the fourth century onwards the common problems of discipline and dogma were discussed and dealt with in ecclesiastical assemblies. At the highest level there were the General Councils, the first of which was convened by Constantine the Great at Nicaea in A.D. 325. All the bishops (or their representatives if they could not come in person) were summoned, and the decisions of these synods were binding on the whole Church. Proceedings throughout were conducted under imperial auspices, and illustrated the close co-operation between Church and State. The sessions ended with acclamations for the ortho-dox rulers and the canons were signed by them, thus ensuring that these would receive the support of the secular authority.

The first seven of these General Councils were recognized by all patriarchates. After the ninth century there was not the same need for general assemblies; the main period of doctrinal definition had passed and problems of discipline could be dealt with on a regional basis. From the mid-eleventh century onwards, there was also another obstacle in the way of fraternal conferences: this was the growing rift between the Latin West and the Byzantine Empire, particularly aggra-vated by the aggression of the Fourth Crusade in 1204.

In the later middle ages the Church had problems of a different nature, but the essential preliminary to any General Council was whether Constantinople would make 'oecumenical' discussions possible by agreeing to ecclesiastical reunion with Rome.

The emergence of Constantinople as the capital of the medieval East Roman Empire and the loss of its rivals Antioch and Alexandria to the infidel inevitably emphasized the importance of the Patriarch of Constantinople, the head of the Byzantine Church. In the face of Rome's protests he had taken the title of 'oecumenical', though it is true that this was not in the sense of ruler over the whole Church. His authority had been increased at the expense of Rome when the Emperor Leo III in 732 transferred the provinces of South Italy, Greece and parts of the Balkans to his jurisdiction. Relations with Rome had been further strained by the papal alliance with the western rulers and the subsequent papal inauguration of a western line of Emperors in 800. The Byzantine Patriarch came into close contact with the Emperor. He received his profession of faith, crowned him, could advise and on occasion admonish.

The Autocrator was the more powerful figure, often largely responsible for the Patriarch's election and capable of procuring his resignation or deposition. Nevertheless the Patriarch had his own place in the closely linked spheres of Church and State, and after 1204 it was usually the Patriarch who took the lead in resisting the Emperor's attempts to achieve reunion with Rome, and in this he was strongly supported by laity, monks and secular clergy. Apart from his priestly functions he was especially responsible for the maintenance of Christian instruction and discipline within the Church. After the settlement of the major doctrinal controversies in the General Councils, the Patriarch worked mainly through the standing synod in Constantinople (*synodos endemousa*).

This had originally been made up of bishops living in the capital but from the tenth century onwards it was attended by metropolitans and auto-cephalous archbishops. Here problems of liturgy were settled, perhaps a new festival instituted, points of controversy dealt with, as for instance whether a particular cult could be permitted or not. Punishment was also meted out to offending churchmen; the synod acted as a court of justice as well as a deliberative legislative body.

Throughout the life of the medieval Orthodox Church the secular and ecclesiastical authorities worked together, the one implementing the other, as is admirably illustrated by the nearest Byzantine equivalent to the western corpus of canon law. Its most important collection of ecclesiastical rulings was known as the 'Nomocanon in fourteen titles'. It consisted of legislation by the Emperor and by the Church, as well as other matter which was regarded as authoritative.

The fourteen titles really applied originally only to the first part which gave canonical rulings on subjects ranging from orthodox faith to the administration of ecclesiastical property. It was followed by texts cited *in extenso,* as the so-called eighty-five canons of the apostles and certain patristic passages, and it concluded with the relevant secular laws. It was originally the sixth century private collection of John the Scholasticus of Antioch, who became Patriarch of Constantinople. On the basis of this work, the 'Nomocanon in fourteen titles' emerged in the seventh century and was accepted by the Council in Trullo (692) and by later councils. In the course of the middle ages it was brought up to date from time to time, and it went through four editions, the last being made by the canonist Balsamon at the end of the twelfth century.

The Patriarch was at the apex of the hierarchy of the Byzantine Church. Under him there were the metropolitans set over the ecclesiastical provinces, each of which was divided into bishoprics. Bishops not under a metropolitan were called autocephalous archbishops. Metropolitans were at first chosen by the Patriarch from three nominees, later by the standing synod in Constantinople. Bishops were chosen by the metropolitan from three names put forward by the provincial synod, and the imperial aim to confirm the election was resisted.

The Emperors did however retain their right to promote or demote by altering the status of a high cleric; thus a bishop might be created metropolitan or autocephalous bishop, often without regard to the radical consequences. The metropolitan had rights of general supervision over his province, but though he could punish offending bishops he had to be careful not to infringe on their rights in their own dioceses. Bishops had to be thirty-five years old and men of some education who knew the Psalter by heart, and if married they had to separate from their wives. Latterly it became usual for bishops to be monks, as also in the case of the Patriarch, in contrast to the days when a distinguished layman and humanist such as Photius could be elected. Within his diocese the bishop was responsible for all ecclesiastical matters, such as the discipline of his clergy or of the monasteries, as also for the spiritual well-being and instruction of the laity. He had certain rights of jurisdiction when clerics were involved and he might be called in to arbitrate by the laity.

In his cathedral church the bishop was assisted by clergy of various ranks, the more important of whom filled special offices connected either with the work of the cathedral or with diocesan administration. Similar arrangements, though on a more elaborate scale, were found in the metropolitan churches. St. Sophia in Constantinople, 'the Great Church' as it was called, had an enormous staff, limited from time to time by patriarchal and imperial efforts. In 612 the Patriarch, with imperial support, reduced the number of its clergy to eighty priests, one hundred and fifty deacons, forty deaconesses, seventy sub-deacons, one hundred and sixty readers, twenty-five cantors and seventy-five door-keepers; and this was in addition to a certain number of permitted 'extras'.

In the Great Church the leading figure after the Patriarch was the *syncellus*. He was the *familiaris* and confidant of the Patriarch, his spiritual father, as also that of the Emperor. There also developed a group of leading officials who shared between them the work connected not only with St. Sophia itself but with the patriarchal administration in general. For instance the Great Chartophylax (the keeper of documents) began by taking charge of the patriarchal archives. He became a kind of librarian, secretary and chancellor rolled into one, for his work expanded to include supervision of clergy, ordinations, episcopal elections, and indeed complete control of the patriarchal chancery. His importance is shown by his place at pontifical mass when he stood near the holy door and at the moment of communion summoned the clergy with the words, 'Priests and deacons, come and receive your King and God.' This group of major officials found its counterpart in the curias of metropolitans and bishops throughout the Orthodox Church. They are the eastern equivalent of the four chief dignitaries *(quattuor personae)* of the medieval English cathedral chapter. Ecclesiastical organization bore a certain similarity at different levels and in different parts of Christendom.

In the Orthodox Church the great majority of the secular clergy, that is, the orders below that of bishop, were allowed to be married, provided this had taken place before they were ordained sub-deacon. They evidently engaged in all kinds of trade until prohibited by canon law. It would of course be unfair to deduce from conciliar rulings that the majority of clergy regularly attended cabaret shows or ran betting establishments.

But their status was often a low one, and many did agricultural work in the fields like the present-day *papas* in the Greek countryside. When property was sold they went with the estate like the *paroikof,* or dependent tenants, in the village. These lower clergy might serve in two different kinds of church: the 'general' or parish church (the *calholicon),* i.e. the church under the diocesan bishop who nominated its incumbent; and the chapel belonging perhaps to a monastery, perhaps to a private person or even group of individuals who had clubbed together to found it. Sometimes the villagers would assist the little nucleus of a new community in building the monastic chapel, as was the experience of the eleventh century St. Dorotheus in Asia Minor. It is evident from various *Lives* of the saints and other sources that the needs of the countryside, as well as the towns, were mostly provided for by monastic or private foundations which far outnumbered the 'catholic' churches.

The Church was not poor, and imperial legislation abounded in regulations controlling the administration of its property. Patriarchal administration was in the hands of the Great Oeconomus. Within the diocese the bishop might appoint an oeconomus steward of property belonging to particular churches or institutions, or it might be controlled by the clergy in charge. Landed property was sometimes granted out on lease, though in practice it was often found that the church lost by this. Church property could not normally be alienated, not even for imperial needs. Sometimes Emperors made laymen the guardians of a monastic foundation, thereby allowing them to take charge of the house's property, provided that they allowed the monks sufficient for their livelihood – a system that readily lent itself to abuse.

In addition to donations and legacies from the faithful, the bishop received a tax, the *canonicon,* which was defined and made compulsory in the eleventh century. The villagers paid partly in money, partly in kind, according to the number of families in the village; priests paid him one gold coin *(nomisma)* a year, and monasteries also had to pay, unless they sent this direct to the Patriarch because they had been founded by him and were under his direct control (such monasteries were called 'stauropegial').

Certain other dues were paid on special occasions, as marriage fees. Dues were also paid on the occasion of an ordination, but not for the ordination. Such gifts were regulated by custom and imperial decree. Simony was strictly condemned (even the eleventh century anti-Greek Cardinal Humbert found something to praise in the Orthodox Church on this account). From his revenue the bishop would normally provide for his cathedral clergy, unlike the western system of separate prebends. He was also responsible for churches which had no endowment. In the later middle ages these *catholica* or parish churches were sometimes provided for by revenue from a special grant of church property *(klerikaton)* which was leased to the incumbent.

Within this framework the Orthodox Church lived its everyday life, preserving its tradition unbroken to the present day. Almost from the beginning the Church had shown itself to be the heir of Graeco-Roman, as well as of East Mediterranean, traditions; it therefore defined its terms and articulated Christian belief, often in an atmosphere of bitter and prolonged controversy. Thus in the days of the early Church and of the early Byzantine Empire the theological foundations of Christianity were laid. By the ninth century the worst dangers – mainly disputes about the nature of the Trinity and of Christ – had been overcome; 'the Church of the seven General Councils' had emerged, firmly convinced of its sacred mission to preserve and spread the true faith.

In common with the rest of Christendom the theological heritage of the Orthodox Church was enshrined in the patristic writings and the canons of the oecumenical councils which interpreted the Scriptures and the liturgical tradition of the Church. The works of the Greek fathers, particularly of the fourth century, constantly shone out as a beacon to guide troubled churchmen through four centuries and more of perplexity and challenge. By the time that the iconoclast controversy was beginning to die down in the ninth century, orthodox teaching had been summed up, restated as it were, by the last of the Greek fathers, John of Damascus, in his *Fount of Knowledge.*

This culminated with an exposition of doctrine known as the *De fide orthodoxa,* which was used in a Latin translation in the West from the twelfth century onwards. It is often assumed of the Orthodox Church, as of the Byzantine Empire, that it 'preserved' rather than developed.

Far from it. Tradition, to be maintained, must develop as it is handed from generation to generation. Byzantium was a Christian Empire in the fullest sense; its passionate interest in theological discussion did not suddenly cease with the restoration of icon veneration and the absence of major theological controversy within its gates. At no period can it be said that Christianity was not a living issue, and Byzantine concern for it was accompanied by a full range of literary activity. The implications of orthodoxy left ample scope for discussion and development, as well as for controversy. Churchmen and laity alike applied their humanist outlook and classical background to the elucidation of the Scriptures and patristic writings.

Commentaries, and treatises on particular points, homilies of every kind were poured out by each generation. Byzantine theological interests varied. In the eleventh century under Symeon the New Theologian there was a marked development of that form of spirituality which was to come to its full flowering in the hesychast movement in the fourteenth century. Hesychasm raised a major theological controversy. The views of anti-hesychast and pro-hesychast are put forward respectively in the histories of Nicephoras Gregoras and John Cantacuzenus, and these one-time friends became so estranged that they could not even bear to speak to each other.

There were many conflicting currents and it is sometimes difficult to disentangle theological and political partisanship, but the movement, though open to misunderstanding, was in reality an integral part of orthodox spirituality. This fruitful development was closely connected with Mt. Athos and is indicative of the extent to which the living wood of Byzantium was now to be found in its Church and not in its political institutions,

There was another aspect to the theological vigilance of the Orthodox Church. The Christian tradition in all its fullness was to be enjoyed by the faithful, but in order to ensure this, it was necessary to keep watch lest heresy crept in. The Byzantine Church, like the Western Church, had to deal both with individuals who had been led astray, often inadvertently, and with popular movements which were far more difficult to eradicate, being widespread and due to a variety of causes. The Church certainly did not forbid the use of pagan authors, but it assumed that these would be read with discrimination.

It was easy for an adventurous or sceptical mind to overstep the bounds and find it was propounding views not in accordance with Christian teaching. Photius in an impish moment is even said to have put forward unorthodox statements to see if he could catch out a Patriarch who affected to do without intellectual weapons. Others, as Michael Psellus in the mid-eleventh century, at once retrieved a false step by a swift profession of orthodoxy. John Italus, an ardent student of Plato and Aristotle, who followed Psellus as professor of philosophy in the university of Constantinople, was not so adroit.

The story of his condemnation for heretical views and his public recantation from the pulpit of St. Sophia is related by Anna Comnena with somewhat smug satisfaction as yet another illustration of her father's care for orthodoxy. Italus' errors are anathematized in the Synodicon (a list of heresies to be abjured) which is read in Lent on Orthodoxy Sunday. He came to grief, it was held, because he failed to realize that classical literature provided intellectual discipline but not the Christian truth. To the end of its days Byzantium had trouble with its intellectuals, down to Gemisthus Plethon who reverted to out and out Platonism.

A more subtle danger lurked in the widespread heresy which threatened to undermine the whole position of the Church in certain areas. This movement was dualist in character, and perhaps originated in Asia Minor, long the home of such heretics as the Paulicians. In the tenth century a form of this dualist heresy developed in the Balkans. It took its name from its leader, the *pop* (i.e. priest) Bogomil. At this time

Bulgaria was in process of being absorbed into the Byzantine Empire and when its conquest was finally achieved under Basil II in the early eleventh century the insidious heresy crept into the very stronghold of orthodoxy. It was doubly dangerous in that it was not only an attack on Christian doctrine and the organization of the Christian Church but had social and economic and political implications.

In Bulgaria at any rate it was allied to anti-Byzantine feeling, and in addition was directed against the wealth of both lay and ecclesiastical landowners. The heresy was vigorously combated, particularly by the Comnenian Emperors working in close co-operation with the Church. But it was never entirely quenched in the Balkans. The Bogomils lingered on until the Turkish conquest and after, and their fantastically grotesque tombs may still be seen in Bosnia. The heresy is said to have affected Mt. Athos itself in the fourteenth century, but this charge may have been part of the anti-hesychast propaganda against the Holy Mountain.

In addition to watching over the religious life of their own household, Orthodox churchmen were aware of their responsibilities towards those of other creeds. Euthymius Zigabenus, at the request of the Emperor Alexius Comnenus, wrote a handbook exposing the religious errors of the major heresies, including the Jews and the Muslims. John of Damascus had regarded Mohammedanism as a Christian heresy; he was well-equipped to write a treatise against it, for he knew Arabic and his refutation could use the Koran at first hand.

Polemic against every form of heresy was in the competent hands of theologians, both lay and ecclesiastical, and was continually being turned out until the last days of the Empire. Other, and perhaps more fruitful, steps were also taken, in personal discussions which took place between bishops and rabbis, between Muslim and Christian, or between Armenian and Orthodox. As far as Islam went the honours were divided, for either side had its converts.

In fact when Archbishop Gregory Palamas was captured by the Ottomans in the mid-fourteenth century and took part in disputation with Muslims, he learnt that Islam was particularly proud of the numbers converted to its faith in Asia Minor. The really constructive missionary work of the Orthodox Church was done in its early days amongst its pagan neighbours, or further afield, when countless church-men toiled to convert Slav or Khazar. Some, like Cyril and Methodius, still enjoy a world-wide reputation for their work. But most remain anonymous, or, like the eleventh century John of Euchaita's uncle who worked in the Balkans, are only known by chance reference buried in a sermon or funeral oration. In missionary work of this kind the Church had a comparatively virgin field, very different from the situation when rival creeds had already hardened in the framework of an older civili-zation, or were perhaps a heretical offshoot of the Christian body itself, as the Nestorian and Monophysite churches.

The Orthodox Church took care to maintain its vigilance within the Empire and lost no opportunity of promoting its cause by public disputation or by published propaganda, and indeed by wars against the infidel, yet this did not preclude diplomatic relations or even the recognition of a rival way of life, particularly with eastern powers. Constantinople could regard Persia or the Saracens as powers which it could respect. An early tenth-century Patriarch of Constantinople even wrote to a Muslim ruler, 'As the two great luminaries of heaven outshine all others, so do the Saracens and the Romans, and so we should therefore live in friendship, in spite of our different ways of life and worship.' (Migne, *Patrologia Graeca* Vol. CXI, col. 28B.)

This may have the ring of diplomacy about it and sentiments of this kind did not prevent the outbreak of frequent wars; but arrange-ments were usually permitted which allowed visitors or merchants or mercenaries of another creed or rite their own place of worship. Thus the Latins had their own churches, in particular the Venetians and Genoese, who became numerous from the twelfth century onwards and acquired their own quarters in the City or across the Golden Horn. Even the distant English (of whom a number served in the imperial body-guard) could find something peculiarly their own in the church founded in Constantinople by a rich fellow-countryman at the end of the eleventh century, where lamps burnt at night before an icon of its two patron saints, St. Nicholas and St. Augustine of Canterbury.

Thus in practice there was a measure of toleration which official relations and the official attitude often conceal. There is a profundity and a warmth of feeling in the remark made by the two patricians from the capital in the story which tells of the finding of the Virgin's robe and its translation to Constantinople. For generations it had been handed down from virgin to virgin within a certain Jewish family. The travellers reached this Jewess's home in a little village in Galilee, and that night besought her to tell them the real reason for the divine power which dwelt in the house, saying, 'For our God and your God is one and the same God.' (See N. H. Baynes, *Byzantine Studies,* p. 247.) Words of this kind are a reminder that the Byzantines were not bigoted. Indeed a measure of toleration was often taken for granted and in no way lessened their devotion to orthodoxy.

The farmer or townsman, housewife or child, would not normally be engaged in polemic or with doctrinal developments, Though the maintenance of right doctrine concerned them as much as it did theologians or statesmen. Like monks and clergy, laity, whether scholars or craftsmen, were part of the body of the faithful, and it was the supreme concern of the Church to care for their spiritual life. Their special needs were provided for within the diocesan framework. Often monasteries and hermits supplemented the work of the secular clergy, but their activities were not part of the normal diocesan provision for parishioners.

The laity, no less than the newly converted, had to be instructed. From childhood upwards they were taught by their priests and by their bishop. It is clear from synodal rulings and other evidence that the clergy taught the Scriptures and otherwise educated young children, and if they were very troublesome they might give them a beating if they wished. It was the special responsibility of the bishop to preach both to his clergy and to the people. The Council in Trullo in 692 laid down that this was expected every Sunday, and if possible on weekdays as well. This obligation was evidently taken very seriously.

The Byzantines were most prolific sermon writers. Many of their homilies have survived. In them, 'the shepherd and pastor' of his flock would explain the meaning of various parts of the Bible, often expounding the patristic interpretation of a particular passage, or speaking of the liturgy and the other sacraments, or the special significance of a patronal festival. This duty was shared by all from the humblest parish priest to the Patriarch. And the Emperors themselves wrote sermons and delivered them before high ecclesiastics and imperial officials on special occasions, as at the beginning of Lent.

Profound understanding of the faith and a deep devotional life is reflected in many sermons, as well as in mystical writings. How far experience of this kind came to most men and women remains unknown. But all were bound together in a living fellowship by the sacraments. The Orthodox Christian was baptized into the Church, confirmed by the sacrament of the Holy Spirit and, when need be, purified by penance. He could understand in some measure the fullest meaning of the Christian life when he took part in the central act of public worship, the eucharist, or, as the Byzantines usually called it, 'the divine liturgy'.

Interior of Hagia Sophia, today as a Muslim museum

Art and theology, music and poetry, were integrated in the celebration of the liturgy. Byzantine artists expressed their awareness of the supernatural world by so representing Christ and the celestial hierarchy in mosaic or fresco on the dome and walls of their churches that the heavenly host seemed present with the faithful in the body of the building below. Byzantine music was closely linked to the words of the liturgy. As this service was enriched by the addition of canticles and hymns, so its music was developed. Liturgical poetry and its tunes grew more elaborate. (Recent research has succeeded in deciphering the different forms of medieval Byzantine notation. Versions of the living tradition may be heard in Greece, or closer at hand in the monastery of Grottaferrata near Rome.) They were often antiphonally divided between precentor and people and were interwoven between the lessons and psalms of the office or the different parts of the liturgy.

The version of the liturgy used in the Greek Church was that of Constantinople, i.e. it was based on the liturgy of St. Basil and of St. John Chrysostom. The liturgy began with that of the Catechumens, when the 'Little Entrance' was made with the singing of the 'Thrice-Holy', followed by the lessons and the sermon. Then came the liturgy of the Faithful, with prayers and the 'Great Entrance', the creed and the commemoration of the living and the dead. After this was the central act of the Holy Sacrifice. It is clear that the liturgy was celebrated frequently. Balsamon wrote that those trying to lead a pure life might communicate daily, whether cleric or layman, though this was not the normal rule.

The Church permeated the life of the people. Its blessing was sought on every form of activity. There were special rituals for blessing the fishing fleet or the harvest, cattle or houses, just as cities and shrines had their own special protectors among the saints, from the Mother of God, the patron of the City, to the humbler guardian angel to whom John of Euchaita dedicated one of his poems.

This desire, like the Byzantine reverence for the ascete, the holy man, was rooted in a belief in the power of intercession and a sense of the close ties between the seen and unseen worlds. Thus the more lowly aspects of human life were sanctified to their right use. Likewise the laity, no less than the monk or cleric, might enjoy the full membership of the Church which was the mystical body of Christ.

One of the best expositions of the meaning of this is found in the fourteenth century Nicholas Cabasilas' *On the Life in Christ.* As he says, it is not necessary to go into the desert to find this life, for it is implanted in every Christian by baptism and is fed by the other sacraments, particularly the divine liturgy.

The Life and Character of Mohammed

W. R. W. Stephens

Some said "He is a good man:" others said,
"Nay, but he deceiveth the people." – (John 7:12)

It will be my endeavor in this set of lectures to gather up the principal points of contrast between Christianity and Islam, the Bible and the Koran; between the religion founded by Jesus Christ and the religion founded by Mohammed – between the book which contains, as the Christian believes, the word of God; and the book which contains, as the Mussulman no less believes, the words of God conveyed through the mouth of His prophet.

I use the word contrast advisedly, in preference to the word comparison. The difference between the two terms is this:

- To contrast is to place two things, which have some resemblances to each other, side by side, in order to detect the points of unlikeness.

- To compare, on the other hand, is to place two things, which present some dissimilarity, side by side, in order to find out the points of likeness.

If two things are exactly alike, there is, strictly speaking, no comparison between them; they are practically identical. If, again, two things are utterly and totally unlike, they cannot fairly be contrasted.

It is possible, for instance, and may be instructive, to contrast a man with an ape, because amidst many differences there are some resemblances between the two animals.

But to contrast a man with a fish, or still more with some inanimate object, would be an idle task, because where nearly all is difference, there are no points to contrast.

The advantage, then, of contrasting is to bring out (where this is desirable) into prominent relief the differences between two objects which in some respects are similar. And I think that an investigation, by this method, of the vital differences between Christianity and Islam is not unprofitable in the present day. Up to at least the beginning of this [19th] century the character of Mohammed and of the work which he accomplished was unfairly depreciated.

In the pages of Prideaux, of Dr. White, and to some extent even of Gibbon, he is represented as a consciously designing and artful impostor, who pretended to be the recipient of divine revelations merely in order to facilitate his schemes of personal ambition.

This view of Mohammed's character has now been abandoned as untenable by all sound critics. But in the eagerness of a better informed and more enlightened age to redress the balance, the danger is that it may be overweighed in the opposite scale. The character of the great prophet of Arabia and of his religion will now no longer be underrated; the fear is lest by many they should be painted in colors too attractive.

It is difficult to doubt that other motives also, besides the praiseworthy desire of repairing past injustice, operate in the same direction.

This is not the time to minutely examine the causes which alienate many in the present day from the Christian faith. With some it may be the bewilderment of the understanding through the manifold difficulties supposed to be experienced in reconciling the discoveries of science or criticism with Holy Scripture; with others it may be that hardening of the spirit against the reception of spiritual doctrine, which is one natural consequence of spending life in the midst of material luxury; with others it may be the aversion of a selfish and impure heart from submission to the severe moral standard of the Gospel; with others it may be that tendency (natural in an age which has made great advances in knowledge) to independence and conceit, which is inclined to dispute the excellence or truth of most things which our forefathers believed and venerated; with others it may be a mixture of some, or all, of these causes.

A fact, however, it remains, that many, in proportion to their disposition to doubt or reject the Gospel of Christ, seem disposed to regard with some favor, even if they do not actually embrace diverse forms of philosophy or religion, a favor which to the careful and impartial student seems greatly in excess of the intrinsic merits of those systems. Simple Materialism, Pantheism, Positivism, Mohammedanism, Buddhism, even the gross and (one would have thought) palpable imposture of spirit-rapping [spiritualism], have found their advocates and patrons among men who fancy they discover insuperable difficulties in accepting the faith of Christ as it was once delivered to the saints.

Now, of all the systems here alluded to, Mohammedanism no doubt presents the nearest parallel to Christianity, both in its origin and progress.

Its beginnings are not lost in the mists of a remote and fabulous antiquity. It was founded, like Christianity, by one person: this person was at first rejected by his own people; gradually he gathered round him a small band of disciples; out of this germ the faith was propagated which in time won Arabia from idolatry, Persia from Magianism, and wrested some of the fairest provinces from Christendom itself. The sacred book, the Koran, might, in sublimity of language, and, to some extent, even in the purity of its teaching, theological and practical, bear comparison with the sacred writings of Jews and Christians.

Finally, the religion thus established has lasted for some 1,250 years, and at the present time [1875] maintains its sway over 120 millions or more of the human race. It is the only other religion besides Christianity which inspires its votaries with much proselytizing zeal; and in missionary success in some parts of the world, it surpasses its rival. It makes fresh advances every year in Africa, Austral[as]ia, and the interior of India which exceed the progress of Christianity in those countries.

Such are a few of the salient points of resemblance between Christianity and Islam. But my aim, as was remarked at the outset, is not to compare but to contrast; to discover the differences which underlie the resemblances, and to estimate their importance.

Let us begin, then, with the origin of the two religions, and consider the circumstances under which each was founded, and the character of the respective founders.

Mohammed

It was an observation of Machiavelli that no man could make himself a prince and found a kingdom without opportunities. What were the opportunities of Mohammed?

To begin with, what was the state of the world when Mohammed appeared? He was born in the year 570 A.D. The civilized world at that epoch was divided between the two great rival empires of [Byzantine] Rome and Persia. Almost incessant warfare was going on between them, and their boundaries were constantly fluctuating. Arabia, being on the confines of the rival powers, was subjugated, so far as the fierce independent spirit of the inhabitants permitted it to be subjugated at all, to each in turn. The religion of the Roman Empire was Christianity, but Christianity on the eastern frontier was distracted and corrupted by a variety of conflicting heresies, which disguised its essential character, and exhausted its vital energy.

As the extremities of the human body are the most quickly chilled, owing to their distance from the heart, as the fringe of a garment is the part most liable to be torn and stained, owing to its friction with other substances, so the pulse of national Roman life beat but feebly in the eastern extremities; the eastern fringes of the empire were constantly torn by dissension from the established religion, by revolt against the political government.

The associations of their old nationality were too strong for them. Neither the religion, nor the laws, nor customs of the Roman Empire had obtained a firm hold upon them. They were ecclesiastically addicted to heresy – politically addicted to rebellion.

The religion of Persia, whatever it may originally have been, had turned to dualism, or the worship of two co-ordinate powers: the spirit of good or light, Ormuzd; the spirit of evil or darkness, Ahriman. But the Sun being venerated as a symbol of the power of light, a superstitious worship of fire and of the heavenly bodies had practically superseded, to a great extent, the purer and more philosophic creed.

As the Arabs were alternately subject politically to their two powerful neighbors, so did they catch some sparks of the religious spirit prevalent in each. Christianity and Magianism each had their votaries in Arabia, and colonies of Jews had settled there more than 600 years before the birth of Mohammed. But the dominant creed of the Arabs was a kind of degenerate Monotheism, the corrupt offspring of the purer faith of their forefather Ishmael.

They believed in one Supreme Deity, but subordinate to Him was a host of inferior divine personages who were supplicated as intercessors. This mixed, mongrel religion had its national home and center in the sacred temple, the Kaaba, in the sacred city of Mecca.

Here was the holy black stone, the relic of an earlier temple built by Abraham and Ishmael, a relic, also, as was believed, of Paradise, where it was originally given to Adam. Once it had been white, but had changed its hue either from contact with sinful lips, or from the repeated kisses of the faithful. There was the print of Abraham's footstep; there was the holy spring, Zemzem, which had burst forth to save Hagar and Ishmael from perishing by thirst.

Thither the devout Arab came to worship the God of Abraham, but also to implore the succor of the 360 intercessory powers whose images were ranged within those sacred walls. Round those holy walls he walked seven times, naked, to signify the putting away of his sins. Seven times did he run to and fro between Mounts Safa and Merwa, to typify Hagar seeking water for her child; seven times did he throw stones into the valley of Mina, in memory of the stones which Abraham flung at the Devil, when disturbed by him in the act of offering up Ishmael; for in Arabian tradition it is Ishmael, not Isaac, who occupies the foremost place.

But, shortly before the rise of Mohammed, a spirit of profound dissatisfaction with the national religion had begun to work among the more reflective and discerning of his countrymen. In the introduction to one of the most ancient biographies of Mohammed there is a chapter inscribed 'an account of four men who without revelation perceived the error of idolatry.'

This is the substance of it. One day the Koreishites, the tribe which was the guardian of the Kaaba, were celebrating a solemn feast in honour of one of the lesser deities. They bowed the knee before the image, walked round it, and offered sacrifices with customary reverence. But four men secretly held aloof from these acts of devotion, and opened their hearts one to another.

'Verily,' said one, 'our tribe does not know the true religion. They have corrupted the faith of Abraham; they worship a stone and walk round about it, though it neither sees nor hears, and can neither do them good nor harm. Friends, let us seek the truth for ourselves, for verily we are not in the right path.'

So they parted and went hither and thither in quest of the pure faith of Abraham.

Of the four inquirers, two it is said became Christians; a third after the preaching of Mohammed embraced Islam, but ultimately he too, on going to Abyssinia, was converted to Christianity, and when he met any disciples of the prophet he was accustomed to say: 'We see, and you attempt to see.'

The fourth, Zayd by name, renounced and condemned all the gross superstitions of his countrymen, more especially the custom of sacrificing before images, and the horrible practice of female infanticide; but he remained in a skeptical condition of mind, ever longing, but never able, to come to the knowledge of the truth.

There is a pathetic story of him in his old age: how he was seen leaning with his back against the wall of the Kaaba, and he cried aloud: 'O, ye Koreishites! by Him in whose hands my soul is, none of you follow the religion of Abraham.' And he continued: 'O Lord, if I knew which form of worship is most acceptable to Thee, I would adopt it; but I do not know it.' Thus he spake, resting his forehead on the palms of his hands. He traveled through Mosul, Mesopotamia, and Syria, seeking repose for his troubled, anxious spirit. In the midst of his wanderings he heard of the growing fame of Mohammed. He started for Mecca, but was murdered on the way.

I have related this narrative, not as considering it in all its details deserving of much credence, but because its very existence, whether true or not, is a proof and illustration of a spirit of dissatisfaction and doubt prevalent at the time to which it refers.

To form any just estimate of the prophet of Arabia and of his work, it was necessary to indicate the conditions, political, social, and religious, of his country. To sum up, then, Arabia was on the edge of two great rival empires, both weakened by protracted and exhausting contests. The crisis of the struggle, indeed, was contemporaneous with the preaching of Mohammed.

Heraclius the Roman Emperor overthrew the Persian power in 629. The Roman Empire was itself weakened in the border provinces by this exertion; the Persian Empire never recovered. The Arabs had been partially subject to one or other power, but never absorbed politically or religiously by either. Gross superstition and licentiousness prevailed, but a spirit of discontent and skepticism was at work. There was no national unity. Each tribe was a separate independent atom.

The opportunity, then, was favorable for the action of some master mind which should first of all weld the jarring elements of life in Arabia itself into a compact body; then proceed to annex to it the great neighboring Empire of Persia, already prostrate by its rival; and finally to subdue the weakened fringes of that very rival, the Roman Empire.

And this was the work of Mohammed. By bringing men to believe in himself as a divinely inspired prophet, he established a theocracy wherever that belief was accepted; he united his followers under a political and religious system all in one, for the Koran was to them alike their code of civil law and their oracle of theological truth.

Having now examined the nature of the field in which the prophet of Arabia planted his creed, we will turn for a few minutes to the contemplation of the man himself, from the soil to the sower and to the manner in which the seed were sown.

Mohammed as a Person

The sketch must of necessity be compressed, but I will try not to omit any incidents of real importance.

Who, then, was Mohammed? Mohammed, the son of Abdallah, and the grandson of Abd-al Muttallib, belonged to the tribe of the

Koreish, the guardians of the Kaaba, and to the family of Hashem, the most honorable family within that tribe.

His father died a short time before his birth. His mother was of a nervous and superstitious temperament. She fancied that about the time of the child's birth she was surrounded by an extraordinary halo of light; and it may have been partly owing to this circumstance that he was named by his grandfather, Mohammed, or "the Renowned." This meaning of the word should be remembered, since it was afterwards turned, as will be seen, to curious account. For the sake of convenience, I follow the more usual European form of the name, and write it Mohammed.

The birth took place at Mecca, on or about August 20, 570 A.D. The child was nursed according to Meccan custom, not by his mother, but by a Bedouin woman, and was reared by her in the desert. When four years old, he had the first of those epileptic fits to which he was liable during all the earlier half of his life.

Such fits were regarded with superstitious awe by the Arabs, as the supposed effects of diabolical possession, and, on the recurrence of an attack when he was five years old, the Bedouin nurse took the young Mohammed back to his mother, and could not be persuaded to resume her charge.

His mother died when he was six, and his grandfather when he was eight; but he was carefully and kindly brought up by his uncle, Abu Talib, for the duties of a kinsman were scrupulously observed among the Arabs. When he was twelve years old, he accompanied his uncle on a caravan journey to Syria. The story that near Bostra, he made the acquaintance of a Christian monk, tarried with him, and returned under his charge to Mecca, may be true; but it occurs in the midst of such strange tales of incredible wonders that it cannot be accepted as a certain fact.

How much of Mohammed's acquaintance with the Gospel history may have been due to this connection, supposing such to have been formed, it is easy to surmise, but impossible in the absence of information to determine. Much more may probably have been learned at the great annual fair held at Ocatz, three days' journey from Mecca, during the sacred month before the pilgrimage to the Kaaba.

Here a mixed concourse of Arabs, Christian and Jewish, as well as Pagan, assembled, partly for trade, partly for amusement, partly to engage in poetical and martial contests for prizes. Here, according to tradition, Mohammed heard Coss, Bishop of Najran, preach on the great facts and doctrines of the Gospel. Here his poetical imagination and patriotic spirit may have been stimulated; here he may have first conceived the ideal of a religion which should combine truths extracted from many diverse sources.

Time went on, and Mohammed became entitled to the enjoyment of a small patrimony, consisting of a house, five camels, a flock of sheep, and a slave.

He showed little aptitude for practical business, but was fond of the quiet and innocent occupation of tending sheep, in which he was afterwards wont to compare his early life with the lives of Moses and of David.

When twenty-five years old, however, he was entrusted, through his uncle's recommendation, with the conduct of a caravan to Damascus, the property of the wealthy widow Khadijah. He discharged his errand to the complete satisfaction of his employer, who rewarded him with her hand in marriage. She was fifteen years older than her husband; but he remained thoroughly faithful to her, and did not wed another until after her death.

Mohammed searches for God

For fifteen years after his marriage – that is, up to the age of forty – Mohammed worshipped the gods of his fathers, but he became increasingly meditative, restless, dejected. He was courteous in company, but spoke little, and with downcast eyes. Gradually he withdrew altogether from worldly business, save such pastoral occupation as milking the goats, or tending the sheep. He spent much time in fasting and prayer in his favorite retreat, a cave on the bare and rugged side of Mount Hira, occasionally even being absent from home all night.

His mind became agitated by doubts respecting the truth of the religion of his forefathers. His seasons of seclusion were more frequent, more prolonged. He renounced the customs which savored of idolatry.

There are several short chapters in the Koran which probably belong to this period. They read like the expression of an earnest, anxious, inquiring spirit, which has grasped some truths, and is searching for more. The vanity of worldly ambition; the sin of covetousness and slander; the inseparable connection between happiness and virtue, misery and vice; the error of supposing that adversity is always a sign of God's displeasure, or prosperity of His favor; the duty of providing for the fatherless, and of almsgiving; the certainty of future rewards and punishments, according to each man's deeds – these are doctrines insisted upon with the earnestness of profound conviction, mingled with prayers for further enlightenment and guidance (Suras 103, 100, 99 and 1).

He was wrought to a high pitch of mental tension, and felt constrained to preach, but he had no commission; he could not point to any credentials to enforce the authority of his messages. By some, indeed, he was respected as a poet or a genius; but by others he was scorned and derided as a soothsayer, a madman, a fool. He began himself to doubt what he was, a prophet or a Kahin, inspired by God or by an evil spirit.

His wife, his cousin Waraca, and a few other intimate friends believed in his divine inspiration. Such pure conceptions of the Deity, and such a lofty standard of moral teaching and moral conduct, could not, they thought, be the offspring of diabolical influence.

When he was yet in the agony of suspense and depression, sometimes even meditating self-destruction, light pierced the clouds. As he was wandering among the solitudes of Mount Hira, he beheld within two bows' length the dazzling figure of the angel Gabriel, and listened with rapture to the memorable command:

'Cry, cry aloud in the name of the Lord; the most merciful God who hath taught the use of the pen to record revelation.' (Sura 96)

Mohammed hastened home, solaced and encouraged by the assurance that the long-desired commission from on high had come;

but for some period, of which the length is uncertain, it was unheeded by all.

At last, as he lay one day on the ground, recovering from one of his fits, and wrapped up in a mantle, he again heard the voice of the heavenly messenger uttering the words:

'O thou that art covered with a mantle arise, and preach and magnify the Lord, and depart from all uncleanness.' (Sura 74)

Mohammed the persecuted prophet

This is the real starting point of Islam. From this date Mohammed's confidence in himself as the accredited messenger of God never wavers, and all the utterances of the Koran are introduced by the words 'speak,' or 'say,' to intimate that they were put into the mouth of the prophet by his Divine Master.

The people, indeed, still demanded some visible evidence of his authority. Let him cause a spring of water to gush forth, or a grove of palms to rise in the desert, or let him ascend to heaven and bring down a book, and they would believe him. But these skeptical taunts no longer harassed the prophet's mind. He could proudly and calmly reply that he was but a man, not empowered to work miracles, but that the divine beauty of his message was its own evidence.

It came from God; and, if men did not listen to it, destruction would as surely overtake them as it overtook the cities in the plain [Sodom and Gomorrah].

The work of conversion, however, was slow in its progress. In the course of three years Mohammed had gained about forty disciples, consisting chiefly of his own relations, friends, and dependents. As in the early days of Christianity, so in the early days also of Islam, many converts were obtained from the slave class. The slaves in Arabia were most susceptible of conversion, not only from their position, but also because, being for the most part foreigners, many of them had received a tincture in early life of Jewish or Christian teaching, which rendered them at least averse from idolatrous superstitions. But, as Mohammed's influence increased, jealousy and alarm began to be awakened in the tribe of the Koreish.

They were the guardians of the sacred temple, and this heretical son was beginning to shake the fidelity of his countrymen to the ancestral faith, of which that temple was the visible shrine. Some of Mohammed's followers had retired for prayer one day to a valley near Mecca, when a party of unbelieving neighbors unexpectedly passed by. Taunts and retorts led to blows. Saad, one of Mohammed's party, struck an opponent with a camel goad; and this, it was commonly said, was the first blood shed in Islam.

Meanwhile Mohammed waxed bolder

He took up his abode in the house of a convert, named Arcam, close by the Kaaba, and there he preached, especially at the time of pilgrimage, to all who would resort to him, and seldom without some success. The house of Arcam was the cradle of Islam, as the 'Upper Chamber' in Jerusalem was the cradle of Christianity. The burden of Mohammed's message was the same to all: the absolute unity of God; the authority of His prophet; the moral duties of prayer, almsgiving, and fasting; the certainty of a future state of happiness or woe.

The hostility of the Koreish grew more fierce. They seized the converted slaves, and tried to force them to recantation by imprisonment, or exposure to the scorching midday sun, and without food or drink upon the gravel of the Meccan valley. Many yielded under repeated application of this torture, but there were others whose constancy was inflexible. No words could be wrung from the slave Bilal in his agony, but 'Ahad! Ahad! one, one only God.'

Mohammed himself was secure under the protection of his uncle Abu Talib. Abu Talib was not a believer in his nephew's mission, but the sacred duty of the kinsman prevailed over all other considerations. 'Beware of killing him,' he said to the leaders of the hostile movement; 'if ye do, verily I shall slay the chiefest among you in his stead.'

For his disciples Mohammed devised a safer means of escape from persecution and possible perversion. By his advice a small party of them sought an asylum in the Christian kingdom of Abyssinia, and their hospitable reception encouraged a larger body to follow their example the year after. This Hegira, or flight to Abyssinia, stands in relation to Islam as the flight of our infant Saviour into Egypt stands to Christianity. It saved the new religion from being crushed in its infancy; and the success of the plan possibly suggested the great Hegira, or migration to Medina some years later. The departure of his converts, however, oppressed Mohammed with a sense of loneliness and isolation, under which his spirits and faith seem for a short time to have given way.

Amidst some conflict of evidence, something like an inclination to make terms with his opponents seems discoverable. He appears to have uttered words which sounded at least like a concession of some intercessory power to the subordinate deities. But the lapse was of short duration; he was probably soon refreshed by good tidings from Abyssinia (like St. Paul, in his loneliness at Corinth, by the good news which Timothy brought from Thessalonica), and the tone of the Koran waxes louder and sterner than ever, in its denunciation of idolatrous worship. 'Why,' it is scornfully asked, 'implore help from images which have no power to move even the husk of a date-stone?'

The malignity, however, of the Koreish increased in proportion. They tried again to induce Abu Talib to abandon his nephew. The uncle remonstrated with Mohammed for his obstinate persistence in heresy. 'If they brought the sun to my right hand and the moon to my left,' replied the nephew, 'to force me from my undertaking, I would not desist from it until the Lord made manifest my cause, or I perished in the attempt.' But, while inflexible in his purpose, the thought of desertion by his kind protector overcame his feelings, and he burst into tears. The heart of Abu Talib also melted. 'Come back,' he said, 'son of my brother,' as Mohammed had turned to depart; 'I go in peace, and say whatsoever thou wilt, for by the Lord I will not in any wise give thee up for ever.'

The Koreish were now thoroughly alarmed, and, to complete their discomfiture, two new converts were won by Mohammed – Hamza and Omar, men of high position, ability, and influence. Omar had formerly been among his bitterest adversaries.

As a last resource the Koreish placed the whole family of Hashem under a ban. The solemn deed of excommunication was hung up in the Kaaba. The Hashemites were assigned an isolated quarter in the suburbs, and all intercourse with them was strictly forbidden. They managed, indeed, to get provisions in by stealth, but were often reduced to great straits for food. The spirit, however, of Mohammed faltered not. At the season of the pilgrimage to the Kaaba, he would boldly enter the precincts and preach, promising temporal dominion and future paradise to all who would become his disciples. But his day was not come, and the people jeered.

The blockade lasted three years (616-619 A D.). At length some of Mohammed's friends heard that the parchment on which the deed of excommunication was written had been almost devoured by insects. An examination of the document proved the truth of the report. It was represented to the Koreish as a divine judgment cancelling their un-brotherly act. Some of the Koreish relented, and five of their chief men let the Hashemites out of durance, and made themselves responsible for their safety.

Fresh troubles, however, were in store for Mohammed. His wise and loving wife Khadijah died, and very soon afterwards his faithful protector, his uncle Abu Talib. Another uncle, also an unbe-liever, but with a feebler sense of the duties of a kinsman, promised him protection; but it did not last long, and the situation of Mohammed was again critical.

But new light began to dawn from Medina. Powerful Jewish tribes dwelt there, and in their contentions with Arab neighbors they were wont to say: 'A great prophet shall one day rise among us; him shall we follow, and then we shall overcome you.' Some pilgrims from Medina were attracted by the preaching of Mohammed at Mecca. They said among themselves: 'This surely is the prophet with whom the Jews threaten us; let us then be the first to follow him.' They declared to Mohammed their conviction of the truth of his claims: they promised to enlist their fellow tribesmen in his cause, and to report progress to Mohammed at the next pilgrimage. (The dramatic details of this account by Ibn Ishac may not be trustworthy, but they forcibly illustrate feelings which most probably were realities.)

A year of anxiety and suspense wore away, and in the spring of 621 A. D. the pilgrims came again. At an appointed spot, the secluded glen [valley] of Akaba near Mina, Mohammed sought his friends, and to his relief was greeted by twelve men, disciples, who plighted their faith to him in the simple formula: 'We will not worship any but the one God; we will not steal, nor commit adultery, nor kill our young children; neither will we slander in any wise, and we will not disobey the prophet in anything that is right.' The pilgrims departed, and Mohammed returned to Mecca.

He still patiently waited his opportunity for decisive action, but the Koran begins to take a wider scope, a sterner, a more defiant tone. The contest between Heraclius and Persia was coming to a crisis; the Koran confidently predicts the triumph of the Roman Emperor (Sura 30).

Vengeance is declared as imminent to those who will not believe (Sura 21); a dearth at Mecca is interpreted as a judgment on unbelief, and a call to repentance. Solemn imprecations are invoked by the prophet on himself if the Koran be not a true revelation (suras 23, 69).

And now another pilgrimage came around 622 A.D., another meeting in the lonely glen. It was an hour before midnight when Mohammed waited there in a flutter of hope. Presently by twos and threes his converts might be seen stealing from behind the dark rocks into the moonlight, until Mohammed beheld a muster of seventy-three devoted believers in his mission. They spoke in low tones for fear of spies. 'Stretch out thy hand, O Mohammed,' said Bara, the aged chief of the party, and he stretched it out, and Bara struck his own upon it, as the manner was when one took an oath of fidelity to another, and all the rest did the like. Mohammed chose out twelve of the chief men, saying: 'Moses chose twelve leaders from among his people. Ye shall be sureties for the rest as were the Apostles of Jesus, and I will be surety for my own people.' And all answered, 'So be it.' Thus was ratified the second pledge of Akaba.

And now Mohammed felt that the hour was come. The memorable command was issued to his disciples in Mecca: ' Depart unto Medina, for the Lord hath given you brethren and a home in that city.' Gradually the believers stole away. The Koreish were startled day by day to see house after house deserted. In about two months none remained in Mecca except the prophet himself, his faithful friend Abu Bakr, and his nephew Ali.

Abu Bakr urged flight, but Mohammed delayed; 'the command,' he said, 'had not yet come from the Lord.' Abu Bakr, however, was determined to be ready when it did come. Two swift camels were bought, and kept tied and highly fed in the yard of his house. A private hoard of money was concealed about his person. The Koreish meanwhile were known to be plotting mischief, and at last Mohammed declared that the decisive hour had arrived.

He and Abu Bakr stole away by night, and took refuge in a cave on Mount Thaur, a few miles to the south of Mecca, in order to delude their pursuers, Medina being 250 miles to the north. As they were crouching in the cave, Abu Bakr looking up saw light through a crack in the rock. 'What if the enemy were to spy us out!' he exclaimed; 'we are but two.' 'There is a third,' replied the dauntless prophet, 'God Himself.'

A goat-herd in the employ of Abu Bakr brought them supplies of milk, and on the third day they were informed that the Koreish had abandoned the search after them as fruitless. The daughter of Abu Bakr brought them the two swift camels, and a guide. Mohammed mounted the swifter of the two, Al Caswa, thenceforward his favorite, and with his friend reached Medina in safety in June 622 A.D., where he was greeted with honour by his new allies, and congratulations by his old disciples.

Success and Mohammed

The Hegira is the epoch in the prophet's career from which his worldly success dates, but it marks the beginning also of a grave deterioration in his moral character. The earnest preacher of a pure theology and a strict righteousness, undaunted in the day of his weakness and danger, becomes in the day of his power a fanatical despot, and is at times cruel with the cruelty peculiar to fanaticism. The single aim of propagating his faith overrides at times all considerations of justice and mercy, and it is often hard to draw the line between religious zeal and personal ambition.

After the flight to Medina the Koran is pitched in a tone of pitiless animosity against the unbelieving Koreish, and the severity of its utterances was matched by deeds of corresponding violence. The prophet would lead the prayers in the mosque, and then conduct a predatory raid upon some caravan of the miscreant tribe.

He became a polygamous pope, and the mosque was his St. Peter's and the Vatican in one. Here he preached, here he received embassies, here he planned his campaigns. The Koran, about the fifth year of the Hegira, becomes little better than a military gazette. It announces victories, bestows commendation on their valiant, and incites to further deeds of prowess.

A fresh revelation was produced to meet every emergency, removing all obstacles to the advance of the faithful which might arise from a too scrupulous deference to ancient customs, or even to the principles of common humanity and justice. By special divine permission, the sanctity of the month Rajan was violated, which from immemorial antiquity in Arabia, had been consecrated to peace (Sura 2); by special permission captives were executed (Sura 47, 48). Obnoxious unbelievers in Medina were assassinated with the connivance, if not by the command of the prophet, and a blessing was publicly pronounced in the mosque by himself on the assassins.

By special revelation, the destruction of some date trees, which interfered with some military operation of the prophet's, was authorized. By special revelation the marriage of the prophet with another man's wife was sanctioned, and he was exempted from confining himself to four wives, the limit placed by himself on the polygamy of his disciples.

The deeds of cruelty which darkened the career of Mohammed at Medina culminated in the cold-blooded massacre of all the men belonging to a hostile Jewish tribe, the Bani Coreitza, and the subjugation of all the women to slavery. To cite the words of Gibbon: 'Seven hundred Jews were dragged in chains to the marketplace of the city, they descended alive into the grave prepared for their execution and burial, and the apostle beheld with an inflexible eye the slaughter of his helpless enemies.'

In spite of these repulsive cruelties few will refrain from a feeling of sympathy with the prophet, when the dream of his life was accomplished and his beloved and native city Mecca opened her gates to him. Few will refrain from admiration as they contemplate him gravely and majestically pointing with his staff to the idols which lined the walls of the Kaaba, commanding their destruction one by one, and exclaiming as the largest fell with a crash: 'Truth has come, and falsehood vanishes away.'

Few can contemplate without interest mingled with awe, the last days and dying moments of the man who had achieved so great and wonderful a work. Two years only after his reception at Mecca, in the sixty-third year of his age, he was smitten with a mortal fever. He anticipated his end: 'The choice hath been offered me,' he said, 'of longer life, with Paradise hereafter, or of meeting my Lord at once; I have chosen to meet my Lord.' He crawled from his bed one night to select a spot for his burial.

For several days he still conducted, but with feeble and fainting strength, the public prayers in the mosque. At last he transferred this duty to his faithful friend Abu Bakr. Yet once more there was a flash of vital energy; he even mounted the pulpit, and, in tones which reached far beyond the outer doors, he called upon the people, like Samuel, to witness that he had not defrauded any, nor taught anything but what God had put in his mouth. This final exertion probably hastened his death. He returned to his bed; he knew the end was near. 'Oh Lord, I beseech Thee assist me in the agonies of death,' he was heard to murmur; and presently in broken whispers, 'Lord pardon my sins .... eternity in Paradise ... pardon, yes! I come .... among my fellow citizens on High.' These were the last words of the prophet of Arabia.

Mohammed contrasted with Jesus

The contrast between the origin of Christianity and Islam is made perhaps sufficiently plain by such a sketch even as I have attempted of the career of Mohammed.

Yet it may be instructive to complete and clench this contrast by summing up a few salient points.

The Human Mohammed or the Superhuman Jesus

Contrast then, first of all, the essentially human character of the career of the founder of Islam with the essentially superhuman character of the life of the Founder of Christianity.

Mohammed did not lay claim to the power of working miracles; such as have been ascribed to him bear on the very face of them the marks of being the dress with which the real personality has been clothed by the adoration of a later age. Strip it off, and the true man stands out clear, consistent, and intelligible. You see a bold reformer who in early life rises to the conception of a purer theology and morality than the mass of his countrymen, who gradually persuades himself that he is the depositary of divine revelations, commissioned to unite the manifold and conflicting elements of national life under one simple rigid religious system. There is nothing miraculous in his career, except so far as all genius rises above the ordinary level of character, and produces extraordinary effects.

But in the life of our blessed Lord, the superhuman is of its essence. His birth is superhumanly announced, superhumanly effected. 'He came by a new and living way!' (Heb. 10:20). Prophecy upon prophecy, uttered ages before His coming, are fulfilled in the circumstances of His life, even to the most minute particulars. Superhuman He is in deed and in speech every day, although inexpressibly lowly in manner of life. Superhuman He is above all in the hour of death and in the resurrection from the grave. And these circumstances do not belong to the accidents, but to the essence, of the life. Take them away, especially, for instance, the Incarnation and the Resurrection, and the whole fabric of the life, so to say, falls to pieces.

We cannot deal with the history of that life as we can with the history of Mohammed or of Christian saints, round whom a parasitical growth of the miraculous has accumulated, concealing the real shape beneath. We cannot expunge the miraculous from the life of Jesus, and leave a consistent and intelligible residuum.

The experiment has been tried, but it breaks down. The rationalizing process which would divest our Lord's life of the miraculous, brings out an irrational result. It leaves us a hazy and shadowy figure, totally inadequate to stand for the founder of a religion which has produced such results as the Rationalist is constrained to admit that Christianity has produced. The phenomena of Christianity remain, but without an explanation. They hang, as it were, in the air, without a foundation to support them.

Self-aggrandizement or self-depreciation?

Take another point: the moral declension of Mohammed, parallel with the advance of his career. The period when he stands on the highest moral level is early in life. The meditative, musing, retiring shepherd lad, pondering amidst the solitude of his native hills, feeling his way to a purer theology and higher morality than his forefathers, then racked by doubts and fears concerning his mission, then, when convinced of it, calmly and tenaciously adhering to his aim, amidst persecution and distress, this is an interesting, an elevating, and beautiful picture to look at. But of the pure, innocent, kindly youth, very much is effaced in the picture of mingled fanaticism and sensuality which Mohammed presents to us in later years.

It is perfectly true that he retained, to the last, many of the simple, frugal habits which were characteristic of his earlier life. To the last he loved to tend the flock and to milk the goats. He was playful and tender in his treatment of children and of his intimate friends. Neither in dress, nor in fare, nor the appointments of his house, did he affect any of the luxury and splendor of an Oriental despot. But the retention of these innocent customs cannot redeem his character from the stains of sensuality and cruelty occasionally very great. Facts are stubborn things, and facts are conclusive on these points. The best excuse for these blots is that Mohammed became fanatic, and that fanaticism unhinges both the mental and moral equilibrium. To the fanatic the end is everything, and he relentlessly pursues it, without misgivings and without remorse. His moral sense at last becomes so confused and perverted that he gets to think whatever he does in promotion of his one great end must be right.

How far fanaticism itself, or at least the tendency to it, may be due to peculiarities of physical temperament is too deep and complicated a subject to enter upon here. It belongs, indeed, rather to the physiologist than to the historian. It will suffice to remark that in the case of Mohammed there were certainly many symptoms common to his epileptical or hysterical fits, and to his fits of supposed inspiration. Both were generally preceded by great depression of spirits, and accompanied by a cold perspiration, a tinkling or humming noise in the ears, a twitching of the lips, stertorous breathing, and convulsive movements of all the limbs, at times communicated by a kind of electric sympathy even to the camel on which he rode.

The Dervish and Fakir testify to the common Oriental notion that a kind of frenzy or ecstasy must be the natural concomitant of the reception of divine revelation.

The most essential mark of high Christian character is enthusiasm, deep, fervent indeed and intense, but sober in its manifestation. This is only the faint reflex where it is found, of the character of the founder of Christianity. A calm, consistent enthusiasm, to be about His Heavenly Father's business, and to finish the work which was given him to do, constitutes the divine, the matchless beauty of that life. Serenely, he moves on, neither with fanatical haste, nor stoical resolution, but in the unwavering enthusiasm of love to His appointed end – the cross on Calvary, the triumph over death and sin, the accepted sacrifice, the return to the place whence He came. The earthly life rises in grandeur, majesty, and beauty as it advances, not because it is not faultless at the beginning, but because, as it approaches the consummation of the great act to which all the prelude has been working up, it naturally takes a deeper, a more awful tone. It is in the final scene that the superhuman character of the great Actor and of the great tragedy itself, as well as the clear perception of its momentous consequences on the human race, is most deeply impressed upon us. Then it is more than ever that we bow our heads, and exclaim with the centurion: 'Truly this was the Son of God.' (The popular 'Life of Jesus Christ,' by Dr. Farrar, seems, in our humble judgment, to labor under a fatal defect in failing to bring out this upward, onward, continuous movement; it presents a series of brilliant pictures, instead of presenting one great picture.)

Selfish worldly victory or altruistic spiritual victory

Take another point. In the beginning of his career Mohammed was a preacher of righteousness and of the unity of God, regardless of opposition and danger. He relied simply, on the intrinsic merits of his message to make its own way. But, as time went on, he appealed to the pride, ambition, and love of enterprise and plunder inherent in the Arab to promote the propagation of this faith.

War, the natural occupation of the Arab, became invested with a sacred character. Religious zeal and military ardor coalesced in the followers of Mohammed to a degree not equalled in the Scotch Covenanters, or the Ironsides of Cromwell. The joys of paradise were dangled before the eyes of the Mohammedan warrior as an incitement to his valor; the horrors of hell were ever urged as a deterrent from faint-heartedness and sloth. In Mohammed's first encounter with the Roman army, one of his soldiers complained of the intolerable heat. 'Hell is much hotter,' was the indignant reply of the apostle.

His flight to Medina was a direct renunciation of purely moral and spiritual influence in favor of more material and carnal aids.

His entrance into Medina savors more of the political than religious leader. The chief men of the town went out to meet him, and conducted him into it with pomp, riding by his side, and arrayed in glittering armor. The disciples of Mohammed have from that day to this relied largely upon force for the propagation of the faith.

Diametrically opposite to this was the method of the Founder of the Christian religion. The opportunity of His coming was favorable for the assertion of pretensions to temporal dominion. The Jews were fretting under the yoke of foreign conquerors. The least spark would have sufficed to kindle the flame of insurrection. They had persuaded themselves that their Messiah would appear as the champion of their freedom, to restore their long-lost national independence, and to extend the dominion and glory of their empire far beyond the limits reached in the golden days of King Solomon.

The Apostles, even, and familiar friends of Jesus, were affected with this material view of the Messiah's kingdom. We see it in the request of St. James and St. John to sit 'the one on His right hand, the other on His left, in His kingdom.' We see it again in the observation of the two disciples walking to Emmaus: 'We trusted that it had been He which should have redeemed Israel,' implying that His death on the cross was in their view the final frustration of the national hopes. We see it for the last time in the question of the Apostles after the Resurrection: 'Lord, wilt Thou at this time restore the kingdom to Israel?' It was the steadfast opposition offered by Christ to this view of His kingdom, coupled with His searching exposure of national sins, which, humanly speaking, cost Him His life.

Had He ever acceded to the Devil's suggestion to command stones to become bread in the sense of using His divine power to obtain material and earthly advantages, or had He yielded to that other temptation to fall down and worship Satan as the price of earthly kingdoms – that is, had He resorted to artifice, to intrigue, to violence – it is plain that He would have been supported by the Jews, and that a worldly kingdom might have been His.

Into such snares of the Devil the founder of Islam fell. The power of Mohammedanism as one of the religions of the world dates from the day when Mohammed, flying from his enemies, was received by his partisans at Medina with all the honors of a worldly prince.

The power of the Gospel dates from the day when its Founder surrendered Himself to His enemies saying; 'If ye seek Jesus of Nazareth, I am He,' when He refused to summon legions of angels to His rescue, and was abandoned by all His earthly friends.

The power of Islam dates from an appeal to the sword of the flesh; the power of Christianity dates from the day when Christ bade His disciple put up the sword into his sheath, because 'all they that took the sword should perish by the sword.'

In the steady decay of all countries under Moslem rule we see the fulfillment of that prophecy. The immediate strength of Mohammedanism is that which ultimately everywhere becomes its weakness – its appeal to material aids for extension and support, its appeal in some degree also to the material and sensual rather than to the spiritual element in the nature of the convert.

Mohammed the Arab and Jesus the Universal

Lastly, the character of Mohammed, however much, owing to the elevation of his genius, it rises above the ordinary type of his countrymen, is yet as a whole thoroughly Oriental, thoroughly Arabian. Oriental dreaminess, Oriental frenzy, Oriental endurance and fortitude,

Oriental sensuality, Oriental despotism, Arabian enterprise, Arabian vindictiveness, Arabian subtlety, all have their place along with higher and nobler qualities in the composition of the great prophet's character.

The pure character of the Founder of Christianity does not bear the mark of any nationality. It was constructed, as has been beautifully said,

> ... at the confluence of three races, the Jewish, the Roman, and the Greek, each of which had strong national peculiarities of its own. A single touch, a single taint of any one of those peculiarities, and the character would have been national, not universal; transient, not eternal. It might have been the highest character in history, but it would have been disqualified for being the ideal. Supposing it to have been human, whether it were the effort of a real man to attain moral excellence or a moral imagination of the writers of the Gospels, the chances were infinite against its escaping any tincture of the fanaticism, formalism, and exclusiveness of the Jew, of the political pride of the Roman, of the intellectual pride of the Greek. Yet it has entirely escaped them all.[1]

Most true words! To those who would fain expunge the miraculous from the life of Jesus we may well reply there is one miracle which we defy you to remove, and that is the character of Jesus himself. In the literal senses of the expression, 'in Christ Jesus there is neither male nor female, Jew nor Greek, Barbarian or Scythian, bond nor free.' He was the Son of Man because His character was not the offspring of any one race, or caste, or class of men; and we may say boldly that no one could be such a Son of Man unless He was also what Jesus declared Himself to be, the Son of God.

---

[1] 'Lectures on the Study of History,' by Professor Goldwin Smith, p. 137.

The Theology of the Bible and that of the Koran [Qu'ran]

W. R. W. Stephens

"Thou hast created us for Thyself, and our heart is not quiet until it rests in Thee." – Augustine, Confessions I,i.

Before attempting to draw out the contrasts between the teaching of the Bible and that of the Koran, it may be instructive to notice the differences between the two in their outward form; in construction and style.

The Bible: many styles, but one purpose

What we call 'the Bible,' is in fact a collection of many books. The common use of the word Bible to designate the sacred volume dates, I believe, from the thirteenth century; and we still very often speak of the 'Sacred writings,' the 'Holy Scriptures,' terms which in the earliest ages of the Church were almost exclusively employed. But the name Bible, 'the Book,' has become the most familiar, and is perhaps the most precious to us, not only as implying the sovereign supremacy of that book over all other books, but also because it expresses the great truth that although 'the Book' be made up of many parts uttered at 'sundry times and in divers manners' (Heb. 1:1), yet its is after all essentially one, inasmuch as the thread of one divine purpose and design runs through the whole.

The writings range over a vast space of time, and are cast into a variety of forms – the plain prose of narrative, the poetry of prophecy or praise, the direct teaching of precepts, of exhortation, of reproof, or the more indirect of parable, allegory, or vision. But the ultimate aim of each and all is the same – to conduct men along the stream of God's truth winding its way to the Gospel, as the last and fullest revelation of His love, and to lead them to fall down before Jesus Christ and Him crucified, as the central figure in that final dispensation.

One consequence of the writings which compose the Bible being cast into such manifold shapes is that the Book becomes in a manner 'all things to all men' (1 Cor. 9:22). It fits into every fold, so to say, of the human mind and the human heart. It can speak to 'all nations, kindreds, and tongues' (Rev. 7:9), and win converts from all.

The Koran: one author, but lacks plot development

In the Bible, then, there is singleness of aim, but variety of expression. In the Koran, on the contrary, there is no continuity of design, but great uniformity in expression. On the one hand it is fragmentary and incoherent; on the other monotonous and level.

Page of a Koran manuscript Sura (Chapter)

The Koran consists of 114 chapters or Suras, each of which pretends to be a verbatim copy of a distinct revelation made to Mohammed. The revelations were written on palm leaves or mutton blade-bones, as Mohammed recited them to his disciples, and were after his death collected into one volume, but without the least regard to chronological order, first by his great friend and immediate successor, Abu Bakr, and afterwards by the Caliph Othman.

There is not much more connection between them than between the several grains in a heap of sand, or the several beads on a necklace. There is in the Koran no movement onwards, as in the Bible, from a definite starting point to a definite goal in the history of God's dealings with man. There is no sequence, no coherence between the parts. The perusal, therefore, may be compared, not to the unrolling of a scroll, but to the picking up of scattered leaves, on each of which some distinct oracle is inscribed.

But while there is no continuity, there is, on the other hand, very little variety. Approximate chronological arrangements of the several Suras have been made by Sir W. Muir and others, based on a careful comparison of their contents and style; and from this some variations in their character may be discovered, corresponding with the tone of the prophet's mind, and the circumstances of his life, when they were delivered. But still there is nothing which approaches the many-colored texture of our sacred volume.

Having been all produced within the compass of little more than twenty years [610?-633], and delivered through one medium, the Koran presents the exact reverse of the 'sundry times and diverse manners' of the Bible. It is all of one time and one manner, and the monotonous reiterations with which the book abounds are exceedingly tedious and dull. Poetry, which sometimes rises to grandeur, alternates with exceedingly dull didactic prose or puerile legend. Of parables there are but few specimens; and these are for the most part borrowed from Biblical sources, and spoiled in transplantation.

In the characteristic words of Gibbon, 'the European infidel will peruse with impatience the endless incoherent rhapsody of fable, and precept, and declamation, which seldom excites a sentiment or an idea, which sometimes crawls in the dust, and is sometimes lost in the clouds.' This language is perhaps rather overstrained, and seems to betray the irritation of one who had but recently risen from the irksome task; but it is substantially true nevertheless, and the only other (so-called) sacred book that I have attempted to read which exceeds the Koran in tediousness is the Book of Mormon. That book is much more nearly the audacious travesty of the Bible, which the Koran is not uncommonly called, than the Koran itself. The term 'travesty' indeed is not fairly applicable to the Koran, since it does not appear that Mohammed was well acquainted, if at all, with the canonical books of the Old and New Testaments.

There is no evidence in the Koran of deliberate invention; it is rather a badly digested compilation of materials, derived from a variety of sources, true and false, historical and mythical. The Book of Mormon, on the other hand, is a direct, though very tame and feeble, travesty of the Bible in style; and though much of the didactic matter is borrowed from the sacred volume, that which affects to be historical is pure and simple fabrication.

A book, however, which has so long remained an object of veneration to so many millions of the human race as the Koran has remained, must possess some intrinsic merits, some singular power of fascination. These are to be found partly in the great truths which it inculcates (of which more presently), and in the tone of high authority in which they are inculcated, but also partly in the style in which they are expressed.

Here, again, the contrast with the Bible is striking and instructive. In the Bible, the matter exceeds in value by a hundredfold the manner in which that matter is expressed. But in the Koran it is to a great extent the other way. Although the exact meaning of a writer must always suffer some detriment by the translation of his thoughts into a language different from that in which they were first conceived and expressed, yet probably there is no book in the world which has lost less by translation than the Bible. This is more especially true of our English translation. The more delicate shades of meaning sometimes disappear, no doubt, in the English translation of the Bible, as they must in the translation of any book; but the beauty of the original is rivalled, is often indeed surpassed, by the beauty of the translation. And this is not surprising, when we consider that the Greek of the New Testament, and, though only in some portions and in a less degree, the Hebrew of the Old Testament, belong to periods when those languages were in a state of decadence; whereas the English of the translation represents the golden era of our national tongue, the era of its greatest fertility, and vigor, and grandeur – the era of Spenser, of Shakespeare, and of Hooker.

The Koran, on the other hand, was originally written in the purest Arabic. Mohammed continually appeals to its extraordinary superhuman beauty and purity, as an evidence of the divine source from which he declared it to flow. He challenged unbelievers to produce, even with the aid of genii, any passage worthy to be compared with a single chapter in the Koran. Those who are acquainted with Arabic inform us that in its purest type it is in the highest degree copious, musical, and elegant; and that these qualities all meet in the Koran.

Consequently there is scarcely any book in the world which loses so much by translation. The charm of its graceful, harmonious, rhythmical, sonorous sentences utterly evaporates, and the matter, stripped of its gay attire, appears to the ordinary reader insufferably dull and commonplace.

Nothing, however, more forcibly illustrates the poverty of the Koran, viewed as what it claims to be, a complete revelation of theo-logical and moral truths, than its inability to stand the test of translation. If it was really a complete treasury of divine truth, the shape of the treasure-house would be of little importance compared with the jewels it enshrined. But such is not the case; and it is to the consideration of these contents that we now turn: from the form of the book to the book itself.

The Koran may fairly be judged by the definition of its purport as laid down in its own pages. At the close of the twelfth Sura we read:

'The Koran is not a newly invented fiction; but a confirmation of those Scriptures which have been revealed before it, and a distinct unfolding of everything necessary in respect either of faith or practice, and a direction and mercy unto them that believe.'

In other words, the Koran claims to be a complete supplement to all preceding revelation, to be the final statement of God's will, both concerning dogmatic belief and practical conduct.

In the remainder of this lecture it is proposed to examine the theological teaching of the Koran by the light of this claim. Does it only confirm the teaching of the Bible respecting the nature of the Divine Being, or does it tell us anything which, supposing it to be true seems an important addition to the knowledge of Mankind concerning the relation of God to man, and of man to God?

The Omniscience and Omnipotence of the One God

The Koran, then, to begin with, teaches a pure, rigid, austere monotheism; a belief in one absolute God, not as a philosophic abstraction, but a living Being, exercising a vital energy upon the world which He has made. The finest passages in the Koran are, undoubtedly, those in which the majesty, and power, and wisdom, of this infinite Being are set forth. Even through the veil of translation some of the grandeur of the original is discernible! For example:

'God! there is no God but He: the living, the self-subsisting: neither slumber nor sleep layeth hold of Him. To Him belongeth whatever is in Heaven or on earth. Who is he that can intercede with Him but through His good pleasure. He knoweth that which is past and that which is to come unto men, and they shall not comprehend anything that He knoweth but so far as He pleaseth. His throne is extended over Heaven and Earth, and the preservation of both is no burden unto Him.'

Or again:

'It is He who hath created the Heavens and the Earth in truth, and whensoever He saith unto a thing "Be," it is. With Him are the keys of the secret things, none knoweth them besides Himself: He knoweth that which is on the dry land and in the sea: there falleth no leaf but He knoweth it; neither is there a grain in the dark parts of the earth, nor a green thing, nor a dry thing, but it is noted in His clear book. It is He who causeth you to sleep by night, and knoweth what ye merit by day: He also awaketh you therein, that the preordained term of your lives may be fulfilled: then unto Him shall ye return, and He shall declare unto you that which ye have wrought.'

The wonders of the natural world as evidences of the existence and power of a Creator are frequently dwelt upon in language of considerable fervor and force, and at times, doubtless in the original language, of high poetical beauty, e. g.,

'Now in the creation of Heaven and Earth, and in the vicissitudes of day and night; in the ship which saileth in the sea laden with things profitable for mankind; in the rain which God sendeth from Heaven, quickening thereby the dead earth; and replenishing the same with all sorts of cattle; in the changes of the winds, and in the clouds that are compelled to do service between Heaven and Earth, there are signs to men of understanding.'

The omnipresence and omniscience of God, and the unerring justice of His future judgment upon men, are declared with earnestness and eloquence.

'There is no private discourse among three persons, but He is the fourth of them; nor among five, but He is the sixth of them; neither among a smaller nor a larger, but He is with them wheresoever they be; and He will declare unto them that which they have done on the day of resurrection; for God knoweth all things.'

'The Lord knoweth the secrets of men's hearts, and there is nothing in Heaven or on earth but it is written in a clear book.'

And again, in one of the earliest Suras:

'When the earth shall tremble with her quaking, and the earth shall cast forth her burthens, and man shall say, "What aileth her?" in that day shall she unfold her tidings, because the Lord shall have inspired her; in that day shall mankind advance in ranks, that they may behold their works, and whoever shall have wrought good of the weight of a grain shall behold it; and whoever shall have wrought evil of the weight of a grain shall behold it.'

We may freely acknowledge the beauty and the truth of these and similar passages, and yet heartily concur in the judgment of Gibbon that the loftiest of such strains in the Koran 'must yield to the sublime simplicity of the Book of Job,' and we may well add the Book of Psalms.

The mercy and beneficence of God, especially as manifested in His bountiful provision for the physical wants of man, and, on the other hand, the too frequent pride and ingratitude of man in demanding, or expecting as a right, advantages which are conceded only as free and unmerited favors, are topics frequently and powerfully handled, but, again we must say, at a distance vastly below the treatment of such subjects in the Psalms and Prophets of Holy Writ.

Predestination of Mankind

On the other hand, the absolute predestination of men to happiness or misery is repeatedly affirmed with a degree of harshness which it is difficult to reconcile with the attribute of perfect mercy assigned in other passages, and which finds no parallel in the pages of the Bible, where God is represented as a Being, Who, in the beautiful words of our Collect, 'declares His almighty power most chiefly in showing mercy and pity.'

Take, for instance, such a passage as this:

'This is a revelation of the most mighty, the merciful God, that thou mayest warn a people whose fathers were not warned, and who live in negligence; our sentence hath justly been pronounced against the greater part of them, wherefore they shall not believe. We have set a bar before them and a bar behind them; and we have covered them with darkness, wherefore they shall not see. It shall be equal unto them whether thou preach unto them, or do not preach unto them; they shall not believe.'

Or again, yet more boldly:

'Whomsoever God shall please to direct, He will open his breast to receive the faith of Islam; but whomsoever God shall please to lead into error, He will render his breast straight and narrow as though he were climbing up to Heaven:'

i.e., attempting an impossible thing.

Place side by side with such passages as these the strongest language to be found in the Bible concerning the impossibility of opening the ears or eyes of some men to the reception of divine truth, and the difference will be at once apparent. In the Koran this impenetrable hardness is represented as the inevitable consequence of an everlasting, immutable decree of God: in the Bible as the inevitable consequence of perverseness and obduracy on the part of man's free will: the working of a natural law whereby powers which are long disused become at last incapable of acting. He who persistently refuses to see or hear God's truth becomes at last unable to see or hear it, just as he who should refuse to move his arm would in time lose all power to move it.

This is the import of such passages as 'from him that hath not shall be taken away even that which he hath;' (Matt. 25:29) or, 'as they did not like to retain God in their knowledge, God gave them over to a reprobate mind' (Rom. 1:28). Or 'because they received not the love of the truth that they might be saved, for this cause God shall send them strong delusions that they should believe a lie' (2 Thess. 2:10-11).

The same meaning underlies those passages also where it is more boldly said that God 'hardened the heart of Pharaoh;' (Exod. 9:12) or, 'He hath blinded their eyes and hardened their heart;' (John 12:40) or, 'whom He will He hardeneth' (Rom. 9:18). A study of the connection in which those passages occur will always show that such hardening or binding is not arbitrary or initiatory on the part of God. On the contrary it is the judicial penalty of long-continued resistance to God's long-suffering efforts to soften the heart and to open the eyes.

The design, the desire of God is that 'all men should be saved, and come to the knowledge of the truth' (1 Tim. 2:4) but man is free; he is not coerced into goodness. God does not reverse His moral law to save a man in spite of himself, any more than He reverses his physical laws. If a man wilfully puts his hand into the fire, it will be burned; if he sins, he will ultimately suffer for it; if he shuts his mental eyes to the light of God's truth, he will not see it.

The power of God, especially in regard to predestination, being brought out into such strong prominence in the Koran, it is not surprising that fear and passive resignation, rather than love and active devotion, appear to be the prevailing attitude of the Mohammedan mind towards Him. This is indicated by the very name of their religion, 'Islam' or 'resignation to the will of God;' ['Submission' (to the will of God), Webster's] and by the designation of the faithful as 'Mussulman' [Turkish, 'Muslim', Arabic] or 'Moslem,' 'the resigned' ['surrendered' (to the will of God), Webster's].

It was the aim of the founder [Abdul-Wahhab, 1691-1787] of the sect of the Wahabees in the last century to restore the faith of Mohammed in its purity and integrity, as taught in the Koran. The absolute power of the Deity is expressed by the Wahabees in the simple formula 'La Ilah illa Allah.' The words themselves seem harmless and true: literally rendered, they merely signify 'There is no God but one God;' but their full import, we are assured, amounts to a great deal more. It amounts to a declaration that this one Supreme Being is 'the only force in the world, and that all things else, matter or spirit, instinct or intelligence, physical or moral, are nothing but pure, unconditional passiveness, alike in movement or in quiescence, in action or in capacity.' (W. G. Palgrave, 'Central Arabia,' vol i., p. 365, cc. viii.) Such is the God of the sect which prides itself on having revived the teaching of the Koran in its utmost purity.

Such, then, is the God of the Koran, the God whom we are there taught to believe was the God whom Abraham worshipped in spirit and in truth, of whom the true knowledge had been lost, which it was the mission of Mohammed to restore. Whether the God of Abraham is more fully and faithfully presented to us in the pages of the Koran or in the pages of the Bible, I leave the readers of these passages which I have contrasted, and others like them, to decide.

Had Mohammed really known the Bible, it seems almost incredible that he should have imagined himself the depositary of a new and special revelation concerning the attributes of the Divine Being; for all, and more than all, which he affects to disclose was to be found already revealed in the Books of Genesis, of Job, and of the Psalms alone. The intervention of the Angel Gabriel would have been a superfluous waste of divine power. But it appears to be very doubtful whether Mohammed could read (7:157); and, if he could, yet more doubtful whether he ever perused the canonical books of the Old and New Testaments.

He may have read, or heard read, portions of the Prophets or the Psalms, which may have suggested some of the grander passages in the Koran about the attributes of the Deity; but, on the other hand, all his knowledge of Biblical incidents and characters seems not derived from the sacred history itself, but culled from a variety of sources, the Talmud, the Targum, and the Midrash of the Jews, the spurious [pseudigraphical] Gospels of the Christians, and Arabian and Syrian tradition, ranging from the beautiful and probable down to the puerile and grotesque.

The history of the most prominent characters of the Old Testament is either totally disfigured in the Koran, or supplemented with long circumstantial stories, which for the most part destroy the consistency and personality of the character. Some of the tales, for instance, related about Abraham are beautiful and instructive, and in harmony with what we read elsewhere about the patriarch, though they may not be actually true; but others are so silly that no sound critic could possibly admit the incidents of both as real occurrences in the life of the same person.

As a specimen of the higher kind, take the following account, borrowed from the Talmud, of the conversion of Abraham from the idolatry of his countrymen:

'When the night overshadowed him, he saw a star, and he said, "This is my Lord;" but when it set he said, "I like not gods which set." And when he saw the moon rising he said, "This is my Lord;" but when he saw it set he said, "Verily, if my Lord direct me not, I shall become one of those who go astray." And when he saw the sun rising he said, "This is my Lord, this is the greatest;" but when it set he said, "O, my people, verily I am clean of that which ye associate with God: I direct my face unto Him Who has created the Heavens and the earth. I am of the right faith, and am not one of the idolaters."'

We may fairly believe that we have here, though cast into that vivid dramatic form which legend commonly assumes, the record of a true fact: the gradual elevation of the patriarch's mind from the superstitious worship of the heavenly bodies prevalent among his countrymen, to a purer and more spiritual faith.

The accounts, on the other hand, of his destruction of the images of ancestral deities, and of the attempt of Nimrod to put him to death by burning, are too foolish to be looked upon as anything but purely mythical.

The life of Moses is not so much distorted as the lives of some other characters, Solomon, for instance, who is turned into a kind of wonder-working magician; but the narrative of the Exodus, and of the settlement in Canaan, is overlaid with such a mass of tedious legendary rubbish, that the mind of the reader becomes fatigued and bewildered, and thankfully escapes from the fantastic shadows of Fairyland into the serene daylight of real history.

Viewing the Koran, therefore, as a compilation, the critical, artistic power of the compiler cannot be ranked high.

Christianity and Judaism in the Koran

It is needless to say that the idea of a plurality of persons in one Godhead was utterly repugnant to the rigid monotheism taught by Mohammed. His vague acquaintance with Christianity seems to have led him into supposing that Christians acknowledged, and even in some degree worshipped, what he calls 'companions' of God, and taught that sons and daughters were born to him. This strange misconception seems to have arisen partly from confused information about the doctrine of the Trinity, which he seems actually to have thought involved the worship of God the Father, Jesus, and the Virgin Mary as co-ordinate deities; partly perhaps from the tendency to saint-worship, which was beginning to grow up in the Church.

The foundation, therefore, of the Christian creed, the divine Sonship and incarnation of our blessed Lord, was emphatically denied and denounced by the apostle of Islam. It is doubtful indeed if the Christian doctrine was ever fairly and reasonably put before him, the

Christianity with which he came in contact being probably tainted with Manicheism [pure soul in an evil body], Nestorianism [Jesus a dual person], and other common forms of Oriental error; but at any rate he conceived it to be a part of his mission as a preacher of pure monotheism to declare that Jesus was not God and that divine honors ought not to be paid to Him.

Mohammed's aim was to show that the life and character of Jesus had been totally misunderstood and misrepresented: that He had really come only as a prophet, only to begin the work which Mohammed himself was destined to complete: namely, the restoration to its original purity of the monotheistic faith of Abraham; a design which the believers in Jesus had frustrated by unduly exalting Him to the level of the Deity.

Against the Jews he maintained that Jesus was, like himself, an inspired prophet and reformer; against the Christians that He was not more than this. Hence the peculiar aversion of Jew and Christian alike from the religion of Islam. Each was irritated by the assumption of superiority on the part of this rival to both, which required the Jew to believe more, and the Christian to believe less, than was contained in the creed of his forefathers. According to the teaching of the Koran, the Jews would be condemned because they rejected Christ as a prophet, the Christians because they adored Him as the Son of God.

The intolerant tone, however, of the Koran towards Judaism and Christianity increases very much with the gradual growth of Mohammed's power, and the extension of his views of conquest. At first the language is mild, almost conciliatory, and, as concerning the ultimate condition of the Christian, hopeful: take the following as a specimen;

'Surely those who believe and those who Judaise, and Christians and Sabaeans, whoever believeth in God and the last day, and doeth that which is right, shall have their reward with their Lord: there shall come no fear on them, neither shall they be grieved.'

And yet more strongly:

'Unto every one of you were given a law and an open path, and if God had pleased, He had surely made you one people; but He hath thought fit to give you different laws that He might try you in that which He hath given you respectively. Therefore strive to equal each other in good works. Unto God shall ye all return, and then will He declare unto you that concerning which ye have disagreed.'

But as time goes on, this mild language is exchanged for stern, uncompromising denunciation alike of Christian and Jew; and as the rule laid down in the Koran itself is that where passages are discordant, the later revelation abrogates the earlier, the moderate passages just cited must go for nothing.

Jesus in the Koran

The references in the Koran to the life of our Lord exhibit a wider and wilder departure from sober history than the references to characters of the Old Testament. In the ages of the Koran the life of Jesus is dressed up with those fantastic and puerile stories of unnecessary and unseemly wonders with which the Apocryphal Gospels abound, and which rob the character of that divine dignity and simplicity which in the genuine Gospels excite our admiration and our love. The events connected with the birth of John the Baptist are related in tolerable harmony with the Gospel narrative. Not so those which concern the birth and infancy of our blessed Lord.

In the Koran the Angel Gabriel not only announces the future birth of Christ to the Virgin Mary, but the conception of the Divine Son is represented as due to his influence (19:16-35). The birth of Jesus is described as having taken place under a palm-tree in the desert, whither his mother had wandered. Being nearly exhausted from want of food and drink, she is directed by Gabriel to shake the branches of the tree, whereupon ripe dates immediately fall from them, and a spring of pure water gushes forth from its roots. She takes the child home, who speaks in his cradle, and announces himself as a prophet of God. When older he animates a bird made of clay (5:110-118), to convince his companions of his prophetical destiny; but it is expressly said that this and other miracles were wrought by the permission of God, not by his own power.

Some hazy account of the Holy Eucharist which had been brought to Mohammed may perhaps have given birth to the curious statement in the Koran, that, at the request of Jesus, God caused a table laden with provisions to descend from heaven, that the day of its descent might become a festival day to his disciples (5:110-118).

The reality of the crucifixion is explained away by the adoption of the common Gnostic theory that God frustrated the design of the Jews by taking up the real Jesus into heaven (4:157-9), while His enemies wasted their rage upon a phantom substituted for Him.

As a consequence of this view, the resurrection disappears altogether as part of the history of our Lord and faith in the resurrection of all men, although an integral part of the Mohammedan creed, is not based in the Koran on the fact of a risen Christ, but on the power of an Almighty Creator to renew and revive that which He originally made. The miracle of re-creation, it is remarked, is not greater than the miracle of creation.

[In the Koran, a "spirit" is a created being like an angel.] Of any notion of the Holy Spirit, not merely as a Person [i.e., as a member of the post-Biblical Trinity], but even as a direct influence or energy from the Deity operating on man [the Biblical understanding], I cannot find any trace in the Koran. The cold, rigid monotheism which Mohammed taught, did not tolerate the idea of such close personal communion between man and his Maker.

The interpretation put upon the promise of the Paraclete in the Gospel according to John (Chapter 16) is the most curious instance either of astounding ignorance or of audacious imposture, to be found in the whole of the Koran. First, 'parakleetos' (Gk., 'advocate') is confounded with 'periklutos' (Gk.), which signifies 'renowned,' or 'praised;' and then this being also the meaning of Ahmed, of which the name Mohammed is compounded, the passage is wrested into a prophecy of the coming of Mohammed.

'Jesus, the son of Mary, said, O children of Israel, verily I am the Apostle of God sent unto you confirming the law which was given before me, and bringing good tidings of an Apostle who shall come after me, whose name shall be Ahmed.'

There are some other passages more dimly alluded to which Mohammed or his disciples conceived to be prophetic of himself, and he asserted that the Bible had contained more, but had been mutilated by Jews and Christians.

Angels and Genii

While, however, the Koran jealously guards the unity of the Godhead, it inculcates a belief in intermediate beings, angels and genii, who are allowed to exercise a very powerful influence upon human beings. The angels are represented in the Koran as incorporeal beings created of fire, the guardians of the throne of God, the messengers of His will between heaven and earth. At the creation of man, they were bidden to worship Adam as the son of God. All obeyed excepting the devil Eblis, who was too proud and envious to fall down before a creature of clay, and became thenceforth the enemy of man. Further, the good angels are described as impeccable and immortal, of various orders and ranks, which are distinguished by the number of their wings.

To each man is assigned his guardian angel; and two who attend him, one on either side, take an account of his actions good and bad which will be produced on the day of judgment. Angels take the souls of men from their bodies; angels will summon men to judgment by the sound of the trumpet; angels intercede with God for the penitent; angels will convey the faithful to heaven, the lost to hell, where they keep guard over the fallen spirits.

The genii of the Koran are almost identical with the daemons of the Talmud. They have more in common with angels than men, yet are inferior in several respects. Like angels, they are made of fire, they have wings, they roam up and down the world, they know future events; but they have some human qualities, they eat and drink, they are liable to human passions, and to death.

Islam – "Austere, Comfortless and Cold"

Such is Islam, viewed as a theological system – a vast advance upon polytheism, fetichism, gross and grovelling superstition of any kind; but how immeasurably below even the Jewish revelation of the nature of God, and of the relation between God and man! It is austere, comfortless, and cold. The Deity is represented not indeed as a mere philosophical abstraction, but yet as a Being, remote, unapproachable in majesty and might, wielding at His arbitrary will the destinies and movements of men, yet far aloof from them; a ruler of overwhelming power, rather than a loving and merciful, though almighty Father. There is nothing to fill up or bridge over the chasm which divides this tremendous Being from man; no divine Mediator, no quickening illuminating Spirit; for the action of angels is too precarious and vague to fulfil these offices.

Islam – resignation to the irresistible will and decrees of God – expresses very well the relation between man and his Maker as set forth in the Koran; the submission of obedient fear to a power, not the devotion of love to a person.

The theology, therefore, of the Koran fails to meet the profoundest religious needs of man; it removes the Creator to an immeasurable distance from the creatures whom He has made, and in the renunciation of all idea of mediation it falls infinitely below not Judaism only, but Magianism and Brahmanism, which in other respects it excels.

All that is good and true in the Koran concerning the nature of God, and worthy of the subject, is to be found in the Bible, if it be not borrowed from the Bible; all that is original is good for nothing, if indeed there be anything purely original, for probably most of the wilder statements could be traced to traditional sources.

The genius, indeed, of Mohammed as the founder of a theological system consisted, not so much in inventing or devising anything actually new, as in piecing together fragments of other creeds, and by his commanding personal influence, tact, enthusiasm, and self-confidence, imposing this patchwork system successfully on so large a number of his fellow-countrymen.

The Koran

In itself, the Koran is a clumsy production. To suppose that an angel [Gabriel, 2:97], was sent from heaven to reveal the truths which it contains, would be unnecessary, for those truths are to be found more amply, more beautifully expressed elsewhere [but not in classical Arabic]; to suppose that Gabriel was sent from heaven to reveal the childish absurdities which it contains, would be an insult to the character and work of angels.

The Doctrine of the Future State

It remains to consider briefly the teaching of the Koran concerning a future state. It may truly be said that if the lofty, though cold, conception of the Deity be the highest point in the teaching of Islam, its doctrine of a future state stands on the lowest level. It is, indeed, not raised much above the belief which has prevailed among many heathen nations.

As the wild [Native American] Indian imagines that the joy of the future life will consist in ranging over well stocked hunting grounds with the bow and the dog, which have been his companions in the chase on earth; as our Teutonic forefathers, ere [before] their conversion to Christianity, looked forward to banquets in the drinking halls [Valhalla] of Odin, as the height of celestial bliss; so did the Arab, instructed by the Koran, anticipate that the joys of Paradise would be of that sensuous and voluptuous nature which to his temperament were most alluring.

'Verdant gardens watered by clear and unfailing streams, rivers of milk the taste whereof changed not, rivers of wine pleasant to them that drink, rivers of clarified honey, perpetual shade from trees ever laden with the most delicious fruits' (47:15, etc.).

These are the things which make up the scenery of the Mohammedan Paradise. Here the faithful, arrayed in costly raiment of silk, and adorned with bracelets of gold and pearls, should repose on soft couches, attended by dark eyed damsels of immortal youthfulness and superhuman beauty.

Life in Paradise, in short, is made up of the most earthly sensual enjoyments, only magnified and intensified to a degree never experienced on earth, and which if they ever could be experienced, must soon cloy the appetite of the most insatiable Arab that ever lived.

Of God there is no mention in these descriptions, nor, indeed, is it easy to see how the Divine Being could with decency be introduced into them. There are, indeed, occasional hints of a beatific vision of the Deity to be enjoyed by the holiest of the faithful, but they are rare and dim compared with the frequent and glowing pictures of more material and corporeal delights.

The pains of hell are, in their grossness, a fitting counterpart to the pleasures of Paradise. One quotation will suffice:

'They who believe not shall have garments of fire fitted to them; boiling water shall be poured upon their heads; their bowels and also their skins shall be dissolved thereby, and they shall be beaten with maces of iron. So often as they shall endeavor to get out of hell because of the anguish of their torments, they shall be dragged back into the same, and their tormentors shall say unto them, taste ye the pain of burning' (22:19-22).

In the description of the resurrection, and of the day of judgment, some of the Scriptural doctrine is reproduced; the archangel's trumpet, the darkening of the sun, the shaking of the earth, the reeling of the mountains, the shrivelling together of the heavens like a parched scroll; but all these are strangely jumbled with the wildest and most fantastical imaginations.

In all these descriptions of the resurrection, the judgment, and the future life, in addition to their intrinsic materiality and coarseness, we see the culminating example of a weakness which pervades the whole of the Koran, and perhaps more than anything else betrays its human origin. I mean the attempt to bring down the most inscrutable mysteries to the level of the human understanding.

The minute circumstantial descriptions of holy places where angels would fear to tread, and of holy places before whom they would veil their faces, savors of a thoroughly human curiosity which imagines or invents where it cannot discover. They are in direct contradiction to the teaching of Holy Scripture, 'eye hath not seen, nor ear heard, neither hath entered into the heart of man to conceive the things which God hath prepared for them that love Him' (1 Cor. 2:9). The reticence and reserve of the Bible concerning many subjects, which most excite human curiosity, is surely of some value in evidence that the origin of the sacred volume is not human, but divine.

With that partial knowledge of the future state which the Gospel vouchsafes to us, the wise Christian is content. To know that 'God hath prepared for them that love Him such good things as pass man's understanding;' (1 Cor. 2:9) to know that though there be a veil between us and the other world, and 'that it doth not yet appear what we shall be,' (1 John 3:2) yet if 'we purify ourselves even as Christ is pure, we shall be like Him, for we shall see Him as He is;' to know that the body of our humiliation, the body of this present fallen nature, liable to sin, to disease, to death, shall be changed so as to be fashioned according to the body of Christ's glorified state (Phil. 3:21); such knowledge, surely, is enough to be thankful for, enough to live by.

Such knowledge is a revelation of truths which we could not have certainly discovered for ourselves, a revelation which discloses light sufficient to guide and cheer us as we plod along the dark and slippery ways of this world's night, while the greater light, which would now only dazzle and bewilder, is held back until the day comes, when the shadows shall flee away and we shall 'know even as we are known' (1 Cor. 13:12).

Moral Teaching of the Bible and the Koran

W. R. W. Stephens

'Allahu Akbar! Prayer is better than sleep! O Thou bountiful One, Thy mercy ceases not! My sins are great: greater is thy mercy! I extol His perfection! Allahu Akbar.' – The Mohammedan Call to Prayer.

The apostolic mission of Mohammed having been once acknowledged, it was natural that he should undertake the regulation, not only of the creed, but also of the moral practice and ceremonial worship of his countrymen. The Koran consequently became the ethical digest, the civil code, the ceremonial hand book, as well as the theological oracle of his disciples. And it is obvious that if Mohammed's aim was to remodel the national life, the most effectual way of attaining it, his prophetic authority once established, was to frame a number of positive precepts touching every department of moral conduct.

A peculiar character is by this method quickly but forcibly stamped upon the recipients. They become 'new creatures,' with new motives, and new purposes. They are capable of being conducted by their ruler to definite ends, because their movements are under control, because the people are more like a disciplined army, than are a people to whom greater freedom of thought and action is allowed.

Nothing less than the imposition of a minute code of rules for practical life could have enabled Benedict [Benedictine Monks], or Francis of Assisi [Franciscans], or Dominic [Dominicans], or Ignatius Loyola [Jesuits] to fix such a distinct and lasting character upon the great religious orders which they created.

The Code of Mohammed and the Code of Moses

It was by their subjection to a system of positive precepts, molding and regulating every department of life, that the Israelites, after their emancipation from Egypt, were trained for that peculiar position among the nations of the world which it was God's purpose to give them. Their long servitude in Egypt had crushed their spirit of independence and self-respect, had lowered their moral standard, and corrupted the pure faith of their forefathers. Nothing less than a stringent minute set of practical laws could have transformed them from a rabble of abject and superstitious slaves into a brave, God-fearing, God-loving host of free men.

Such a code was given to them in the hands of their mediator, Moses; it became to them, what the Koran has become to the Mussulman, the theological, moral, ceremonial, and civil code, all in one; it taught them what to believe, how to worship, how to live.

Having been converted, under the influence of their heaven-sent law, into a valorous and puissant people, they took forcible possession of the land of Canaan ; and the promise made ages before to their ancestors Abraham, Isaac, and Jacob, was at last fulfilled.

Thus far there certainly seems some analogy between the effects of the law given to the Jews from God, as they believed, through Moses, and the effects of the law given to the Arabs from God, as they no less believed, through Mohammed. The aim of Mohammed was to revive among his countrymen the Arabs, as Moses revived among his countrymen the Jews, the pure faith of their common forefather Abraham. In this he succeeded to a very great extent.

For a confused heap of idolatrous superstitions, he substituted a pure monotheistic faith; he abolished some of the most vicious practices of his countrymen, modified others; he generally raised the moral standard, improved the social condition of the people, and introduced a sober and rational ceremonial in worship.

Finally he welded by this means a number of wild independent tribes, mere floating atoms, into a compact body politic, as well prepared and as eager to subdue the kingdoms of the world to their rule and to their faith, as ever the Israelites had been to conquer the land of Canaan.

But the danger of a precise system of positive precepts regulating in minute detail the ceremonial of worship, and the moral and social relations of life, is that it should retain too tight a grip upon men when the circumstances which justified it have changed or vanished away; that the movements as it were of full-grown men should be impeded and cramped by garments fitted only for children; or to speak more correctly, perhaps, that the moral growth of those who live under such a minute system of restraints should be stunted and retarded.

Icon of the Prophet Moses

Amongst the Jews there was a provision made against this danger. It was one peculiar part of the mission of the Prophets to counteract that tendency to narrowness, formality, and hardness, which was the consequence of living under a rigid system of positive precepts. They kindled the spirit of worship and of morality, as opposed to the letter; they prepared the way for the purer, loftier, more free dispensation of the Gospel.

The earlier system of exact and positive laws had been necessary, first to transform the character of the people, and then to maintain it; first to mark them off from all other nations as God's chosen, peculiar possession, and then to fence them round and preserve their creed and morals intact, and undefiled by the mass of heathenism which surrounded them. But lest they should confound virtue as identical with obedience to the outward requirements of the law, the voices of the Prophets were ever and anon lifted up to declare that a strict conformity to practical precepts, whether of conduct or ceremonial, would not extenuate, but rather increase, in the eyes of God the guilt of an unpurified heart and an unholy life.

'To what purpose is the multitude of your sacrifices unto me? Bring no more vain oblations; incense is an abomination unto me; the new moons and sabbaths, the calling of assemblies, I cannot bear: it is iniquity, even the solemn meeting. ... Wash you, make you clean; put away the evil of your doings from before mine eyes; cease to do evil, learn to do well; seek judgment, relieve the oppressed, judge the fatherless, plead for the widow' (Isa. 1).

It would be unnecessary to multiply citations of similar passages, which are familiar to us all. They are all anticipations of the moral teaching of Him who pronounced woe on those hypocrites that paid tithe of mint, anise, and cummin, but omitted the weightier matters of the law, judgment, mercy, and faith (Matt. 23:23).

It is obvious to any reader of the Koran that it does not contain, except perhaps in a few stray passages, any teachings analogous to the moral teaching of the Hebrew Prophets which might act as a corrective to the cramping and hardening influence of its positive precepts. Nor has any school of teachers arisen in Islam who have made it their aim to accomplish this salutary object. There have been Scribes (and probably Pharisees) in abundance, but no Prophets.

In the reformation which Mohammed effected among the Arabs, by persuading them to adopt as of divine institution a set of theological doctrines and moral precepts, it has been admitted that there seems some analogy to the reformation effected among the Israelites by Moses.

The Use of Force

It has often been considered that in the propagation of the creed of Mohammed by the sword, there is a further parallel to the forcible occupation of the land of Canaan by the Jews.

There are critics who will compare the extermination or subjugation of the inhabitants of conquered territory alike by Mohammed and Joshua, and maintain that it is equally difficult to reconcile either with sound principles of morality. The supposed analogy, however, breaks down upon examination, and the case turns out to be one, not for comparison, but contrast.

In the Koran, the Mussulman is absolutely and positively commanded to make war upon all those who decline to acknowledge the prophet until they submit, or, in the case of Jews and Christians, purchase exemption from conformity by the payment of tribute (9:29).

The mission of the Mussulman, as declared in the Koran, is distinctly aggressive. We might say that Mohammed bequeathed to his disciples a roving commission to propagate his faith by the employment of force where persuasion failed. 'O prophet, fight for the religion of God' – 'Stir up the faithful to war,' such are commands which Mohammed believed to be given him by God. 'Fight against them who believe not in God nor the last day,' 'attack the idolatrous in all the months,' such are his own exhortations to his disciples.

We need hardly stop to point out that such a charge is diametrically opposite to the commission of Christ to His Apostles, who were commanded to preach the Gospel to every creature, but were expressly forbidden to support their preaching by carnal weapons.

It is more important to show that the Jews had no roving commission to go about the world making proselytes, and presenting the alternatives of tribute or the sword to such as would not accept their creed. They were commanded to take possession of only a narrow strip of land, promised ages before to their ancestors, to extirpate the inhabitants on account of their singular wickedness, and then to keep themselves aloof from their neighbors in order that the light of a pure monotheistic faith might be maintained burning undimmed amidst the darkness of surrounding heathenism. Again and again the people are

77

reminded that the land is given them as a step towards the fulfillment of the promise made by God to their forefathers, that through their seed all nations of the earth should in the ages to come be blessed; again and again they are instructed that in destroying or expelling the inhabitants they were only instruments used for the removal of wickedness instead of some inanimate force, such as earthquake, or plague, or the fire which consumed Sodom and Gomorrah.

> 'Understand this day that the Lord thy God is He which goeth over before thee; as a consuming fire shall He destroy them, and bring them down before thy face. .... Speak not thou in thine heart after that the Lord thy God hath cast them out from before thee, saying, for my righteousness the Lord hath brought me in to possess this land. .... Not for thy righteousness or for the uprightness of thine heart dost thou go to possess their land; but for the wickedness of these nations the Lord thy God doth drive them out from before thee, and that He may perform the word which the Lord sware unto thy fathers, Abraham, Isaac, and Jacob' (Deut. 9:3-5).

The two purposes for which the Jews were permitted to take forcible possession of Canaan are here distinctly stated: the immediate purpose was the expulsion of wickedness; the ultimate far reaching purpose was, retrospectively, the fulfillment of the promise made to their forefathers; prospectively, as a part or consequence of this fulfillment, the bestowal of a blessing on all families of the earth.

Meanwhile the Jews, having been once established in their country, were to abstain from aggression upon surrounding nations, and as far as possible from intercourse with them. They were to act on the defensive, to keep themselves separate and undefiled; not to compel others to accept their faith, but to wait patiently God's own time, and God's own way of extending it.

Instructions to Rulers

In the Book of Deuteronomy (Chapter 17) there are some principles laid down for regulating the character and conduct of kings who might in future be appointed. They all aim at repressing the acquisition of military power, the display of military pomp, the indulgence in luxury, and the accumulation of riches to which the Oriental despots of the world were addicted. The Jewish king was not to multiply horses to himself, or wives or silver and gold. The career of Solomon was in direct disobedience to these commands, and initiated a disastrous policy of worldly greatness and ambition in his successors, which ended in the overthrow of the Empire.

In the Koran, on the other hand, there is no such condemnation of these elements of earthly luxury and ostentation, and the later caliphs certainly indulged in them to their hearts' content.

The latitude of toleration allowed to the Jews towards nations alien in creed or birth, or both, was as great as possible compatibly with the necessity of keeping the chosen nation free from contamination; and much greater than many from a superficial view of the Jewish position are apt to imagine.

'Thou shalt not abhor an Edomite, for he is thy brother; thou shalt not abhor an Egyptian, because thou wast a stranger in his land' (Deut. 23:7).

Edomite or Egyptian children of the third generation were to be admitted as members of the congregation (Dent. 23:7, 8). The league of peace made with the Gibeonites was to be observed forever, notwithstanding they had obtained it by a fraudulent artifice. This scrupulous adherence to a pledge once given, this 'swearing to a neighbour, and disappointing him not, though it were to their own hindrance,' (Psalms 15:4) presents a striking contrast to the acts of treachery which were not only connived at by Mohammed, but in some cases expressly sanctioned.

Nothing, again, is more continually and solemnly reiterated in the pages of the Pentateuch than the duty of showing kindness to strangers. The command is always based upon a touching appeal to the recollection of their own former condition as strangers and sojourners in Egypt.

'Thou shalt not oppress a stranger, for ye know the heart of a stranger, seeing ye were strangers in the land of Egypt' (Exod. 23:9).

'Thou shalt neither vex a stranger nor oppress him, seeing ye were strangers in the land of Egypt' (Exod. 22:21).

The Koran also enjoins repeatedly and in very emphatic language the duty of showing kindness to the stranger and the orphan, and of treating slaves, if converted to the faith, with the consideration and respect due to believers.

The duty even of mercy to the lower animals is not forgotten, and it is to be thankfully acknowledged that Mohammedanism as well as Buddhism shares with Christianity the honour of having given birth to Hospitals and Asylums for the insane and sick.

Slavery

But ardent admirers of Islam are so much captivated by these laudable traits that they sometimes unduly magnify them, and underrate the teachings of the Bible in reference to the same subjects. To take the case of slavery, for instance; persons filled with admiration of the humane treatment of the slave inculcated in the Koran, and as a rule practiced in Mohammedan countries, are apt to forget that slavery after all is distinctly recognized by the Koran as an integral part of the social system; that the Mohammedan slave could not look forward like the Hebrew to his release in the seventh year (Deut. 15:9); and that, while the Koran enjoins kindness in general terms, there are not such often repeated and touching warnings as we find in the Pentateuch against oppression of slaves and hired servants, not such distinct and minute provisions for their happiness and welfare.

'Thou shalt not oppress an hired servant that is poor and needy, whether he be of thy brethren or of thy strangers that are in thy land within thy gates: at his day thou shalt give him his hire, neither shall the sun go down upon it, for he is poor and setteth his heart upon it .... thou shalt remember that thou wast a bondman in Egypt, and the Lord thy God redeemed thee thence' (Deut. 24:14).

If a master struck a slave so as to cause the loss of an eye or a tooth, the slave was to go free for his eye's sake, or his tooth's sake; if he caused his death, the master was to be punished. When the slave was released in the seventh year, his wife and children accompanied him unless the wife had been given him by his master. In that case, and in that case only, the master could retain her (Exod. 21:1). The runaway slave was not to be restored to his master.

'Thou shalt not deliver unto his master the servant which is escaped from his master unto thee: he shall dwell with thee in that place which he shall choose in one of thy gates where it liketh him best: thou shalt not oppress him' (Deut. 23:15).

By such like enactments did the law of Moses mitigate the condition of slavery. The Gospel has done more. It did not violently interfere with any of the existing social or political institutions amongst which it arose; it accepted them, it made the best of them. It did not preach rebellion against the slave-owner, or the despot; but it was ever slowly, yet surely, sapping the despotism alike of the slave-owner and the political tyrant at its roots by proclaiming principles of justice and mercy, and infusing a spirit of brotherhood, which were inconsistent with oppression in any form.

The conduct of St. Paul towards the slave Onesimus and his master Philemon is a typical illustration of the general attitude of Christianity towards the institution of slavery as a whole. He sends back the fugitive, but requests Philemon that he may be received, not as a slave, but as a brother beloved, because like the master, he had become a Christian, was a member of the same spiritual family, an inheritor of the same Heavenly kingdom (Philem. 16).

Treatment of Enemies

To pass from the treatment of slaves to the treatment of enemies, 'Islam, tribute, or the sword,' is the well-known formula which sums up the teaching of the Koran concerning this matter.

'When ye encounter the unbelievers, strike off their heads until ye have made a great slaughter among them; and bind them in bonds, and either give them a free dismission afterwards or exact a ransom until the war shall have laid down its arms' (47:4).

This is mild compared with many other passages where the alternative of release is not suggested. The Israelites, as was observed just now, were to abstain from aggression, except upon the inhabitants of that land in which they were to act as God's instruments for the extirpation of wickedness. The capture of towns in Canaan, therefore, but in Canaan only, was to be followed by complete destruction of all that breathed therein.

If forced into war with more distant countries, when the Jewish army came before a city peace was to be proclaimed. If this was not accepted and the city was besieged and captured, the men only were to be put to the sword; the women and children were to be saved alive (Deut. 20.).

Under the Mosaic law women taken captive in war were not to be degraded to the condition of slave concubines. If a man wished to make one his wife, she had first to go through a kind of religious ceremonial of purification, and then she was allowed a month of mourning for her old home before she was married. If the husband afterwards wished to put her away, she was free to go wherever she pleased; the man was not to sell her or in any way to make merchandise of her (Deut. 21.).

These provisions for the honor of female captives form a striking contrast to the law of the Koran, which, while it endeavors to alleviate the evils of polygamy by restricting the number of a man's wives to four, places no limit whatever to the number of his concubines, and makes no provision for the mitigation of their unhappy lot.

Of course we do not forget that the regulations of the Penta-teuch concerning war were frequently violated, like many other par-ticulars of the moral law; yet the deeds of the most merciless kings of Israel and Judah will hardly offer a parallel to one act of barbarous cruelty approved, if not actually ordered, by Mohammed.

Omm Kirfa, an aged woman, chieftainess of a tribe which had molested and plundered the caravans of the faithful, having been made captive, was tied by the legs to two camels, which were then driven in opposite directions, so that her body was literally torn asunder. I am not aware that the exploits even of modern Bashi Bazouks and Circassians can rival such an 'atrocity' as this, committed under the sanction of the founder of Islam.

If it be scornfully observed that things as horrible have been done by men bearing the name of Christians, and sometimes professedly in the name of Christianity, we of course admit what every Christian with shame and sorrow must confess.

Only such alleged parallels prove nothing. The 'te quoque' [You too!] argument is always a poor one, and in this instance it is peculiarly unfortunate.

Wars undertaken in the name of religion by Christians are in direct disobedience both to the spirit and letter of the Gospel; whereas religious wars undertaken by Mohammedans are in conformity with the practice and precept of the founder of their religion.

Christianity, therefore, cannot be made in any way chargeable with cruelties committed in wars which are themselves in contravention of the command of Christ. That men have (sometimes with a sincere zeal for God, only not according to knowledge, Rom. 10:2) attempted to propagate the Christian faith by war with its concomitant horrors, in direct disobedience to the command of Christ, does not improve the position of the Mussulman when he propagates his creed by war in direct obedience to the command of Mohammed.

Destruction of Trees

One more illustration may suffice to close the contrast between the Pentateuch and the Koran respecting the conduct of war. In the book of Deuteronomy the destruction of such trees in an enemy's country as bore edible fruit is expressly forbidden: 'Thou shalt not cut them down to employ them in the siege, for the tree of the field is man's life' (Deut. 20:19).

On one occasion when some palm trees (one of the principal sources of food to the Arab) were an impediment to some military operation of the prophet, he produced a special revelation authorizing their removal.

'What palm trees ye cut down or left standing were so cut down or left standing by the will of God, that He might disgrace the evil doers.'

The vices most prevalent in Arabia in the time of Mohammed which are most sternly denounced and absolutely forbidden in the Koran were drunkenness, unlimited concubinage and polygamy, the destruction of female infants, reckless gambling, extortionate usury, superstitious arts of divination and magic. The abolition of some of these evil customs, and the mitigation of others, was a great advance in the morality of the Arabs, and is a wonderful and honorable testimony to the zeal and influence of the reformer.

The total suppression of female infanticide and of drunkenness is the most signal triumph of his work; yet it may be observed that the excesses of cruelty and licentiousness of which Mohammedans can be guilty, notwithstanding abstinence from wine, proves that total abstinence from one evil thing is not in itself so good a security for virtue as the Christian principle of soberness and temperance in all things.

Women

The condition of women in Arabia seems to have been improved in three ways by the provisions of the Koran.

The transmission of a man's wives to his heir as part of his property, like his furniture or any other household chattel, was forbidden. The right of a woman to a share in her father's or husband's property was declared, and, as already stated, the legal number of wives for any one man was limited to four. Mohammed himself was exempted from this restriction by a special revelation in his favor (33:50) [He was monogamous from age 25 to 50. Later he had 9 wives simultaneously, now rationalized as "taking pity on widows"].

Under the Jewish law, polygamy was tolerated; but it was not distinctly sanctioned, as it is in the Koran, by the definition of a fixed allowable number of wives, and therefore no impediment was placed in the way of the ultimate removal of the system by the gradual growth of purer and truer views respecting the married state and the position of women in society.

The laws respecting divorce in the Koran are vile, and reveal the condition of the wife as suffering under the extreme degradation and servitude common in all Oriental countries. The husband might put away his wife and take her back again at pleasure; but if divorce had been thrice repeated she could not return to her husband except on one revolting condition, that she should first be married to another man and live with him for one whole day and night (2:230).

We read of one follower of the prophet who had offspring by sixteen wives. As he could not have possessed more than four at any one time, his case is a remarkable illustration of the facility of divorce.

With these abominable customs contrast the command in Deuteronomy (24:4), which expressly forbids a man to take back a wife who has been once divorced and married to another. In Deuteronomy Chapter 21, we find a law directed against the effects of that favoritism and jealousy which are among the many banes and curses of polygamy.

'If a man have two wives, one beloved and the other hated, and they have borne him children, both the beloved and hated, and if the first born son be hers that was hated; then it shall be when he maketh his sons to inherit that which he hath, that he may not make the son of the beloved first born before the son of the hated, but he shall acknowledge the son of the hated for the first born by giving him a double portion of all that he hath: the right of the first born is his' (Deut 21:15-7).

Almsgiving

The exhortations to almsgiving as a solemn duty commanded by God and owed to man are, as is well known, very numerous in the Koran. It is perhaps the point on which the teaching of the Koran may most fairly be compared with the teaching of the Pentateuch, yet there are not such careful and particular instructions in the Koran as in the Pentateuch for ministering to the necessities: of the 'stranger, the fatherless, and the widow.'

The certainty of a rich reward in the life to come to those who bestow alms is promised in the Koran in terms which sound rather like a bribe to benevolence, and which might not improbably foster pride in the almsgiver. Future punishment is predicted with equal positiveness on those who should neglect the duty. 'Unto such as believe and bestow alms shall be given a great reward,' but he who did not pay his legal contribution of alms would have a serpent twisted about his neck on the day of resurrection.

Prayer and Fasting

The duties of prayer and fasting are inculcated in the Koran as co-ordinate with the duty of almsgiving; and the punctual and scrupulous observance by the Mussulman of the appointed hours of prayer, and the appointed season of fasting, is notorious and edifying.

According to the traditional account of Mohammed's nocturnal journey to the seventh Heaven, he was commanded by the Almighty to impose on his disciples the obligation of saying prayers fifty times a day. By the advice of Moses, he supplicated and obtained a mitigation of this intolerable burden, and the number was gradually reduced to five. The observance of these hours was indispensable. The prayers might be shortened on the march or in the camp, when some emergency demanded action without delay; but the omissions were to be made up afterwards when the pressure of danger or haste was at an end.

Cleanliness was designated by Mohammed as the key of prayer, even as prayer was the gate of Paradise; and accordingly his disciples were forbidden to enter on their devotions without having washed the face, hands, and feet. In the absence or scarcity of water, the believer is by a special permission in the Koran to use sand as a substitute.

In the beginning of his career, when he was cultivating friendly relations with the Jews, Mohammed instructed his disciples to turn their faces, when they prayed, towards Jerusalem; but after all hopes of conciliating the Jews were at an end, Mecca was established as the Holy City, the center of attraction to which the eyes and thoughts of the faithful worshipper were to be directed.

The temple indeed at Mecca, the Kaaba, was considered by Mohammed, in common with the rest of his countrymen, as far exceeding Jerusalem in antiquity and sanctity as a spot consecrated to pure worship. It was supposed to be almost coeval with the world. The original [temple] having been destroyed by the deluge, the temple was rebuilt, according to Arabian tradition, by Abraham and Ishmael; but the black stone [in the Kaaba] was venerated as a genuine relic of the primeval building, having been let down, it was said, by God to earth at the request of Adam, after his expulsion from Paradise.

The duty of visiting this holy place is urged in the Koran with no less frequency and solemnity than the duties of almsgiving and prayer. Every Mohammedan, as he values the prospect of happiness in the life to come, is bound to make the pilgrimage once, at least, in his lifetime, and those who are able should make it every year in the appointed month.

If prevented by sickness or any other pressing necessity, the omission was suffered to be redeemed by offerings and a ten days' fast.

The Koran prescribes that one month in the year, the month Ramadan, should be observed as a very strict fast. From sunrise to sunset, neither food nor drink must pass the lips, but after sunset the natural appetites may be moderately gratified. As the Arabian year is lunar, each month in the course of thirty-three years runs through all the different seasons. Consequently when the month Ramadan falls in the middle of the summer, the length of the days and the severity of the heat cause such vigorous abstinence from sunrise to sunset to be extremely mortifying.

Summary of Moral Teaching

We have now touched upon the main precepts, ethical and ceremonial, contained in the Koran. The following passage is perhaps the best summary of the moral teaching which could be picked out of the whole book, especially showing that Mohammed himself did not value ceremonial unless it was attended by that real devotion on the part of the worshipper which all ceremonial is intended to express:

'There is no piety in turning your faces towards the east or the west; but he is pious who believeth in God, and the Last Day, and the Angels and the Scriptures and the Prophets, who for the love of God dispenses his wealth to his kinsfolk, to the orphans, and to the needy, and the wayfarer, and to those who ask, and for ransoming, who observeth prayer, and payeth the legal alms, and who belongs to them that are faithful to their engagements, when they have engaged in them, and are patient under ills and hardships and in time of trouble; these are they who are just and those who fear the Lord.'

We get here a taste, a gleam, of that higher and more spiritual moral teaching which, as was pointed out at the beginning of this lecture, is the most salutary counterpoise to the stiffness and hardness of bare ethical precepts and ceremonial regulations, and to their tendency to contract men's notions of morality. Yet if all the sublime teaching of the Hebrew Prophets did not suffice to rescue the Jews from formalism, if our Lord had to denounce pretentious prayer-making, ostentatious almsgiving, superstitious ablutions, an inordinate veneration of Jerusalem and the Temple as the only spots where prayer would be acceptable, it is impossible to forbear thinking that the minute directions of the Koran concerning the times and places of prayers, and fasting, and pilgrimage, concerning the amount of almsgiving, and its consequent reward, must be perilous to the preservation of a large-minded, large-hearted piety.

The tendency of the human heart to self-deceit and formalism is so strong that when men are tied down to the performance of certain religious functions, minutely and precisely fixed in respect to time and manner, so that neither less nor more is required of them, they will very commonly (though perhaps often unconsciously to themselves) fall into the error of imagining that there is a peculiar intrinsic merit and virtue in the mere discharge of those duties. Morality is viewed not in the abstract, but in the concrete, as consisting in a bundle of religious observances rather than in a certain disposition of the heart towards God and man.

Thus, in contrasting the moral teaching of the Koran with the moral teaching of the Old Testament, and still more of the New Testament, the point which cannot fail to strike the careful student is this, that it deals much more with sin and virtue in fragmentary detail than as wholes. It deals with acts more than principles, with outward practice more than inward motives, with precept and command more than exhortation.

For instance, there are commands to give full measure, to weigh with a just balance, to abstain from wine and gambling, to treat certain persons with kindness; but on the graces of truth and honesty, of temperance and mercy, as principles of wide application, the Koran does not dwell.

I have failed to discover a single passage which touches on the virtue of meekness properly so called. Patience is inculcated, but chiefly as a condition of success in propagating the faith of Islam; for unless the believer was patient under insult and adversity, the cause of his religion might be injured by the provocation of an attack.

It is, however, only fair to give a specimen, which may be a sample of many more like it, of the check which reverence for the precepts of the Koran could place upon angry passions. As one of the sons of Ali, Mohammed's nephew, was dining, a slave dropped by accident a dish of scalding broth upon him. The poor creature fell prostrate before his master, and, to deprecate his rage, repeated a verse from the Koran 'Paradise is for those who command their anger;' 'I am not angry,' was the reply. 'And for those who pardon offenses;' 'I pardon your offence.' 'And for those who return good for evil;' 'I give you your liberty and four hundred pieces of silver.'

Sin

Nowhere in the Koran, as in the Bible, is sin set forth as the subtle leaven, the moral disease, pervading and corrupting human nature, as the evil principle of which all particular forms of wickedness are the outcome. The Koran prescribes the practice of certain virtues, and condemns the practice of certain vices; it encourages by promising rewards, it deters by threatening punishment; but it does not hold up before man the hatefulness and ugliness of all sin as a whole. It does not depict vividly and forcibly the sinfulness of his fallen nature and of the impossibility of his really cleansing himself in the sight of God. Of the need of propitiation for daily and inevitable transgressions, there is not a word.

This places at once a vast interval between the standpoint of the Mohammedan and the Jewish religions. The essence of the Biblical ethics is the insufficiency of man to fulfil the divine law of righteousness, the hopelessness of his obtaining the favor of God, or opening the gates of Heaven by the strength of his own merits.

The necessity, therefore, of propitiation and atonement runs through the teaching of the Bible from beginning to end. Every offering under the Jewish Law was an acknowledgment of the offerer's inability to meet God's demands; it was a cry for mercy [or an expression of thankfulness and devotion]. All the offerings were summed up and completely discharged for man [in some respects, but not others, for Christians are to be "living sacrifices"] in the Life crowned by the Death of Jesus Christ; and the attitude of the Christian towards God is that of humility and hope, his moral motive is gratitude and love.

The moral motive of Islam is a solemn sense of the duty of obedience and submission to an Almighty Ruler; whereas the moral motive of Christianity is love to an Almighty Father, an all-sympathizing Redeemer, Brother, and Friend.

The moral teaching of the Koran, put into a few words, seems to amount to this:

Obey these rules for moral conduct, and conform to this pre-scribed ceremonial in worship, because they are commanded by God and His prophet, and you will be rewarded with everlasting bliss in the life to come: (not, indeed, because you deserve it. Mohammed is careful to say that future bliss is the gift of God's mercy; but yet it is as confidently asserted that this gift will follow the discharge of certain prescribed duties, as if it were the price paid for them) disobey them, and you will be rewarded with everlasting torment.

Such a system is not calculated to inspire hope in the sinner, or to foster humility in the righteous, and is, to say the least, not unlikely to gender the delusion that the whole of practical morality and piety is enclosed within the narrow compass of a fixed number of precepts. There is no foundation laid in the Koran for that far-reaching charity which, under the Gospel regards all men as equal in the sight of God, and recognizes no distinctions into races and classes; there is no foundation for that keen sense of sinfulness, unworthiness, insuffi-ciency, for that distrust of self, and that reliance on one higher and mightier than ourselves, which has enabled all God's saints to do and to suffer things beyond their natural power, making good the saying of St. Paul, 'When I am weak, then am I strong' (2 Cor. 12:10).

The Practical Results of Christianity and Islam

W. R. W. Stephens

'By their fruits ye shall know them.' – (Matt. 7:20)

We have considered Islam hitherto in itself; the nature of its origin, and the character of its Founder; its Sacred Book, and the teaching theological and moral therein contained. But the best test, after all, of the truth and worth of a religion must be the practical one. What has it effected? Is mankind the better for it or the worse? What are its fruits? Men do not gather figs from thorns, neither from a bramble bush gather they grapes. Caution, however, must be observed in the application of this test.

It is not always easy to trace how far the prosperity or the depression of any given country is owing to the religion which prevails there or to other causes: race, climate, foreign invasion, and the like. Nor is it the primary object of religion to secure man's happiness in this world, but to guide him in his aspirations to the world above. But it seems safe to take our stand upon this principle, which may be called the law of concomitant variations: that if prosperity has followed the establishment of a certain form of religion, increasing where it is strong, and decreasing where it is weak, and this in a multitude of instances, - that is to say, in divers countries, and in divers ages of the world, - there must be something in that religion which is conducive to prosperity; and, in like manner, that if the reverse follows, there must be something in that religion adverse to prosperity, and consequently that such religion cannot as a whole be divine.

'The light which leads astray is not the light from Heaven.'

In Arabia

Let us, then, briefly survey what has taken place in those countries where Islam has been planted. First of all, it must be freely granted that to his own people Mohammed was a great benefactor. He was born in a country where political organization, and rational faith, and pure morals were unknown. He introduced all three. By a single stroke of masterly genius, he simultaneously reformed the political condition, the religious creed, and the moral practice of his countrymen; in the place of many independent tribes he left a nation; for a superstitious belief in Gods many and Lords many he established a reasonable belief in one Almighty yet beneficent Being; taught men to live under an abiding sense of this Being's superintending care, to look to Him as the rewarder, and to fear Him as the punisher of evil doers.

He vigorously attacked, and modified or suppressed, many gross and revolting customs which had prevailed in Arabia down to this time. For an abandoned profligacy was substituted a carefully regulated polygamy, and the practice of destroying female infants was effectually abolished.

The Middle East

As Islam gradually extended its conquest beyond the boundaries of Arabia, many barbarous races whom it absorbed became in like manner participators in its benefits. The Turk, the Indian, the Negro, and the Moor, were compelled to cast away their idols, to abandon their licentious rites and customs, to turn to the worship of one God, to a decent ceremonial and an orderly way of life. The faith even of the more enlightened Persian was purified; he learned that good and evil are not co-ordinate powers [Magianism], but that just and unjust are alike under the sway of one All-wise and Holy Ruler, who 'ordereth all things in heaven and earth.'

Primitive Cultures

For barbarous nations, then, especially, nations which were more or less in the condition of Arabia itself at the time of Mohammed - nations in the condition of Africa at the present day [1870], with little or no civilization, - and without a reasonable religion - Islam certainly comes as a blessing, as a turning from darkness to light, and from the power of Satan unto God.

Advanced Cultures

But the imposition of a system good for barbarians upon people already possessing higher forms of civilization, and the principles of a purer faith, is not a blessing, but a curse. Nay more, even the system which was good for people when they were in a barbarous state may become positively mischievous to those same people when they begin to emerge from their barbarism under its influence into a higher condition.

The danger, as was remarked at the beginning of the last lecture, attaching to a system which minutely regulates every department of social life, moral conduct, and religious ceremonial, is that it should be held rigorously in force upon men when they have outgrown the need of it.

It may be good as far as it goes; good relatively to certain circumstances, and perhaps, for the circumstances under which it was first devised, the best possible; but if it be not absolutely and perfectly good, good for all times, places, and persons, it must at some time, in certain places, and to certain persons become not a help, but a hindrance, to civilization and moral progress.

The immediate effect, then, of the introduction of Islam among barbarous races, is to raise them considerably in the scale of humanity. Its action in this respect is probably more speedy than the action of Christianity, owing to that definiteness, positiveness, minuteness, with which it is brought to bear on practical life, of which we have already spoken; it lays down rules and enforces conformity to them, and consequently a more immediate return is yielded in a visible reformation of manners, than is possible in the case of a religion which inculcates large principles for the due application of which much must be left to the individual conscience.

But when we turn to consider the effects of the introduction of Islam among nations already acquainted with the civilization of the Roman Empire and the light of the Christian religion, the picture is very different. We are compelled by the facts of history to decline believing that in these cases Islam, viewed as a whole, has been anything but an enormous evil.

Arab Conquests

Claiming, as it did, to be the truth, the whole truth, and nothing but the truth, it tolerated no rival; Christianity and Christian civilization were voluntarily or by compulsion to bend the knee before it. The most effectual plan was to make a clean sweep of both. Let us see how far the first Mohammedan conquerors acted upon it.

I will quote the words of that most eminent and trustworthy historian of the Byzantine Empire, Mr. Finlay. 'The Arab conquest,' he says, 'of Palestine and Syria, not only put an end to the political power of the Romans, which had lasted seven hundred years, but it also rooted out every trace of the Greek civilization introduced by the conquests of Alexander the Great which had flourished in the country for upwards of nine centuries' (Vol. i. p. 445, 2d edition).

The celebrated reply of the Caliph Omar, when asked what should be done with the library of Alexandria, illustrates the policy of the Saracens in Egypt as elsewhere. 'If,' said he, 'these writings agree with the Book of God [Qu'ran], they are useless and need not be preserved; if they disagree, they are pernicious, and ought to be destroyed;' and accordingly the library was burned. Here, again, Mr. Finlay remarks, 'political sagacity convinced the Arabs that it was necessary to exterminate Greek civilization in order to destroy Greek influence. The Goths, who sought only to plunder the empire, might spare the libraries of the Greeks; but the Mohammedans, whose object was to convert or subdue, considered it a duty to root out everything that presented any obstacle to the ultimate success of their schemes for the advent of Mohammedan civilization.' [And this continues in 2001 in Afghanistan, etc.]

Tracing their career of conquest along the northern coast of Africa, he concludes by observing 'The Saracens were singularly successful in all their projects of destruction; in a short time, both Latin and Greek civilization was exterminated on the southern shores of the Mediterranean' (Vol. i. pp. 450, 451. 2nd edition).

Moors in Spain

In Spain, after the establishment of the Caliphate of Cordova in 936 A.D., order succeeded a state of anarchy, which had been disastrous alike to the conquerors and to the conquered, and under a happy succession of vigorous, and in many instances, upright and enlightened Caliphs, commerce and agriculture, science, literature, and the arts, were carried to a higher degree of perfection than in any other country under Arabian rule. I am not just yet going to discuss the question, how far Arabic science and art were original, how far borrowed from the lower Greek Empire. What I wish to point out at present, is that although in Spain a high order, as it seemed, of prosperity grew up, yet it was only partial, it did not extend to the whole of the population; the subject Christians were never conciliated, or assimilated; they were not happy or content; and their resistance to the Moors, as they were called, never ceased, from the day the first Moor set foot in the land until the day the last was expelled from it [ca. 1490 A.D.].

The Byzantine Roman Empire

From this rapid survey of the early conquests of the Saracens, two facts seem abundantly plain: first, that the claim of Islam to supersede every other form of faith and of civilization was so absolute, that it could not tolerate their presence side by side with itself; and that, as a consequence, it never could get a permanent hold upon any country which had become thoroughly leavened with the Christianity, the civilization, and the law of the Roman Empire. It is a very inexact way of speaking to say that it 'crumpled up the empire;' (Bosworth Smith, Lect. i, p. 26, 2nd Edition) it would be more correct to say that it grated on the edges. Countries like Syria, Palestine, Egypt, and northern Africa, on the fringe of the empire, countries whose inhabitants were regarded as rebels by the Emperor, and as heretics by the Greek Church, fell before Islam, but on the heart of the empire it made no impression. Once it menaced Constantinople [later to fall to the Turks, in 1453 A.D.], but it was hurled back by the might and valor of Leo the Isaurian.

The second fact is this; that in those countries on the skirts of the empire where it did succeed in planting itself, this was accomplished at the cost of uprooting as far as possible the religion and civilization which it found there. To quote again from Mr. Finlay:

'Of all the native populations in the countries subdued, the Arabs of Syria alone appear to have immediately adopted the new religion of their co-national race; but the great mass of the Christians in Syria, Mesopotamia, Egypt, Cyrenaica, and Africa, clung firmly to their faith, and the decline of Christianity in all those countries is to be attributed rather to the extermination than to the conversion of the Christian inhabitants. The decrease in the number of the Christians was invariably attended by a decrease in the number of the inhabitants, and arose from the oppressive treatment which they suffered under the Mohammedan rulers of these countries - a system of tyranny which was at last carried so far as to reduce whole provinces to unpeopled deserts' (Vol. i. p. 452).

Persia, now Iran

Looking now beyond the limits of the Roman Empire, the country where we might most reasonably expect Mohammedanism to have accomplished great things is Persia. There Islam had a fair field to work upon; it became the national religion; there were no infidel Europeans to resist and hinder its free development. But, as if by a strange perverseness, Islam never seems to flourish so well as when it is attacked or attacking. Left to itself unmolested it loses energy, or wastes its strength upon internal strife. In Persia it split into a multitude of contending sects, more occupied in devouring one another than in promoting the welfare of their common country.

The Persian is probably the most polished, well educated, and literary, of all Mohammedans; yet his country is the most deplorable specimen of mismanagement, political, commercial, and everything else. Fertile as the country is, and scanty as is the population, there is none which has suffered more cruelly from famine; and, as a last resource, the helpless government was reduced to the ignominious necessity, a short time back [1870], of calling in the aid of a foreigner, a European, to save the country from becoming a total wreck.

India and Pakistan

Incomparably the most favorable example of Mohammedan rule is to be found in the Empire of the Great Moguls. The greatest man of that illustrious dynasty as far surpasses the best Caliphs of Cordova, as they excel the Shahs of Persia. The wise and noble Akbar, the third Mogul Emperor, presents to us the extraordinary spectacle of an Oriental despot, who during a long reign of nearly half a century was unblemished by a single crime worthy of record. In warfare he was humane, forbidding the sale of captives as slaves, dispensing when possible with the punishment of death, and forbidding it to be inflicted with unnecessary pain, or prolonged torture.

In legislation he was liberal; he abolished the capitation tax hitherto imposed upon the Hindus, he admitted men of all creeds to the highest offices of state. But, unfortunately, it cannot be maintained that this splendid example of an enlightened Moslem ruler was himself a veritable Mussulman. He was in fact an eclectic, and, beyond the doctrine of the unity of God, he paid but little attention to the teaching, theological or practical, of the Koran. He treated Christianity with marked respect, and even permitted one of his sons to be instructed in the Gospel.

The Moslem, too, was free to drink wine, to eat pork, to play at dice, and to withdraw, if he pleased, from the Mosque.

In short, Akbar was so sorry a Mussulman that he incurred the displeasure of his Moslem subjects, not, we may suppose, so much from the indulgences which he allowed to them, as for the lenity and impartial justice which he observed towards all other creeds. None of his successors were equally tolerant, and in Aurungzebe Moslem bigotry again mounted the throne.

The mild and equitable rule of Akbar is emphatically the case of an exception which proves [i.e., tests or demonstrates] the rule.

Still it is to be freely granted that the lot of the Hindus under Mussulman rule in India has never been so unhappy as the lot of the subject Christians in other countries. While this has been partly due to the character of the rulers, much, no doubt, has been owing also to the character of the ruled. The Hindu was naturally more passive and submissive than the native of western countries, and the mild tolerance of his religious creed inspired him with no earnest zeal either to propagate his own faith, or to resist the faith of his conquerors.

Turkey

But if there have been a few Moslem dynasties which present some passing gleams, more or less bright, more or less prolonged, of civilization and righteous government, there is one which, from the beginning of its career to the present day, has acted the part of the destroyer and the oppressor with the most fearful and unrelenting consistency. No country under Moslem rule is permanently prosperous, but the Ottoman Turk has succeeded beyond all others who have professed the faith of Islam in making the countries subject to his rule permanently miserable [written when the Ottoman Empire still flourished].

The land may be 'as the Garden of Eden before him, but behind him it is a desolate wilderness' (Joel 2:3). There is no country, perhaps, which Providence has blessed with a more bountiful store of natural resources than Asia Minor, especially on the sea coast; its rivers ran with gold, its mountains yielded copper and iron, and costly marble; its plains waved with all manner of crops, and the sides of its hills were clad with the vine and the olive. In the days of Greek and Roman enterprise the coast was thickly studded with populous and opulent cities. Under the care of an industrious people, it once was, and might be again, a paradise of beauty, and a treasure house of wealth.

But now the traveller wanders through a dreary region rich only in ruins, the melancholy relics of departed splendor, and inhabited only by roving bands of Turcomans, and their herds of goats.

Travellers also in Palestine [then part of the Ottoman Empire] tell us that the sacred soil would be prodigal in its gifts; that it might be again 'a land of wheat, and barley, and vines and fig trees and pomegranates, a land of oil olive and honey; a land wherein men might eat bread without scarceness; they should not lack anything in it; a land whose stones are iron, and out of whose hills men might dig brass;' (Deut. 8:8) (see especially Captain Warren's 'Underground Jerusalem,'. chap. xx.), but the curse of Turkish Mohammedan occupation is upon it, and, save in the neighborhood of Christian villages, the once fruitful land has become barren. [This was before the major Jewish immigration into Palestine started in 1881 A.D.]

Engraving of the Golden Horn and the city of Istanbul

The Balkans

The condition of European Turkey [the Balkans, still a major trouble-spot] is too notorious, unhappily, at the present time to require any description or comment. The conclusion to which we are brought by this rapid survey is that sooner or later, in less degree or in greater, historians and travellers have the same tale to tell of all countries under Moslem rule - the tale of lost fertility of the soil, of a diminished and degraded population, of ruined towns, of poverty-stricken villages.

Muslim Culture and Human Character

Turning now from the effect of Mohammedanism upon the countries where it was introduced to its effect on human character, some analogy is, I think, discernible between the two. The immediate effect is surprisingly great, and for the most part exceedingly admirable, but it does not last.

The first successors of Mohammed himself were splendid examples of the character which his religion could produce. Abu Bakr and Omar, Othman and Ali, were patterns of temperance, justice, and honour, for parallels to whom we look in vain among the corrupt and effete rulers of the Roman Empire in their day. But this early and speedy promise is followed by a no less rapid deterioration and decay. In the course of a few generations the noble breed of men who founded the Empire of Islam, partly warriors, partly statesmen, partly even saints, has vanished away.

The Christians in the Syrian province of the Roman Empire almost welcomed their Saracenic conquerors as affording them the prospect of a happier lot than that which they endured under the evil administration of a decadent power; but in a few generations these hopes were frustrated: the conquerors became oppressors, and the province was transformed into a desert.

In like manner the earlier Ottoman princes, although never approaching the Saracenic Caliphs in nobility of character, were not destitute of many fine qualities, and Othman at least had some true notions about the duties and obligations of a sovereign to his people. 'Rule mercifully and justly,' were the last words he spoke to his son. But his successors quickly degenerated into merciless tyrants, and have finally dwindled into the abject and despicable creatures whom we have now beheld for generations, seated on the throne of Constantinople, and in whom it is often difficult to say whether wickedness or weakness is the more distinctive feature.

Muslim Civilization

With regard to the science, literature, and art of the Saracens, of which one hears and reads so much, I would not for a moment question their reality or underrate their value; but that they were in any sense direct products of Islam is, I think, very much to be doubted.

Where did the Saracens get these things? Did they evolve them from their 'own inner consciousness'? They certainly did not bring them with them from Mecca and Medina. The fact is, that though they succeeded in destroying much of Greek and Roman literature and art, they could not destroy all. They could not destroy every copy of Aristotle and Hippocrates; they could not break down every Roman arch, nor did they demolish the mighty dome of St. Sophia at Constantinople [recently converted from a Mosque to a museum, and which still bears Christian inscriptions].

And there were men among the Arabs who were wise enough to study these Greek and Roman masterpieces of thought and art, and clever enough to turn their study to good practical account. They taught in Persia and in the Western part of the Roman Empire what they had learned in the Eastern part of it; and reproduced, perhaps with improvements, in Cordova or Baghdad, what they had seen in Byzantium. Their range of study amongst Greek authors was limited, and confined to translations of books on physical and metaphysical science.

The research of Gibbon failed to discover a record of any Arabic translation of any Greek poet, orator, or historian. We cannot rate very highly the literary genius of a people who neglected the richest treasury of human thought in these departments which the world possesses. Their native literary productions may be of a very high order; but it is difficult to believe that what is so very insignificant in translation, can be positively first rate in the original, at least in matter, though it may be in style.

Of the value of Arabian contributions to astronomy, mathematics, and medicine, I am quite incompetent to decide. Astronomy, we may say, is indigenous in the East, where the climate favors and facilitates the study. The so-called Arabic numerals appear to be of Indian origin.

What if?

If, then, it be true that the Mohammedans picked up their science and art, for the most part second-hand, from those fragments of both in the Roman Empire which escaped destruction from the early Mohammedan invaders, this question naturally occurs – supposing Eastern and Western Christianity had been left to pursue their course unmolested in Syria, Palestine, Asia Minor, Egypt, Northern Africa,

Spain, and Turkey, would not science, literature, the arts, and everything else which makes up civilization, have flourished as well as they have done in those countries under Moslem rule, or do now in those whose are still under it? It is hard to believe that they would not have flourished, not only as well, but a great deal better.

At any rate, they could not have flourished less than they do in most of those countries at the present moment. Mr. Palgrave bears strong testimony to the high intellectual and practical qualities of the Arabs; he sees capacities and aptitudes in the race for accomplishing great things in science and art, but he adds:

> 'When the Koran and Mecca shall have disappeared from Arabia, then, and then only, can we expect to see the Arab assume that place in the ranks of civilization from which Mohammed and his book have, more than any other cause, long held him back.'

Here again, then, we see, as in the case of Persia, that Islam left to itself has somehow the unpleasant knack of consuming energy and retarding progress.

Great Muslims weren't Muslim!

And this brings me to the last point in connection with this part of our subject. As the greatest and noblest specimen of a so called Mohammedan sovereign, Akbar was not, strictly speaking, a Mohammedan at all, so we find that, in all Mohammedan states, many of the most eminent men in all departments, politics, war, and literature, belonged, originally at least, to an alien race, and an alien creed, most commonly Christian or Jewish.(He who thinks it worth while to plod through the lists of learned men in the pages of Abdulpharagius may soon convince himself of this fact.)

Janissaries

The most remarkable illustration of this fact, because it is one which lasted for several centuries, was the employment by the Ottoman Turks of the corps known by the name of the Janissaries. From the end of the fourteenth up to the middle of the seventeenth century, the great military conquests of the Turks were mainly due to this celebrated body of soldiers.

And who were the Janissaries ? They were the offspring of Christians in the provinces which the Turk had already subdued - Greece, Albania, Bulgaria, and Romania. They were a human tax levied by the conqueror on his victims; the very flower of their strength. Torn at an early age from their homes, they were carefully trained up as Mussulmans, in ignorance of any home but the camp, and of any earthly power to whom allegiance was due, save the representative of the great prophet of Islam.

'From the seminaries of the Janissaries,' says Von Hammer, 'issued the greatest men of the Ottoman Empire. As long as the yearly levy of Christian children continued, their most famous statesmen and generals were for the most part born Greeks, Albanians, and Bosnians; seldom native Turks.' 'And thus,' he proceeds in cogent and indignant language, 'thus the strength of Turkish despotism repaired itself in the heart-blood of Christendom; and by means of this cunning engine of statecraft Greece was compelled to tear herself to pieces by the hands of her own children.'

The words of Von Hammer are only a repetition of an observation made centuries before, in 1573, by a Venetian diplomatist at the court of Selim II. 'It is in the highest degree remarkable,' he said, 'that the wealth, the administration, the force, in short the whole body politic of the Ottoman Empire rests upon, and is entrusted to, men born in the Christian faith, converted into slaves, and reared up as Mohammedans.'

The saying remains in a great measure true to the present day. Whatever vital energy there is in Turkey, whatever agricultural industry, whatever commercial enterprise, appears to depend upon Jews or Christians; in fact upon any people but the Turks; and though the common Turk can fight with courageous obstinacy [as in WWI Gallipoli], the conduct of the fleet and army of that poor shadowy thing men call the Sublime Porte, appears to be entrusted in a great measure to foreigners.

We do not say that the barbarism of the Turk is the product of Islam; far from it. It is, no doubt, in a great measure inherent in the

Tartar race; but we do say that Mohammedanism has not cured it, or even improved it. As he was barbarian in the beginning, so is the Turk barbarian now, and so, as long as he remains Mohammedan, barbarian to all human appearance he will continue to be.

On the other hand, experience warrants the assertion that there is no race, barbarian or civilized, of which Christianity has taken a firm hold, that has not advanced, and that does not manifest capacities of further progress to an indefinite extent. (I use these words advisedly because Abyssinia [Ethiopia] is an instance of a state which has long professed Christianity, and yet is barbarous; but Christianity in Abyssinia is so very imperfect and impure that it can hardly be said to have more than touched it.)

This is the real answer to those superficial remarks often made that the Russian or the Bulgarian is as barbarous as the Turk, that the Turk 'is a gentleman,' and so on. It is not indeed true, even now; but if it were true, we might be quite sure that it would not remain true, because history and experience teach us, that while in Christian states, there is an indefinite power of advance, Mohammedan states, after quickly reaching a certain point, become stationary, or else retrograde.

In the most degraded, the most barbarian Christian state, there are untold germs, endless possibilities of growth. Is it thus with Mohammedan nations? Let the past history or the present condition of Arabia, of Persia, of Syria, of Egypt, of Northern Africa, of Spain, of Asia Minor, of Turkey in Europe supply the answer.

It is easy to point to individual Mohammedans who have been better than individual Christians, just as it is easy to point to special eras when some Mohammedan states have been more civilized than some Christian states. But this proves nothing. The question is, not whether Islam has produced here and there fine types of character, or splendid eras of civilization, but whether, as a system, in the long run, it promotes a higher and ever increasing order of civilization and virtue. Are Mohammedan countries, as a rule, prosperous and progressive, or are they depressed, stationary, retrograde?

Take a practical test. Would any one as willingly live in the London, the Paris, the Vienna, the St. Petersburg, of 200 years ago, as he would live in the London, the Paris, the Vienna, the St. Petersburg of the present day, notwithstanding all the abominations which yet remain there? I think not. This is because the countries of which those cities are the capitals have advanced in civilization.

Could we apply the same test with equal confidence to cities under Mohammedan rule, Smyrna [in Turkey], for instance? In fact, from a review of the past history, and a survey of the present condition, of the principal countries in the world, there seems no escape from the conclusion that Christianity and real civilization are practically co-extensive; where the one ends, the other ends also.

And if this be the case; if, though with occasional gleams of sunshine, the presence of Mohammedanism acts like an east wind on prosperity and progress, the question yet remains why is this?

The three worst elements of Barbarism

The explanation may be found in the fact that three of the worst elements of barbarism, three conditions the most fatal to human civilization and moral improvement, are incorporated in Islam as integral parts of the system. The three evils to which I allude are polygamy, despotism, and its counterpart, slavery. They are indigenous in the East; Mohammed alleviated them indeed, but they are distinctly adopted in the Koran, and consequently are invested with a kind of divine sanction.

They stamp upon the religion of Mohammed an essentially Oriental character. Christianity and the Western nations abhor and repudiate these three evil things, and consequently Mohammedanism has ever been the most implacable foe to Christianity and the Western nations, the most impervious barrier to the advance of Christianity and Western civilization in an eastward direction.

The establishment of a regulated polygamy by Mohammed was, of course, a great advance upon the unrestrained licentiousness which in Arabia had preceded it; but then polygamy, although controlled, is established, with all its concomitant evils: degradation on the side of the woman who belongs to the husband, while the husband does not belong to her: jealousies on both sides, an overgrown and divided household. Yet all who acknowledge the Koran must accept polygamy as a divinely sanctioned condition of life.

Under the law of Moses, polygamy was tolerated; under the law of Mohammed it is established. All honour to him for endeavoring to mitigate its evils by restriction. The practice was so deeply rooted in Oriental life that this was probably all which he could venture to attempt.

The divine wisdom of the Mosaic law is manifested in the fact that while it seems to do less for the evil, while it tolerates and places no defined limitations on the practice, it thereby left the way more clear for its ultimate abolition.

To the votary of Islam, again, there is no escape from the recognition of absolute despotism as a divinely ordered form of government. By virtue of his alleged commission from God, Mohammed claimed the right to regulate every item in the life of his disciples; and his successors are suffered [allowed] to inherit his divine right of absolute power, only limited in their case by deference to the directions of the Koran. That sacred volume is the only groundwork of jurisprudence for nations professing the faith of Islam ["Islamic Law"]. It is for the Mussulman his code of civil law, as well as of theology and ethics.

The ultimate appeal in every question of law in any Mohammedan nation, whether it be in the East or the West, whether it be in the ninth century or the nineteenth, is to some sentences inscribed on a palm leaf or mutton bone in Arabia in the middle of the seventh century.

The rigidity of the Koran is often so incapable of adaptation to the necessities of particular cases that, in order to prevent a deadlock, an ingenious method of evasion is adopted. To quote the words of Gibbon:

'The Kadi respectfully places the sacred volume on his head, and substitutes a dexterous interpretation more apposite to the principles of equity, and to the manners and policy of the times.'

Should the employment of this subterfuge become more common, as in some Mohammedan countries seems probable, the way will be indefinitely opened to moral and social, if not religious reformation; but then Islam will cease to be Islam.

Where the religion of Mohammed is maintained in its integrity, the sciences of divinity and law coalesce; the jurist and divine is the same person, only looked at from different points of view, and one name is common to him in both capacities. In like manner the functions of monarch and chief pontiff are united in the same person [i.e., the Ayatollah].

Such is the impotence of the Ottoman Sultans at the present day, that the administration of government (if the word government can be so far dishonored as to be applied to what is, in fact, merely a system of rapine) must practically be conducted by other wills than theirs; yet the Grand Vizier and the Mufti are in theory only the ministers, and obedient slaves of the Sultan's will in temporal and ecclesiastical affairs.

And in the early days of Saracenic and Turkish power, the great Caliphs and Sultans exercised a despotic power exceeding that of any Roman Emperor or Pope; for the will even of the most despotic emperors or popes was subject to the control of some forms of constitutional law, and that law, again, was leavened more or less by the principles of the Gospel. Even the tyranny of the first [Napoleon] Bonaparte was not that purely arbitrary will, that mere personal agency, which in its origin is essentially Oriental, and which is embodied in the religious system of Mohammed.

In describing the effects of the early Saracenic conquests, Mr. Finlay remarks:

'No attempt was made to arrange any systematic form of political government, and the whole power of the state was vested in the hands of the chief priest of the religion, who was only answerable for the due exercise of this extraordinary power to God, his own conscience, and the patience of his subjects. The moment, therefore, that the responsibility created by national feelings, military companionship, and exalted enthusiasm ceased to operate on the minds of the Caliphs, the administration became far more oppressive than that of the

Roman Empire. No local magistrates elected by the people, and no parish priests connected by their feelings and interests both with their superiors and inferiors, bound society together by common ties; and no system of legal administration, independent of the military and financial authorities, preserved the property of the people from the rapacity of the government. Socially and politically the Saracen Empire was little better than the Gothic, Hunnish, and Avar monarchies; and that it proved more durable with almost equal oppression is to be attributed to the powerful enthusiasm of Mohammed's religion which tempered for some time its avarice and tyranny.'

We may add, that where the conscience of the sovereign and the patience of the people are the only bounds to the exercise of his power, conscience is apt to become hardened, and patience amazingly enduring. Inured to subjection, and deprived of any ready means of discussing their wrongs, or concerting resistance, the people are apt to lapse into apathetic indolence, and stupid resignation.

Slavery

It is unnecessary to add that where polygamy and despotism exist, there also slavery must be found. Slavery, in fact, pervades the whole social and political life of a people under Moslem rule. The wife is the slave of the husband rather than his partner; the domestic servant is the slave of both. The Pasha is the slave of the despot; he is a despot himself over the province which is in bondage to his rule.

Slavery appears to be mild in Mohammedan countries, and so it is; not only because kind treatment of the slave is enjoined in the Koran, but also because where all are reduced more or less to the condition of slaves, servitude is no disgrace. Where all are equally subject to the absolute will of the monarch, the sharp distinctions of rank are removed. Servitude becomes no barrier to the elevation of a man to the highest offices in the State.

The favor of the despot indeed is more likely to be bestowed on a slave than on a man of noble origin; the policy of the despot being to depress the aristocracy, who might by their position become leaders of rebellion, and to reduce all ranks as much as possible to one dead level of subjection. And, as a matter of fact, the men who have risen to the highest offices in Moslem States, especially at Constantinople, have been commonly men who began by discharging the most menial and often the basest and most disgraceful functions about the court of the sovereign.

Islam tied to Middle Eastern ethics

We repeat that we do not affirm these evils to be the direct products of Islam. They are indigenous in the East, and are deeply rooted in Oriental [Middle-Eastern] habits of life; but we do say that they are the concomitants of Islam; that where Islam is established they are established, and further that, though alleviated in degree, they are more closely riveted upon Mohammedan countries than any others, because they are there invested with a divine sanction.

Islam has taken up into itself and consecrated these evil forms of Oriental life, and consequently it opposes the most solid obstacle to the reception in the East of Christian and Western civilization.

Where, on the other hand, the Mussulman rules over a population which is Christian and European, he can never assimilate them or be assimilated by them; the Koran forbids him to treat an infidel as his equal; the alien invader can maintain his conquest only by becoming an oppressor; the two elements may live centuries side by side, but like oil and vinegar they will not fuse; the one is Mohammedan, Asiatic, stationary; the other Christian, European, progressive.

Christianity is International

As the character of the Great Head of the Christian Church, when He became incarnate, was Catholic [=International], so is the character of the Church which He founded. It is capable of adaptation to human nature everywhere, because it is not like an inanimate machine which, once made, can work only in one way, but is a living organism instinct with a divine life, even the spirit of its Head. It can move in a hundred different ways according to His direction, and accommodate itself to every race, and to every form of social or political condition; it can live under a despotism or a republic, amongst the rich and the poor, the Teuton, the Celt, the African, the Indian, the Melanesian.

Engraving showing the Golden Horn and the Suleymaniye mosque

On the other hand as the character of the founder of Islam was essentially Oriental, so is the character of the religion which he founded; it is acceptable to the Oriental nature, but repugnant to the Western; it has made rapid progress and obtained a firm footing among Eastern countries; and, as it will not easily recede from its pretensions to the possession of absolute truth it is the most formidable rival which Christianity has to encounter in the East.

Relations between Christianity and Islam

And what tone, it may be asked, ought the Christian Church to assume towards its rival? Certainly not that of denunciation or defiance, nor, on the other hand, of approbation and concession.

In the face of the fact that Christians never have been able to live peaceably and happily under Moslem rule, although at the present day Mussulmans live in great peace and prosperity under Christian rule, it is, we think, rather hard that Christians should be reproached as inclined to an attitude of harsh hostility or contempt towards the

Moslem faith (Bos. Smith, Lect. iv. p. 259, 279, and Preface to second edition, p. 9.).

By all means let us recognize to the full what was great and noble in Mohammed himself and in the work which he accomplished; let us recognize to the full all the good which the religion of Mohammed has done, as well as all the evil, all its truth as well as all its error; let us hold out the right hand of fellowship to the Mussulman as a brother, though an erring brother, whom we are bound to honour, to respect, and even to love.

But, on the other hand, do not let us disguise or gloss over the fact that there is error, and most mischievous error in his religion; do not let us talk of it as if it were almost as good as Christianity, or because Mohammed had a sort of reverence for Christ, go to the ridiculous length of calling Islam 'a form of Christianity;' (Bos. Smith, Lect. iv. p. 260) although it expressly denies the very essence of Christianity, the Divinity and Incarnation of our blessed Lord.

Do not let us make apologies for praying that the Mussulman may be brought to the knowledge of a nobler and purer faith than his own as if it was an insult (Ibid. p. 259.).

To cultivate friendship and good-will with men of a different creed it cannot be necessary, because it cannot be right, to surrender one jot or tittle of the essential principles of our own faith; conscientious unbelievers would despise us if we did. What is needed is the exercise of that large-hearted charity which seeks their good in every possible way; endeavors to win them to the truth; acts with them where it can, and, where it cannot, stands respectfully and courteously aside.

It was a common saying of one of the most uncompromising Churchmen, the late Dean Hook, to Dissenters with whom he was brought much in contact and always lived on the most friendly terms: 'There is a line between us, but across that line we shake hands.' The saying would equally illustrate the proper attitude of Christians towards the Mussulman, or any other kind of unbeliever. There is a line between us; if we can persuade them to cross the line and to be one with us, we will receive them with open arms; if they will not cross it, let us shake hands over the line, and work hand in hand whenever they will move in a parallel direction with us.

But do not let us pretend that there is no line, that Christianity is only a few shades better than Mohammedanism, the Bible only 'as a whole' better than the Koran, and that the difference between the two religions is one not of kind, but only of degree (Bos. Smith, Lect. i., p. 64, 67.). In short, in our laudable anxiety to make our Christianity pleasant and attractive to men of another creed, let us take heed not to dilute Christian doctrine so far as to find some day that we have lost what was of vital value for ourselves, and only bestowed on others a residuum which was hardly worth their acceptance.

Christianity and Islam in Dialogue

Address of His Beatitude
Petros VII
Pope and Patriarch of Alexandria and All Africa
to the 12th International Meeting "People and Religion"

31st August 1998

It can be said that dialogue between Christianity and Islam springs from the essence of Christianity, which is the foremost religion of dialogue. God Himself in the Old Testament, as the God Creator, speaks with man (cf. Gen. 1:28; 17:1-2, Exod. 3:4-6) and reveals the uniqueness of His divine existence (cf. Deut. 6:4); and the same God, in the New Testament, in the person of the incarnated Logos of God, reveals Himself to the world (cf. John 1:14) and calls everyone to repentance (cf. Mark 1:15) and salvation (cf. John 1:13-19).

There are basic and essential differences between the religions of Christianity and Islam, which cannot be ignored, but there are also common elements which can be discussed. Subjects concerning man and the world, especially matters which deal with everyday problems, can lead in this dialogue. The existence since the 7th century A.D. of both religions in the same geographical locality, for example, in the Middle East and North Africa, can inspire mutual respect and the peaceful acceptance of the beliefs of both religions.

Christianity, through and within dialogue, aims to learn more about Islam, its teachings, its history and traditions, always in the spirit of truth, pure love and respect. Today, more than ever before, each religion feels the need to proclaim its existence and authenticity in the contemporary world. Communication and co-operation between religions make an essential contribution to the abolition of religious fanaticism, an intellectual sickness of the religious person, to friendship between nations, and towards the encouragement of the rule of the ideals of freedom and peace in the world. Our co-operation in finding solutions to the contemporary problems of mankind, will assist in our peaceful coexistence and common understanding.

The religions of Christianity and Islam are two individual fountains, from which their faithful receive the inner strength to follow their faith and grow spiritually. According to this principle, each religion claims its autonomy when confronting any theoretical or practical problems faced by their flocks.

Unfortunately, racial and religious discrimination often aggravate the minds of men and bring back the painful past. As a result, Christian and Muslim communities often have reservations about approaching one another and about the feasibility of peaceful coexistence.

Religious fanaticism can bring only new social and religious problems upon the people who are ruled by it. Religious confrontations and clashes are the result of this sick religious phenomenon. Christians and Muslims alike are obliged to turn their attention towards the future, so that they can bring about the vision of God's peace upon Earth.

But why, although these two religions have coexisted for such a long time, does the smallest political disturbance inflame religious intolerance? It is here that dialogue between Christianity and Islam can offer a great deal to mankind. Productive dialogue can help realise heavenly peace on Earth, and protect the holiness of life and man's dignity. Religions do not enforce peace, but can mark out the man of peace, and adapt his mission to the needs of his time.

Dialogue which is based, not only on theological matters, but on worldly issues, can be both hopeful and fruitful. The secularity, coldness and anonymity of society, the destruction of the environment, the lack of world justice and peace, hunger, poverty, nuclear threat etc., are issues which touch the soul of the unfortunate man of our time. The world is tired of religious wars and conflicts.

Let us not forget that many local Churches, such as the three ancient Greek Orthodox Patriarchates of the East (Constantinople, Alexandria and Antioch), live today in the Islamic world. Orthodoxy coexists and seeks dialogue with Islam; dialogue which presupposes freedom of speech and equality between the two parties.

In Eastern Christianity one sees respect towards the religious experience of others, forbearance and mutual understanding. Basic theological faith held that the "calling" and the "desire for God" guide all men. Man, even after his Fall, had the ability to receive the divine presence. St. Paul emphasised this by saying: "And had made of one blood all nations of men for to dwell on all the face of the earth, and had determined the times before appointed, and the bounds of their habitation; that they should seek the Lord, if haply they might feel after him, and find him, though he be not far from every one of us" (Acts 17:26-27). Religious experiences do not represent only an insistent inner movement of man towards a higher reality, but an acceptance of the divine radiance within this world.

For the Greek Orthodox Patriarchate of Alexandria, which for thirteen centuries has lived in the friendly country of Egypt, dialogue with the Islamic world has special and vital meaning. Islam is our close neighbour and the Patriarchate is not alien to it. Alexandria, where the ancient Patriarchate was founded by St. Mark the Apostle and Evangelist, is alien neither to the West nor to the East, because it is a Greek environment from where Greek civilisation and the theological thoughts of the Fathers of the Church have been channelled. The meeting and coexistence of the second-ranking Patriarchate of Orthodox Christianity with the eastern civilisations has its roots deep in history.

For centuries, a large part of Orthodoxy lived in the Islamic world, although not always as an equal member of its society. Despite difficult times, confrontations and misunderstandings, the bonds between them were never broken. This productive spiritual communion between the Greek and Arabic world, between the Christian and Islamic civilisations, is in itself a dialogue of centuries which has enlightened and benefited the people of both East and West.

In conclusion, we must say that dialogue is necessary, and indeed, is the only acceptable way to bring our two religions closer. It is our common desire that all misunderstanding and preconceptions be put aside. We must cultivate mutual trust in order to achieve a better understanding. Dialogue is necessary if we are to overcome the past and the present of alienation, confrontation, enmity and hatred. Those who are responsible for this dialogue must make every effort to solve the prevailing problems of our world, to build a more human society characterised by justice and fraternal love.

While being fully aware of our common responsibility, Christians and Muslims are duty bound to respect absolutely each others religious beliefs and overcome antagonistic feelings. We must strive for solidarity if we are to resolve the problems facing the world, for the Earth is the common home of all nations wherein we are called to worship the One True God.

Arab-Christians in the Arab and Muslim World

What is Our Mission?

Patriarch Gregory III
Melkite Greek-Catholic Church of Antioch, Alexandria, Jerusalem and All the East

Christianity is not an identity, nationalism, or community, or even a church in the institutional sense, although Christians are united in a Church of flesh and of stone.

Christ did not come to found a religion, a nation, a group, a society opposite other groups, although he wanted to gather around Himself the college of Apostles, saying to Peter: "You are Peter, and upon this rock I will build my church, and the gates of the netherworld shall not prevail against it" (Matt. 16:18, NAB).

Christ did not want to suppress Jewish religion in order to establish another religion in its place. He went beyond it without renouncing it, because Christ is Love, and He cannot hate that which He desired with His Father, He, the Word, through Whom everything was made and without Whom nothing was made. In Him is life, and Christ is of the race of David, hence of Jewish and divine origin at the same time. This is why He is for everyone and of everyone.

Christ goes beyond, in this sense, all values, all categories, all measures, all boundaries between one land and another, between one group and another, between one tribe and another, between one nation and another, between one community and another, between one gender and another, as St. Paul says: "There is neither Jew nor Greek, there is neither slave nor free person, there is not male and female; for all are ONE in Christ Jesus" (Gal. 3:28, NAB, emphasis added). This is found in the prayers of the Akathist of the Theotokos, where one speaks of the "new creature" (Ikos 13: "The Creator has appeared for us, a new creature, to us, his new creation").

Christianity is thus this new creation, which exceeds all the frameworks, all the categories, all the predications of philosophy and of human, nationalist, sectarian thought. Indeed, Christ is in the world, but He is not of the world. Jesus prayed before His passion: "[Father,] I do not ask that you take them out of the world but that you keep them from the evil one" (John 17:15, NAB). This does not mean that Christianity, a new creation, exceeds other religions, or even that it is superior or preferable to them. It is something else, a new category, a new predication. Likewise, true Islam goes beyond everything: "you are the greatest nation," says the Qur'an. This does not mean that it is better than the others, but a new category. Likewise the true Judaism is that of the Prophets, which goes beyond human categories, beyond all the sinful values of "my" religion and "your" religion.

In this sense, being a new creature, the Christian cannot be for himself. He cannot be limited to his group, his community, his nation, or even his Church. I, as an Arab-Christian bishop, am not only for Christians. I am for "man," in order to bring him the Gospel, whoever he may be, not as the Book of a given group, but rather, as the etymology of its name says, "a spiritual, universal, global, open Good News." One can understand that Christians, throughout their history, have little by little institutionalized this Good News of the Gospel, but this framework must not stifle this message, limit it, obscure it or hide it as clouds hide the sun. This is the understanding behind the statement I made in the summer of 1990 at the Congress for the Patrimony for Christians and Muslims in the Holy Land: "I am a bishop for Christians and Muslims." I can complete this: "I am a bishop for Jews, for every person," and Christians cannot be Christians if they are not such for Muslims and with Muslims, and with every person.

Hence, what is the mission of Christian Arabs in the Arab and Muslim world? Must we place ourselves into a ghetto? Curl ourselves up upon ourselves? Is it necessary to put forth all our efforts in order to preserve our presence as a community, a nation, a group versus other groups? Is it necessary to concentrate our efforts on keeping and preserving what we unfortunately call " our privileges and rights," and "our status quo," especially in the Holy Land? Must we continually fear Muslims and Islam, as is the case for many of us Christians? Must we either content ourselves with a dialogue that often goes nowhere, when what we want is a dialogue about religions, or convince ourselves and others of their religion? Dialogue, in that sense, "to win the other over to me," is a dialogue of the deaf. Is this so? Or, unable to realize everything I come to propound, we emigrate in the vast regions of God's earth and leave this land and this Arab-Muslim milieu...?

How can we renew the leaven of our Christian societies with these ideas? What can we do with respect to the responsibilities of the Christian churches? With respect to the clergy? To the monks and nuns? To all sorts of centers of formation? To engaged Christian laity? Do they not have an important role to play in the Christian mission, in the Arab-Muslim world?

What is this mission? This role? This is the difficult question to which I propose some elements of a response further on. We are co-citizens of the world and of Arab-Muslim society. Each Christian is this co-citizen, in his own city, in his own country, in Palestine, in Israel, in Jordan, in Lebanon, in Syria, in Egypt, etc. We are, purely and simply, Arab citizens. We are of and for these countries in which we were born and in which we live, and we have obligations toward this country of ours. We likewise have rights, like all the citizens of our countries. We are citizens like others, without distinction and without privilege and without special rights because we are Christians. Moreover, we must not permit anyone to practice against us any kind of discrimination, division on the basis of race, religion, group, community, or church. We require this for ourselves and for others. We demand this for us, not on account of a different religion or on account of our different community, but solely as citizens, and we do not allow any sort of racial, social, or religious discrimination against anyone, since we know that neither our religion, nor the Gospel, nor Islam, nor any other religion can accept such discrimination; and we know that our Muslim brothers, if they are faithful to Islam, cannot permit any discrimination.

We are members of this Arab society, and we are Arabs. If we, as Christians, are not Arabs, then many, many are no longer Arabs as well, since many among them are of Christian origin and have passed over from Christianity to Islam in the course of the centuries. We are Arabs, of the Arab world and for this Arab world, and we refuse that

Christians not consider themselves Arabs or Arabized. I say that without chauvinism or prejudice, but as a truth, a reality.

We are of the Arab world and for the Arab world, for this Arab society, for this Islamic world, although without being Muslims. We ought, perhaps, to consider ourselves as Muslims, being obliged to engage ourselves totally, entirely, existentially vis-à-vis this Arab world. St. Paul says: " I have become all things to all" (1 Cor. 9:22, NAB) in order to gain all for Christ. I wonder who is responsible for bringing the message of the Gospel to our Muslim brothers, not to convert them, but to bring the Gospel to them, if not we who have lived with them for centuries, for 1, 414 years. I do not speak of conversion to Christianity, which may come in secondary fashion; what is important is the spiritual, interior witness of the Gospel and not the passing over from one group to another with the same spirit of the group and of the clan. Bearing witness to the Gospel can assume many different and varied forms and has nothing to do with proselytism, which has conversion as its goal. It is to bear the message of the Good News to our Muslim brethren without harming them in any way whatsoever. Bearing the message is an act of love, a splendid, radiant, transfigured human act. To bear to this Muslim world the Christian message while leaving it free, respecting it, and thereby gaining its love, too; to serve this Muslim world, at the cost of greater and greater sacrifices, even if we ourselves are not served.

To bear the message is the foundation of the work of God, who converts whom He will, as the Qur'an says; and Christ Himself has taught: "In my Father's house there are many dwelling places" (John 14:2, NAB); "many will come from the east and the west, and will recline with Abraham, Isaac, and Jacob at the banquet in the kingdom of heaven, but the children of the kingdom will be driven out into the outer darkness" (Matt. 8:11-12, NAB).

It is for that reason that it is not necessary to see the fruits of the message that we bear to others, but we must enliven this Muslim society by the spiritual leaven of the Gospel, and likewise through the elements of Islam and of the Qur'an that we find in their sacred Book, in Muslim spirituality, and in our Muslim brethren who know us and who love us. It would be very desirable to have, here in the Holy Land, an Islamic-Christian circle, with a human, spiritual, religious, and open character outside the official dialogue of Al Liqa, and to reflect, with them, on the manner in which they see the mission of the Arab Christian in the Arab Muslim world. To live a spiritual life with a small Muslim group would be an extraordinary thing.

We should unite our efforts to those of the Muslims in thousands of ways and thousands of means. We work together as faithful believers for the same goal of reinforcing faith, building a society that will be our society for everyone, Muslims and Christians. We should not fear the Muslims, or any Muslim group whatsoever. We must not isolate ourselves from any group at all, regardless of its orientation, even from a "fundamentalist" group. The important thing in all of this is to keep on erecting bridges, to build them with our Muslim brothers and Muslim society, in this vision that I am about to propose. Building bridges is an integral, extremely important, truthful, and fundamental part of the evangelical message. It is an essential component of the meaning of our mission in the Arab and Muslim world. We have no right, whatever the conditions and the social, political, and economic situations, to stop this Christian opening to Islamic thought, as well as to Islamic culture, society, and personality. We cannot be Christians without our Muslim brothers in the Arab-Muslim world.

That said, it is necessary that we be circumspect, prudent, and careful to preserve Christian identity and personality through this work of building bridges and of going out toward this Arab-Muslim world. We must make our Muslim brother feel that we have no aim or intention of destroying this Islamic identity and personality, nor to change, uproot, or diminish it. The Muslim has his personality, his mentality, spirituality, and way of life. In and through all of this we must bring to him the evangelical message of the Good News. There should be osmosis with the Arab-Muslim world, a reciprocal activity full of respect, consideration, and esteem, a mutual exchange of sincere, complete, and simple efforts, without either an inferiority complex or fear.

It is necessary, in order to realize this goal, for our efforts to be coordinated with those of our European brothers who often have a rather negative stance toward Islam and Muslims, especially with regard to fundamentalist movements. Quite often, Europe nourishes sentiments of fear, hatred, and lack of respect toward the Arab world. It is our duty to help our Christian brethren to understand us and to support us in this mission. We will thus be "bridge-builders" with regard to Muslims and between European Christians and Muslims. It is a very important mission.

Likewise, it is urgent to find adequate means to influence the nations of Europe and America, the so-called Christian states, or at least to influence Christian politicians, Catholics in particular, such that they have this openness toward Islam and Muslims and conduct themselves according to the spirit of the Gospel in their relations with the Islamic world.

Moreover, new bonds could arise between a reunified Europe and the Arab world, better understood, after the terrible upheavals of the Gulf war.

Is it not an opportune time to establish an East-West, European-Arab, Christian-Muslim collaboration on a grander scale and, thus, to realize together peace, religious freedom in mutual respect, reciprocity among people, as well as the realization of a true democracy, respectful of the Christian presence in the Arab-Muslim world?

It is indispensable to study all of this at different levels: the laity at the level of Liqa, of the Cenacle, of pastoral councils of different churches, of schools, at the same time as at the level of the heads of the churches in each country, and within the framework of the Council of Churches of the Middle East. This process is already underway in certain cases.

The time has come to study seriously the meaning of our presence and of our Christian mission in the Arab-Muslim world: this is a challenge of the Gospel for us; we have to raise the consciousness of our brethren, of our faithful, of our parishes on this subject. It is very important to help the faithful get rid of feelings of fear, prejudices, complexes, and isolationism toward Muslims.

It is important to do this at the threshold of the third millennium, and of what we hope is a new, effective, and inspired stage of development for the Palestinian cause. This is very important in our Palestinian country and in our relations with the Israeli Jewish world. We, as a Christian community, do not have the right only to follow, to lag behind, to be without color, without a true Christian personality reflected in a luminous visage, in clear thinking at the service of the involvement of our people at the present hour, which is crucial for the region.

Can we do something practical in order to put these ideas to work? By means of open discussions within the Cenacle of Jerusalem. Might it be the time to reflect on the future of our country and of our Palestinian church in order to see how we might continue down the road together?

It is possible to present these ideas to the next Holy Synod of our Greek-Catholic Church.

It is perhaps important to present these ideas, after ripening and sharpening them, to the West.

It is necessary to ripen these thoughts, these propositions, these ideas that have come to be of extreme importance at the time of the settling of the Gulf war, at the time of the new world order, of the perspectives and prospects of a better future for the whole region.

*View of the Hippodrome, Sultanahmet mosque and Hagia Sophia
(in the distance) of present-day Istanbul*

The Coptic Orthodox Church under Islam

Metropolitan Seraphim of Glastonbury

The Arab Conquest

In Egypt, the last years of Byzantine rule were characterised by inter-Christian strife arising from the continuing rejection of the Council of Chalcedon (451) by the Coptic majority. Having just regained Egypt from Persian occupation (618-628) the Emperor Heraclius (610-641) appointed Kyros, Bishop of Phasis in Kolchis, as Melkite Patriarch of Alexandria in 631. In order to achieve religious unity within the Empire, Patriarch Kyros was also appointed *Dioiketes* (effectively viceroy) of Egypt giving him almost absolute power to impose his will on the non- Chalcedonian Copts.

The vigour with which he did this led to ferocious persecution. His Arabic sobriquet *Al-Mukaukas*, is still a byword for brutality. The Coptic Patriarch Benjamin I (622-661) was forced to flee into the desert and his brother, Mina, having been tortured in an effort to discover his hiding place was drowned in the Nile in a sack filled with stones. For ten years the persecution raged under the tyranny of Kyros who was likened to "a wolf devouring the flock and never satiated."

It is against this background that the Arab invasion (639-643) took place. Following the capture of Jerusalem and the ongoing conquest of Syria, the Muslim general Amr ibn al-Asi turned his attentions to the wealth of Egypt, which the recent Persian conquest had shown to be vulnerable. In December 639, with a force of only 3,500 to 4,000 soldiers, Amr secretly entered Egypt and within a few weeks had captured Pelusium, the city guarding the eastern edge of the Delta. Without reinforcements he might have easily been driven back by the Imperial army but he was able to advance towards the strongly fortified fortress of Babylon meeting little resistance until Heliopolis, where he won a decisive victory.

The siege of Babylon lasted seven months and was successfully holding up Amr's wider plans for conquest when Kyros proposed acceptance of a shameful treaty, which involved the surrender of the fortress and payment of tribute in return for the evacuation of the Imperial garrison and their safe passage to Alexandria. Permitted to leave the fortress to seek the Emperor's ratification, Kyros returned to Alexandria before being summoned to an angry reception in Constantinople. The rejection of the treaty by the Emperor Heraclius and the exile of Kyros brought the truce to an end and assaults on the besieged citadel were resumed. Weakened by plague and unsure whether reinforcements had been despatched or not, the final blow to the defender's morale came with news of the Emperor's untimely death and the resultant chaos in the struggle for the succession. The defenders held on for a further month before accepting even less favourable terms than those previously proffered, whereby they retired by river carrying only a few days' subsistence whilst their treasure and arms were to be surrendered to the Arabs. However, before they left Babylon following the Paschal celebrations, they found time to scourge and mutilate those Copts still languishing in their dungeons.

Having secured the strategically important apex of the Delta, the Arabs soon began their advance northwards, defeating imperial forces at Terenouti and moving against the fortified city of Nikiou. The cowardly and weak commander Domentianus (who was married to Kyros' sister) fled for his life and when the Arabs arrived they found the panic-stricken garrison in chaotic retreat. Having slaughtered the helpless defenders they took the city unopposed and celebrated their victory by a cruel massacre of all its inhabitants.

Over the next weeks the Arabs steadily advanced towards Alexandria, engaging in battle with imperial forces at several stages but each time pushing them back as they moved relentlessly forwards. Although both armies would have received reinforcements, the numerical advantage was still with the defenders. At Alexandria Amr failed to take the city and faced another long siege without all the paraphernalia of siege engines and other necessary equipment of destruction. In September 641, however, Kyros returned to Egypt, charged by the Empress Martina with reaching terms with the invaders. He was joyfully received by the dispirited Alexandrians and one of his first acts was to resume the persecution of the Copts, which had somewhat relaxed during his absence.

Travelling to Babylon in November he concluded a secret treaty with Amr which effectively surrendered the province without a battle. It provided for an eleven-month armistice during which both armies would maintain their positions but all military operations would cease. This period would enable the garrison at Alexandria and all troops there to depart by sea, taking their possessions and treasures with them. Soldiers departing by land would be subject to a monthly tribute on their journey and no Roman army would return or attempt the recovery of Egypt. The Jews were to remain in Alexandria, a fixed tribute was imposed and hostages were provided by the Romans to ensure the terms of the treaty. The only concession extracted from the Arabs was that they would refrain from seizing churches or interfering in any way with the religious affairs of the Christians.

The first that the general populace knew of what had been agreed was when an Arab force appeared before the walls of Alexandria, having come to collect the first instalment of the promised tribute. Kyros died the following March leaving a legacy of bitterness and betrayal. His policies contributed in no small measure to the loss of Christian Egypt. In September 641 Amr, at the head of his army, took possession of the city and inaugurated Islamic rule.

The accusation that the Copts had aided the Arab invaders was long ago explored by A. J. Butler in his study *The Arab Conquest of Egypt* (1902). They were in fact too weakened by persecution and lacking in leadership to play any significant communal rôle at this stage, whilst the ineptness and cowardice of the Byzantine administration was the Arab's greatest asset.

Pope Benjamin I was still in hiding and had to be recalled by Amr, who promised him "safety and fearlessness." Impressed with his dignity as a 'man of God', Amr authorised him to "freely administer the affairs of his Church and people." Although Christians were now counted as *dhimmis*, subject but protected people, by comparison with the last years of Byzantine rule, this was a time of peace and safety. They were free to practise their religion and in those early years churches were built and restored without any difficulty.

The Years of dhimmitude

The new rulers were anxious to secure their latest conquest as well as finance their standing army through regular taxation and this was best achieved by maintaining the social stability of the Coptic majority. The Copts therefore enjoyed considerable freedom in the administration of their internal affairs and the incidence of conversion was remarkably low in the first centuries under Islam. The imposition of the *jizyah* (literally meaning 'penalty') or poll tax, payable by all non-Muslims, was at first no worse than the high taxes imposed previously. The hegemony of an Arab élite meant that even those who converted were still of inferior status and the time of Umar II (717-720). Converts to Islam continued to pay the *jizyah* so there was little incentive to abandon both faith and community. As a military government, the day to day administration was entrusted to Coptic officials and notables.

Under the first caliphs and their successors of the Umayyad (661-750) and Abbasid (750-868) dynasties, Egypt was ruled as a province by ethnic Arab governors appointed by the caliphs in Damascus or Baghdad. A turnover of 108 governors during this period was hardly conducive to either imaginative or creative rule. Their interest in Egypt was largely fiscal: the rich income deriving from agricultural taxation as well as the poll tax on the dhimma.

It was not too long before the social disabilities and humiliations began to bite as the reality of *dhimmitude* began to be felt. Only gradually did its burdens become greater as corrupt and greedy officials steadily squeezed more and more from the legendary riches of Egypt. If Amr began his rule justly, his master, the Caliph Umar (634-644 showed little gratitude for the great prize he had been given, accusing Amr of "protecting Egyptians" and slyly implying that this was done for his own profit rather than his master's.

The assurance that the Coptic Pope could "freely administer the affairs of his Church and people" was soon betrayed. When Pope Isaac (686-689) was discovered to have arbitrated in a dispute between his spiritual subjects, the emperor of Ethiopia and Nubia's king, the Arab governor was so infuriated by his "meddling" that the Pope was placed under house arrest and churches despoiled of all crosses, especially those made of silver and gold. He ordered large posters to be fixed to the gates of churches declaring Mohammed to be the apostle of Allah whilst Jesus was only a prophet of God and not his son.

Arab governors were notoriously mercurial in their dealings with the Church. The same 'Abd al-'Aziz ibn Marwan who imprisoned Pope Isaac also executed a sorcerer who tried to poison Pope Simon I (689-701) and granted him land to build churches and monasteries. It was when he was succeeded as governor by his son, al-Asbagh, that the full scale of Coptic subjection seriously began to be felt. An insatiable thirst for money, abetted by a Coptic quisling named Benjamin who revealed all places where Copts had concealed their wealth, led to extraordinary taxation, confiscation of treasure and the extension of the *jizyah* to monks. A levy of 2,000 dinars was imposed onto the existing land tax (*kharaj*) for all bishops. This heavy imposition led to the first serious wave of conversions by Coptic notables anxious to escape such burdens. Yet finance was not al-Asbagh's only motivation as it is recorded that he reviled Christ and spat at the ikon of Our Lady when it was carried in procession at Helwan.

When the Copts complained to the Umayyad Caliph 'Abd al-Malik (685-705) he arrested their spokesmen, confiscated their wealth and sent an even more disastrous governor. On going to greet him, Pope Alexander II (705-730) was abruptly arrested and a ransom of 3,000 dinars set for his release. Churches and monasteries were pillaged, sacred vessels despoiled and monks carried away as slaves to either serve in the Caliph's navy or to erect palaces for his governors. Those who did not convert fled their homes to avoid the crippling taxes but were brutally treated when apprehended, being flogged and branded, returned in chains, their limbs amputated and property subject to confiscation. The heirs of those who died were disinherited. Even short periods of respite under moderate caliphs were cut short by the rapacity of local governors anxious both to enrich themselves and gratify the caliph during their brief tenure of office. Outbreaks of plague and ruinous taxes to finance the war with Byzantium brought Egypt to the verge of ruin. The Copts had profound grievances but a number of Muslims were also among the rebels.

Insurrection was inevitable and between 725 and 832 Copts rose against their oppressors on several occasions but were speedily crushed. Only in al-Bashmur, in the marshlands of the northern Delta, were they able to resist pacification and engage in periodic attacks on the Muslim army. In 749 the last Umayyad Caliph Marwan II (744-750) brought an army to support the forces already engaged under his governor and carried away in irons Pope Kha'il I (744-767) to Rashid (Rosetta) as a hostage. Undaunted the Copts defeated his forces and destroyed Rashid. In the resulting chaos of the Abbasid overthrow of the Umayyads the caliph fled and the Pope and other imprisoned clergy gained their freedom. In 767 an expedition against the rebels was defeated and the government retreated. It was not until 830 that the Caliph al-Ma'mun (813-833) despatched an army under al-Afshin to subdue them and sought the assurance of Pope Yusab I (830-849) that he would act as a mediator for peace. His efforts were to no avail and a further army under the caliph himself finally prevailed amidst great slaughter, wholesale deportations and wasting of entire villages. Describing the Copts, the Muslim historian al-Makrizi wrote:

"From that time they were in subjection throughout the Egyptian territory, and their power was definitely crushed. None of them had the power to revolt or even resist the government; the Muslims were in the majority in the villages."

The Church was now weakened both economically and socially. An incident during the papacy of Pope Mina I (767-774) records that their churches had only glass and wooden utensils for sacramental use, and that they possessed no gold or silver vessels since they had already been plundered by former governors in times of persecution. Pope Kha'il III (880-907) found himself imprisoned by the governor Ahmad ibn Tulun (868-884) who was misled into believing that he had great hidden wealth. When nothing was forthcoming the Pope was freed on the stipulation that he would pay 10,000 dinars within the month and a further 10,000 within four months. The first instalment was raised from ten bishops but the second sum was never needed as ibn Tulun was struck down in battle.

Direct conversion to Islam as well as intermarriage became the way of joining the new ruling class. It is said that in 744 some 24,000

Copts embraced Islam when the governor promised them relief from the *jizyah*, which was periodically rescinded. For the first time since the Conquest the Copts were now the minority.

In the time of Pope Cosmas II (851-858) a periodic wave of oppression went beyond increasing taxation and extended to an assault on religious observances. Crosses and bells were smashed; the sale of wine prohibited; churches destroyed and others desecrated with mocking graffiti of the devil and pigs; Copts were prohibited from riding horses and a law was introduced requiring them to dress in black. All Copts were dismissed from the administration and their places were to be taken by Muslims or Islamicised Copts. Once again, considerable numbers of Copts converted to Islam. However, the loss of so many experienced and skilled administrators brought the administration close to economic collapse and many Copts were reinstated.

The Fatimids (969-1171) were a Shi'ite dynasty, whilst the majority of Muslims in Egypt remained Sunni, so during their time the Copts and Jews enjoyed significant positions in their administration, as well as the essential positions as clerks, accountants and scribes.

With the exception of the rule of the mad tyrant al-Hakim (996-1021), when Muslims as well as Jews and Christians were persecuted, the Church hierarchy enjoyed a rare interval of religious tolerance. Caliphs even participated in Christian festivals. Pope Abraham (975-978), in whose pontificate the celebrated Mokhattam miracle occurred, enjoyed close relations with the Caliph Al-Mu'izz (969-975) when old churches were renovated and new ones constructed. More remarkably those who had converted to Islam under compulsion were allowed to revert to their original faith; a recently restored church in Minyat-Zifta converted to a mosque by an anti-Coptic mob was later restored and Muslim converts to Christianity were not always punished.

Yet their very success with the rulers led to the envious hatred of the lower class Muslims for what they regarded as *dhimmis* who had over-reached themselves. During the reign of the Armenian vizier of the caliph al-Hafiz (1132-1149) the position of Christians was so comfortable that it was feared that some Islamicised Copts might revert. This may have been a factor in the rebellion of al-Hafiz's son and the caliph's brief deposition when Pope Gabriel II (1131-1145) was imprisoned and restrictive measures against the employment of Christians in the administration introduced. However, such measures were unenforceable and a Copt continued as chief scribe with his fourteen assistants comprising twelve Christians and two Muslims. Nevertheless there was a steady increase in the financial burden imposed on the Copts. State intervention in an internal church squabble, which led to the arrest of Pope Christodoulos (1047-1077) and the seizure of his 6,000 dinar fortune, resulted in his prompt release but not the reimbursement of his coins. Under his successor, Cyril II (1078-1092), the *kharaj* cost the church 4,000 dinars a year whilst the *jizyah* and other taxes rose and under Pope Gabriel II the *jizyah* was doubled to appease the mob.

As Fatimid rule began to disintegrate and a general anarchy developed the mob once again showed its dislike for the Christians. Churches were destroyed and monks executed if they refused to accept Islam. The restoration of order brought about by the triumph of Salah ad-Din and the establishment of the Ayyubid dynasty (1169-1252) brought an end to Coptic dominance of public services. Suspicious that the Copts might act as third columnists in the war against the Frankish crusaders, laws were enacted forbidding them from holding office and enacting the sort of petty humiliations which had been introduced briefly under al-Hakim. Bells and crosses were to be taken down from churches, whose walls were to be painted black, and religious processions were banned. Riding horses was forbidden to Copts and ridiculous sumptuary laws introduced. However, once Salah ad-Din had decisively defeated the Crusaders at the Battle of Hittin in 1187 we find the Copts returning to prominence. The Cairo Citadel was built by Coptic builders, Copts and Jews were allowed to practice as doctors and punitive taxes were either reduced or abolished. Copts were distinguished for their skilled workmanship and records exist of Coptic architects and shipbuilders as well as officials managing the estates and finances of their masters.

Pope John VI (1189-1216) was previously a much travelled and wealthy merchant of the Karimi Guild and his candidacy was urged as much by Muslims as by Copts. His position reflects the relaxed spirit of this period when the social differences between Copts, Arabs and Jews were insignificant. Through the close contacts between the Sultan and the Ethiopian emperors the Coptic Pope was treated with high respect. Yet a curious incident during his papacy indicates the ambivalence of the Muslim authorities. When the monk Abuna Yuhanna al-Makary converted to Islam he was rewarded with the lucrative post of tax collector in the city of Mit-Ghamr. After three years he approached Sultan al-Kamil (1218-1238) clutching a shroud, asking to revert or suffer the penalty of execution. The sultan not only agreed but even issued a decree granting him protection against Muslim fanatics. However, when another Islamicised Copt requested the same treatment, the sultan, fearing he had established a dangerous precedent, sent a messenger to Abuna Yuhanna offering him Islamicisation or decapitation. Not being martyr material he rapidly resumed his former position as tax collector.

Although Arabic had been designated the official language for the administration as early as 706 it was slower to take root among rural Copts. However, as even Coptic peasants were forced to use Arabic for economic survival its spread was inexorable. If it enabled the differences between Christians and Muslims to be blurred it also facilitated conversions. It was during this period that Coptic began to give way to Arabic. Previously Arabic-Coptic dictionaries and Coptic grammars in Arabic had been compiled to preserve the vernacular, but now Arabic was being used for Christian purposes and use of Coptic declined.

A nineteen-year interregnum (1216-1235) coincided with the decline of Ayyubid rule. When Cyril III ibn Laqlaq (1235-1243) finally secured the papacy it was by the appointment of the sultan as a result of his friendship with ibn al-Miqat, the Coptic chief Scribe. The standing of the papacy suffered badly with widespread simony. Attempts by a Church Council to address these issues led to sharp criticism of the Pope but 12,000 dinars artfully distributed as bribes ensured an acceptable verdict. Another interregnum of seven years (1243-1250) was followed by the papacy of Athanasios III (1250-1261) under whom the Mamluks began their long oppressive rule (1250-1517). In the six centuries since the Conquest the number of Coptic dioceses had shrunk from one hundred down to forty and the trend was not going to change.

The Mamluks ruled according to a feudal system and therefore needed traditional Coptic skills in administration and finance. A Copt was appointed vizier in the early years of the Mamluk sultans. Although they appeased public resentment to Coptic dominance in these areas by the traditional face-saving wholesale dismissal of Copts, in reality they were essential to their own control of society and were soon surreptitiously reinstated. Eight times they resorted to this subterfuge! There is no doubt that the sight of rich Copts aroused deep resentment against Christians. An incident in 1293 began when a well-dressed Copt was seen mounted on his horse and leading a Muslim debtor behind him bound with a rope. The crowd erupted and murdered the Copt before setting out on a general massacre of Copts with looting and destruction of their homes. Such outbreaks recurred regularly: in 1301 the Sultan ordered all churches to be closed because of the fear that they were accumulating wealth through the purchase of land and in 1321 some sixty churches and many monasteries were destroyed. A threat by the Ethiopian emperor to come to the defence of the Copts during the papacy of Pope Benjamin II (1327-1339) brought a period of calm when churches could be restored but in 1354 another Coptic administrator was lynched by a rampaging mob. In 1365 the Sultan, needing additional finance for a war in Cyprus, confiscated church properties; in 1389 a number of Copts who had nominally adopted Islam, were publicly executed for reverting to their Christian faith. It is hardly surprising that conversions to Islam became a flood.

When Sultan Selim I (1512-1520) brought Egypt under Ottoman rule in 1517 the Copts had already become a marginalised minority. A modern historian observes, "Recorded Coptic history came to an end by the fourteenth century. This means that between the fourteenth and the nineteenth centuries we are dependent largely on occasional references by Muslim authors or observations by Western pilgrims and travellers."

Modern times

During the brief but significant French occupation of Egypt (1798-1801) Copts played a significant rôle and inevitably one served as minister of finance. Although Bonaparte had declared himself a Muslim to curry favour with his new subjects, Christians were given prominence and Copts undoubtedly hoped that their circumstances would change. As usual, once the French had departed and Ottoman rule was restored, the Copts were accused of collaboration with the invaders and Christian homes and churches attacked. However, what might have been false hope of a new dawn for Copts in reality turned out to be the beginning of significant and beneficial change as it was the catalyst for the destruction of the Mamluks and Mohammed Ali's assumption of power.

The new dynasty which ruled Egypt from 1805-1952 not only saw the modernisation of Egypt but the lifting of the worst burdens of *dhimmitude*, although there was always obvious Islamic ascendancy. The testimony of a *dhimmi* against a Muslim was inadmissible in court and this led to much injustice. In 1844 Sidhom Bishay, a government clerk in the port of Damiette, was falsely accused of cursing Islam and offered the options of either forsaking Christianity or suffering death. Refusing to abandon his faith he was flogged before being martyred in molten tar. It is reported that the Khedive 'Abbas Hilmi (1849-1854) actually contemplated the idea of transporting the Copts *en masse* to the Sudan and Ethiopia, thereby rendering Egypt completely Muslim. When informed of this project the Islamic authorities issued a *fatwa* rejecting it and reminding the Khedive that the Copts were the original inhabitants of Egypt whose deportation would be both wrong and impractical.

At the beginning of the twentieth century the Copts were described as "the surveyors, the scribes, the arithmeticians, the measurers, the clerks, in a word, the learned men of the land. They are to the counting house and the pen what the fellah is to the field and the plough." The dismantling of the Ottoman *millet* system, whereby each religious community was administered internally, helped in opening up new career opportunities for Copts. The experience of the Copts stood them in good stead in the expanding civil service, although under the British occupation (1882-1936) many Copts were purged, obliging them to find new openings in the professions. The only Copt to become Prime Minister was Butros Ghali, who was assassinated by a Muslim nationalist in February 1910.

The Copts feared Pan-Islamic tendencies of the nationalist movement and at a Coptic Congress at Assiout in March 1910 called for an end to discrimination & full equality. This was not immediately forthcoming but as the movement for independence became truly nationalist it had the effect of uniting Christians and Muslims in a way never known before. The Wafd Party founded in 1919 under Sa'ad Zaghlul (c.1850-1927) for a brief period enabled sectarian barriers to be transcended. The cross and the crescent side by side became the symbol of this short-lived unity. Coptic clergy spoke in mosques and mullahs stood in Coptic pulpits.

The 1952 Revolution promised the abolition of all discrimination based on race, language or religion and at the outset it cultivated good relations with the Coptic authorities. The Nationalist spirit was re-ignited and in the face of the British invasion over Suez, religious leaders proclaimed an "Islamic-Christian union." The Church authorities voiced no objections to Nasser's socialist alliances and vigorously adopted a patriotic stand over Egypt's championship of justice for the Palestinians. In 1954 an attempt by the Muslim Brotherhood to challenge the new government led to their suppression, although this merely drove them underground and led to their infiltration of the armed forces.

In 1970 Anwar al-Sadat (1970-1981) became President. He had been the liaison officer between the officers who had brought about the 1952 Revolution and the Muslim Brotherhood. As a result he regarded the Brotherhood not only as "a useful ally to our revolutionary movement" but also felt that "the dogmas of Islam must be inculcated into all branches of the Army." A year later Pope Shenouda III became the head of the Coptic Church and energetically encouraged the spiritual renewal, which had begun under his predecessor, Pope Kyrillos VI (1959-1971). Attacks on Coptic churches by Islamic extremists were growing and Sadat's reversal of Nasser's pro-Soviet position in favour of closer links with conservative Arab states meant that Islamic groups proscribed under Nasser were now fêted. In 1977 the Coptic Church spoke out strongly against a Ministry of Justice proposed Islamicisation Bill which would have imposed *sharia* law. Faced with serious economic and domestic unrest at home Sadat pursued a policy of disengagement from conflict with Israel, culminating in the Egypt-Israel Peace Treaty in March 1979, although this alienated the Islamacists he had previously been courting. In 1980 an amendment (Part 1, article 2) to the Constitution was introduced stating that "the principal source of legislation is Islamic Jurisprudence (*Sharia*)." Inter-communal strife persisted with Coptic properties throughout Egypt being bombed and awareness that the government was not actively protecting Copts. In 1981 three days of religious riots left at least seventeen Copts and Muslims dead and more than a hundred injured. When the Coptic Holy Synod protested by cancelling the traditional festivities associated with Easter and American Copts vociferously demonstrated during Sadat's visit to the USA in May, he responded by intemperately accusing the Pope of wanting to erect a separatist Coptic state in Upper Egypt. Eventually Sadat was forced to clamp down on religious extremists and in September 1981 a number of groups were dissolved, the Muslim Brotherhood proscribed and over 1,500 people arrested. These included Coptic bishops and priests and, most notably, Pope Shenouda, who was placed under house arrest at Saint Bishoy's monastery in the Wadi al-Na'trun. A month later Sadat was assassinated by Muslim extremists who felt he had betrayed them.

Over the next few years international pressure was brought to bear on the Egyptian government and on 2 January 1985 Pope Shenouda was freed without having made any form of concession or deals to achieve this. He returned to Cairo in time for the Christmas festivities and received a rapturous reception. His treatment and his dignified behaviour throughout had immeasurably enhanced his standing in the world and in the Coptic community. Under Hosni Mubarak, who became Sadat's successor, Pope Shenouda has re-established a sound relationship with the state as well as maintaining excellent contacts with moderate religious leaders, especially the Grand Sheikh of Al-Azhar, Dr. Tantawi. At the recent celebrations to mark the thirtieth anniversary of his enthronement Pope Shenouda said, "Love generates love and separation generates separation. Seek to love everyone, everywhere and on every occasion."

Restoration of churches and construction of new ones has continued at a steady pace in the last two decades but the growing needs of the Coptic community have been frustrated by the antiquated administrative procedures required before even the most trivial repair can be authorised. Under the Ottoman *Hamayoni Decree* of 1856, as amplified by a Ministerial Rule of 1934, Christian congregations are required to submit petitions for any form of building, repair or renovation of church buildings to the head of state, the Egyptian President. As such rules do not apply to the erection of mosques it is clearly a discriminatory law.

Eventually, widespread criticism of this law and the derisory images conjured up at the thought of a head of state concerning himself with such administrative trivia, resulted in President Mubarak delegating this responsibility to provincial governors. Although intended to go some way towards resolving the issue, this was not viewed as especially satisfactory as some governors are seen as hostile to Christians.

Equally, the Egyptian government's attempts to suppress fanatical Muslims intent on undermining the state have not always left Copts confident that their security is an equal priority. Since 1990 Islamic extremists, who have imposed an unofficial *jizyah* in some villages, have murdered many Copts. The British Coptic Association has published details of some 85 Copts who were murdered for non-payment between September 1994 and November 1997. Elsewhere random shootings of Copts are recorded in Nobareia, Alexandria (May 1990); Dayrut, Manshiyat Nassir (May 1992); Al-Moharak Monastery (March 1994); Mere village, El-Joseaa (October 1994), Badari, Ezbat Al-Aqbat (February 1996), Tahta (August 1996), Abu-Quorqas (February 1997), Kafr Zuhair (March 1997), Mahjoura, Nag Hamadi (March 1997), Al-Minya (April 1997) and account for a further 62 Copts killed.

In August 1998 in the village of El-Kosheh in Upper Egypt, where 70% of the population are Christian, two young Copts were murdered. Although the identity of the murderers was common knowledge the local police force rounded up large numbers of local people and subjected them to brutal interrogation and torture. Instead of apprehending the criminals the local Coptic bishop was charged with sedition. To calm the rising communal tension Pope Shenouda issued a simple declaration calling for prudence and expressing faith in the legal investigations, which the government had promised. Unfortunately when it transpired that the police officers against whom charges of brutality were brought were not only exonerated but also promoted, confidence in the government's resolve was shaken. It was little wonder, therefore, that on New Year's eve 1999, a further outbreak of violence in the same village left 21 people brutally murdered (19 Christians and two Muslims), 33 wounded and 81 shops and homes destroyed in an orgy of looting and fire bombing. The local police not only failed to intervene promptly but the local Security forces even apprehended the

Pope's secretary on his way to attend the victims' funeral and accused him of bringing weapons to arm the Christians. He was eventually rescued by a different contingent of police officers. Once again the police tried to blame the local clergy and a priest was charged with "attempted murder, conspiracy to commit murder, leading a gang that attacked a number of residents and planned destruction of property."

This time the Pope was not content merely to say that he had confidence in the authorities in Cairo. A special edition of *El Keraza*, the church's official journal, clearly coming from the pen of the Pope himself, spoke of "Our Martyrs in El-Kosheh" and left no-one in any doubt as to his views, "The problem will not be resolved by covering-up, or by painting the victims as criminals !" He called for truth and declared that true reconciliation could only take place "after the blood of these victims receives justice."

However, in recent months there have been some encouraging signs. In July President Mubarak received Pope Shenouda at Ras El-Tin Palace in Alexandria where they had "a constructive and frank meeting". The Pope thanked the president for condemning a scandalous attack on the Coptic Church, which had appeared the previous month in a gutter press newspaper, *Al-Nabaa*. Three weeks later the Egyptian Supreme Court intervened to overturn the verdict of the court in Sohag concerning the violence in El-Kosheh. Commenting on the decision, Bishop Wissa of El-Balyana said, "We think justice can now prevail. There were killers and there were victims and we only want to know who was who."

In October, Pope Shenouda flew to Al-Tour in South Sinai to lay the foundation stone of the first *official Coptic Church in the area. Although there are several major cities in South Sinai, local Copts were forced to travel about 280 kilometres to their nearest church. Requests to build a church had met with repeated refusals. Eventually a small church was erected on top of a cafeteria in Al-Tour owned by the church but in February 2000, only hours after Pope John Paul II had left Sinai, this was stormed by the police, its altar destroyed, the vessels and vestments confiscated and it was forcibly closed. Twenty months later the presidential decree was forthcoming and the governor himself assisted Pope Shenouda in the stone-laying ceremonies.*

Today the Copts are the largest Christian community in the Middle East, numbering more than ten million and comprising about 16% of the Egyptian population. Their very survival is a remarkable testimony of fidelity to their Faith. The manner in which the Coptic Church has responded to oppression has only enhanced its moral standing in the world. A government that can redress the injustice of centuries by enabling Copts to stand equally with their Muslim brothers would be a wise one indeed.

Remnants of the walls around Constantinople

Our Lady, Fatima and Peace

Bishop Basil H. Losten of Stamford

What I write in this short essay is the product of my thoughts, observations and ruminations based on the readings I have done. These words come from one who is both open to learning and willing to carry out a dialogue in the hope of arriving at an understanding where Christian and Muslim can walk together in peace.

In my readings, I discovered that whenever any Muslim mentions Mary, she is refered to as "Our Lady Mary (May the peace of God be upon her)" or as abbreviated, "Our Lady Mary (pbuh)." These words reflect a respect that would be a desirable usage from any Christian. She is held in this respect because she has attained "the perfection of human spiritual attainment" and as being "among the first group of prophets to enter Paradise." Muhammad himself in honoring his daughter Fatimah said, "The best women in all the world are four: the Virgin Mary, Aasiyaa, the wife of Pharoah, Khadihah, the mother of the Believers, and Fatimah, daugher of Muhammed." Mary is the "spiritual example for mankind." She is seen as the faithful servant of the Lord who allows God's Word to bring Jesus to life in her miraculously, and so give the world a prophet whom Muslims revere.

While both Christians and Muslims have respect for our Lady because she is the mother of Jesus, our understanding of the who and what of Jesus differ. While as Christians, Catholics and Orthodox hold that he is the Son of God; Muslims hold that he is just a human being. He is a prophet, a great one, but not as great as Muhammed who is the Paraclete, the one who is to come, of which Jesus refers to in the Gospels. While Christians hold that Jesus was crucified, died and rose from the dead, Moslems hold that he did not die but was rather raised by Allah and is still living in order that he come again in his old age. There would seem to be no common ground for discussion of Christology here.

The common ground could be our Lady Mary. We both hold that Mary gave birth to Jesus as a virgin so his birth was miraculous.

When his mother Mary was betrothed to Joseph, but before they had lived together, she was found with child through the Holy Spirit (Matthew 1:18).

And (remember) he who guarded her chastity: We breathed into her of Our spirit, and We made her and her son a sign for all peoples [Qur'an 021.091].

Mary, the Mother of God, and Jesus

We both hold that Jesus did not have a human father.

We both hold that an angel spoke to her.

In the sixth month, the angel Gabriel was sent from God to a town of Galilee called Nazareth to a virgin betrothed to a man named Joseph of the house of David, and the virgin's name was Mary (Luke 1:26-27).

She placed a screen (to screen herself) from them; then We sent her our angel, and he appeared before her as a man in all respects. She said: "I seek refuge from thee to (God) Most Gracious: (come not near) if thou dost fear God." He said: "Nay, I am only a messenger from thy Lord, (to announce) to thee the gift of a holy son. She said: "How shall I have a son, seeing that no man has touched me, and I am not unchaste?" He said: "So (it will be): Thy Lord saith, 'that is easy for Me: and (We wish) to appoint him as a Sign unto men and a Mercy from Us:' It is a matter (so) decreed." So she conceived him, and she retired with him to a remote place. [Qur'an 019.017-022].

Eastern Christians have a great love for the apocryphal work of the Protoevangelium of James because of its stories of Mary and the Temple, which have become part of the church's liturgical calendar. There are stories in the Qur'an that bring new understanding to some fundamental Christian teachings. When Joseph asks Mary how she as a virgin could have conceived, Mary answers, "Do you not know that God, when He created the wheat had no need of seed, and that God by His power made the trees grow without the help of rain? All that God had to do was to say, 'So be it, and it was done.'" This is not to say that the Qur'an is "gospel." Rather, as a Christian one can find in it a meaningful expression of our Christian faith. There is nothing in the quotation here that is contrary to our teachings. This does not mean that the entire Qur'an is a text upon which Christian teaching is faithfully presented, because it is not.

The Muslim love of Mary is seen in the fact that one chapter of the Qur'an is named Sura Maryam "Chapter Mary" (XIX) named in honor of Mary, the mother of Jesus Christ. This chapter contains 41 verses on Jesus and Mary. Interestingly, this is used as "proof" that Muhammed himself did not write the Qur'an, not only because he is thought by many to have been illiterate but also because there is not a chapter on his mother, or any of his wives, nor on the daughter Fatimah, whom he loved so dearly.

One of the reasons given in the Qur'an for the Jews' condemnation is "that they uttered against Mary a grave false charge [Qur'an 4: 156].

The only woman in Islam to come close to Mary is Fatimah. Muhammed said, "You shall be the most blessed of all the women in Paradise, after Mary." In a variant of the text, Fatimah is made to say, "I surpass all the women, except Mary." Muhammed once said, "Whoever pleases Fatimah has indeed pleased God, and whoever has caused her to be angry has indeed angered God." Fatimah was given the name, "az-Sahraa," which means the "Resplendent One." This is because her face seemed to radiate light.

Her words have been an inspiration to the Muslim people. Fatimah gave this speech in a mosque:

> Praise be to Allah for that which he bestowed (upon us); And thanks be to him for all that which he provided; From prevalent favors which he created, And abundant benefactions which he offered and perfect grants which he presented; (such benefactions) that their number is too much too plentiful to compute; bounties too vast to measure;

> Their limit was distant to realize; he recommended to them (his creatures) to gain more (of his benefactions) by being grateful for their continuity; he ordained himself praiseworthy by giving generously to his creatures; I bear witness that there is no God but Allah Who is One without partner, a statement which sincere devotion is made to be its interpretation; hearts guarantee its continuation, and illuminated in the minds is its sensibility. (Fatima the gracious compiled by Odeh A. Muhawesh.)

Her life and her example have been an inspiration to the Muslim people and her influence upon the Muslim world has been significant.

The Muslim people had under their dominion for centuries a large portion of what is now known as Portugal. The last Muslim chief over the area had a beautiful daughter, named Fatima. A Catholic young man fell in love with her and as the Muslim people were driven out, she chose to stay behind with the man she loved. She became a Catholic. The young husband, so in love with his wife, changed the name of the town in which they lived to Fatima. Is it no wonder then when Mary, under the title of the Immaculate Conception, would choose a place to appear that she would choose a place where love had joined together a Catholic and a Muslim?

It is for this reason that Mary can be the point of debarkation for true dialogue between Muslims and Eastern Christians. In October of 1996 in Indianapolis, Indiana there was the First Regional Midwest Islamic-Catholic Dialogue. The program was hosted by Father Thomas Murphy of the Archdiocese of Indianapolis and Shahid Athar, M.D. As part of the program there was a discussion of a paper by William Cardinal Keeler of Baltimore on "How Mary Holds Muslims and Christians in Conversation." Many were moved with what Cardinal Keeler had to say about the status of Mary and Jesus shared by both faiths. This group decided to develop a joint booklet informing Muslims and Catholics about the Muslim concept of Jesus, Mary, Mohammed, Prophets of God and the Word of God. Dr. Borelli of the United States Catholic Conference was to review the available literature and put something together which will be acceptable and easily understood by both faiths.

At the time Archbishop Fernando Capalla of the Southern Philippines was in the midst of the Mindanao Conflict. Catholics and Muslims of the area together turned to Mary for peace and justice. Peace was achieved. At the peace conference that followed Tabang Mindanaw, co-chair of the conference reported that to preserve peace certain initiatives were being taken. He said that Archbishop Capalla and Alim Mutilan [Muslim] would launch a program to honor Mary in the Holy Scripture and Miriam in the Qur'an, as she is the most respected woman of both the Christian and the Islamic faiths. He said that this will open a seventh path to peace through Miriam who is closest to the hearts of all Filipinos, Muslims and Christians alike. He interestingly went on to say, "It occurred to me when I heard of this new peace initiative, that this might be the beginning of the fulfillment of a prophecy that, one day, the Blessed Mary will unite the Muslims and Christians of the world. It is said that this is why our lady appeared at Fatima in Portugal which is named after the daughter of Mohammed."

In these two previous examples, we see that Mary is a serious basis for dialogue, and that when Christians and Muslims come together to honor Mary, peace can be achieved.

Icon of Our Lady of Vladimir

At this time in the world serious dialogue is needed and peace must be achieved. If together Catholics and Muslims could with joyful hearts welcome the pilgrim statue of our Lady of Fatima when it came to India, Africa and particularly Mozambique, can she again be the instrument for bringing Muslims and Christians together in prayer?

Further, as an Eastern Christian, I have a special devotion to Mary as "Protection." Whether it be her covering of the city of Constantinople or any one of numerous other cities with her mantle people were saved from natural calamities and from wars. Can we not at this time, pray that our Lady throw her mantle over the entire world to protect all innocent persons from war and injustice? May she bring peace. This peace though can only be sustained if we who honor her as the Mother of God and the Muslims who honor her as our Lady can come together and come to an understanding that will allow us to co-exist in peace and harmony. When these two great religions view each other as satan, the only winner is Satan.

From a Catholic perspective the Pontifical Council for Interreligious Dialogue has produced *Guidelines for Dialogue between Christians and Muslims*. This work reminds the Christian that we have to dialogue not from the perspective that things of the West are better. Rather it calls us to point out differences of emphases and interpretation and to put them along side the genuine Muslim aspirations and moral ideas, and then to dialogue.

This document language is the language of faith, hope and love. It does not allow us to sit back in our complacency nor does it underestimate our ability to have respect and esteem for others while holding ourselves responsible.

The living out of this document is seen in the personal ministry of Pope John Paul II. In March 2000, the Pontiff met with Mohamed Sayed Tantawi, the Grand Sheikh of al-Azhar, the highest authority for Sunni Moslems. Together they have followers of over two billion people. Most of the world's Moslems follow the rites of Sunni Islam; Shi'ites, concentrated in Iran and Iraq, are in a minority. Ironically, it was a conquering Shi'ite dynasty known as the Fatimids who founded al-Azhar in their capital of Cairo in 971 AD, over a century before Pope Urban II launched the First Crusade.

The Fatimids named the mosque-university after the Prophet's daughter from whom they traced their lineage. Al-Azhar outlasted Fatimid rule to become the top source of authority in Sunni Islam. Today, the fatwas, or religious rulings, of the Grand Sheikh still resonate far beyond Egypt.

In recent decades the Vatican and al-Azhar have begun to dispel the distrust arising from centuries of struggle between Christianity and Islam which at different times saw Crusaders ruling Jerusalem and Ottoman Turks at the gates of Vienna.

It is this pontiff with his devotion to Our Lady of Fatima who is in the position to lead the Catholic faithful, a significant part of Christianity, to openness and dialogue with Muslims. This Holy Father's papacy seems to be sustained by the message of Fatima. This proclamation may have been the background for the fall of communism. As Pope John Paul II is quoted by Aura Miguel in her book, *The Secret That Leads the Pope*,

"Perhaps this is also why the Pope was called from a faraway country, and perhaps this is also why there had to be the assassination attempt in St. Peter's Square on the very day of May 13, 1981 ... so that all would become more transparent and understandable ... so that the voice of God, which speaks in the history of men through 'the signs of the times' could be more easily heard and understood."

Maybe the signs of the times continue to unfold and with a focus on our Lady of Fatima the path for the future will become clear and understandable.

It is time for the American Church with the Muslim community living within our borders to dispel distrust and begin dialogue in peace and truth. Together looking to our Lady of Fatima, we can walk together in peace, justice and harmony. May Mary (pbuh) protect us.

Between Western Crusades and Islamic 'Crescades'

Father Alexander F. C. Webster, Ph.D.

The media flap over President George W. Bush's innocent use of "crusade" to describe the American response to the terrorist atrocities on September 11, 2001, revealed astounding degrees of ignorance in the media and hypocrisy among his Muslim critics. To be sure, the medieval Crusades to recover the Holy Land from its Muslim conquerors have earned a place of dishonor among modern Roman Catholics and Protestants, as well as people of other faiths. What is not as familiar to Americans, however, is the general disdain for crusades and other "holy wars" by the Orthodox Christians of the Byzantine Empire and its successor kingdoms and the fundamental embrace of the concept and practice of holy war by Islam since its inception.

For eight centuries after the rise of Islam in the Arabian peninsula in AD 622, the Byzantine Empire was flanked in the West by the rising political and religious power of the papacy and in the East by the Islamic empires of the Arabs and the Turks. In his seminal 1993 essay, "The Clash of Civilizations?" Samuel P. Huntington actually factored out of western civilization an historic buffer civilization that he labeled "Slavic-Orthodox" (although "Greco-Slavic Orthodox" would have been more accurate).[1] The fault line between the West proper and this Orthodox Christian civilization is the eastern boundary of Western Christianity circa AD 1500, which, in the Balkans, conformed closely to the division of the Roman Empire into eastern and western halves by Emperor Diocletian in AD 283. The other fault line for the Slavic-Orthodox civilization skirts the current borders of Islamic states from Turkey to the Caucasus and along the southern Russian frontier. Islamic civilization still prevails in the equatorial belt of the

---

[1]   Samuel P. Huntington, "The Clash of Civilizations?" *Foreign Affairs* 72:4 (Summer 1993), 22-49, esp. 29f.

world's Eastern Hemisphere, from Morocco on the Atlantic Ocean to Indonesia on the Pacific Ocean.

This historical geography has provided the setting for the unique moral and cultural roles that Eastern Orthodox Christianity has exercised on the global scene. Nowhere is that uniqueness more in evidence than in the matter of crusades and holy wars. This essay will demonstrate how Orthodoxy has stood squarely and defiantly in the path of both Western Christian crusades and, to coin a term, Islamic "crescades" – shorthand for crusaders for the crescent moon, the perennial symbol of Islam.

Three's a Crowd

The vast literature on the subject of war and peace generally yields three classic moral positions that are most aptly described as "holy war" or "crusade," "just war" or "justifiable war," and "pacifism."[2] What appears to differentiate the "war ethic of the crusade," as Protestant theologian Edward LeRoy Long, Jr., labeled it, from the "justifiable war" position is its intense, explicit religious content and lack of reasonable restraint. Long detected four peculiar characteristics: (1) religious motivation as the sole, or at least primary, justification for military action; (2) "extrinsic religious rewards" (such as a plenary forgiveness of sins or admission to Paradise as a martyr) for the soldier's work; (3) an erosion of restraints against hostility toward the enemy (including noncombatants such as women and children); and (4) an absolutist spirit that tends to justify all means, however extreme or otherwise immoral, to achieve objectives.[3]

Though shrouded in religious language or the quasi-religious language of modern ideological movements such as Nazism and com-

---

[2]   Roland H. Bainton, *Christian Attitudes Toward War and Peace: A Historical Survey and Critical Re-Evaluation* (Nashville: Abingdon Press, 1960), 13-15.

[3]   Edward LeRoy Long, Jr., War and Conscience in America (Philadelphia: The Westminster Press, 1968), 22-47. See also LeRoy Walters, "The Just War and the Crusade: Antitheses or Analogies?" *Monist* 57 (October 1973): 584-94, 593.

munism, the unrestrained quality of this kind of human enterprise from time immemorial was categorized by Carl von Clausewitz as "total war" – literally whatever it takes to compel the enemy to do one's will. The military alternative is "real" or political war, which consists in the "continuation of political activity by other means," with a reasonable proportionality of violent means to political ends.[4] Clausewitz's terminology is especially apropos. For the ostensibly "religious" motivation of the "holy war" obviously provides an unnatural, surreal dimension to the sheer carnage and destruction in total war.

Although the history of Eastern Orthodoxy is checkered in this respect, it is safe to discard the holy war position as non-normative in Orthodox moral tradition. Like other Christians, as well as the Jews, naturally, and Muslims who respect the Bible, Orthodox have to come to grips with the disturbing presence of holy wars in the Old Testament. Whether intended as a sacrifice of non-Hebrews to secure God's aid in battle or to purify the Hebrew community by eradicating injustice and evil outside the people of faith, the "ban" (herem in Hebrew) enjoined Israel to exterminate all human beings – irrespective of age, sex, or non-combatant status – in its numerous wars of conquest and survival in Canaan.[5] Such military campaigns appear as "Yahweh's wars" in the Hebrew text (see, for example, Numbers 21:14 and 1 Samuel 18:17). The phrase "holy war" arose among the ancient Greeks, particularly Thucydides' Peloponnesian Wars. The German scholar Friedrich Schwally first applied the phrase to the Old Testament in 1901, and he, ironically, derived it from the Arabic jihad![6]

---

[4] Carl von Clausewitz, *On War*, ed. and trans. Michael Howard and Peter Paret (Princeton: Princeton University Press, 1976), Bk. 1, Ch. 1, esp. 75, 81, 87.

[5] Susan Niditch, *War in the Hebrew Bible: A Study in the Ethics of Violence* (New York: Oxford University Press, 1993), esp. 28, 35, 77.

[6] Gerhard von Rad, *Holy War in Ancient Israel*, ed. and trans. Marva J. Dawn (Grand Rapids: William B. Eerdmans Publishing Company, 1991), 5f. See also Peter C. Craigie, *The Problem of War in the Old Testament* (Grand Rapids: William B. Eerdmans Publishing Company, 1978), 49.

In any event, the Old Testament tradition of holy war, like many other doctrines and practices, developed through the centuries of ancient Israel's turbulent history. One need only compare the extreme divine command in Deuteronomy 20 to the limited use of violence that appears in new texts from the Greek version of the Old Testament (the Septuagint) in the second century BC. For example, in 1 Maccabees 5:28, 35, 51, only the males suffer the wrath of victorious Israel. And in the New Testament, of course, there is not even a hint of holy war. Orthodox moral tradition allows for such development in the holy scriptures as "salvation history" – that is, God leading His people from primitive barbarism to ethical civilization and on to the perfect holiness revealed by Christ in the gospels. On this view, the practice of holy war as it appears in the Old Testament has – or ought to have – no claim on Christians whatsoever.

To be sure, Eusebios of Caesarea's controversial encomium to St. Constantine the Great exalted the emperor's military conquests and forcible conversions of those who "defied" God." As early as the fourth century, therefore, a uniquely Christian theological/spiritual foundation was in place for the forcible extension of Church and Kingdom by Christian civil authority.[7] Fortunately from a moral standpoint, this nascent crusader mentality, which in the Christian West blossomed into full-blown aggression in the anti-Donatist holy war in the fourth century[8] and later in the medieval Crusades, was stillborn in the Christian East. Only in isolated incidents and movements do we catch so much as a glimpse of a holy war ethic among the Orthodox.

Sometimes anti-heresy holy wars marred the entire reign of a Byzantine emperor such as St. Justinian the Great in the sixth century,[9]

---

[7] The rest of this section is adapted from Alexander F. C. Webster, The *Pacifist Option: The Moral Argument Against War in Eastern Orthodox Theology* (Lanham, MD: Rowman & Littlefield Publishing Group, 1999), 84-87.

[8] For a detailed comparative ethical analysis of this case, see Alexander F. C. Webster, "Just War and Holy War: Two Case Studies in Comparative Christian Ethics," *Christian Scholar's Review* 15:4 (1986): 362-71.

[9] Demetrios J. Constantelos, "Religious Minorities and the State in Sixth Century

or arose when powerful leaders were stirred by a spirit of retribution, such as the vengeful holy war against the brutal Persian invaders of Palestine waged by Emperor Heraclios from AD 622 to 630.[10] The most massive movement of fratricidal Orthodox persecution was the internal conflagration that erupted in Russia in the seventeenth century, when Patriarch Nikon of Moscow attempted to extirpate the "Old Believer" schism.[11]

Also possibly falling under the category of holy war are the occasional military ventures to liberate captive Orthodox nations in the Balkans from the Muslim Turkish yoke. They began with the ill-fated "Insurrection of St. Sava" in AD 1593, which was "directly stimulated" and formally blessed by Serbian Orthodox Patriarch Jovan II,[12] and the equally star-crossed rebellion of Michael the Brave of Romania in AD 1595 on behalf of the anti-Turkish "Holy League" headquartered in Vienna.[13] These feeble attempts at liberation finally succeeded on a grand scale in the nineteenth century as one Orthodox nation after another achieved national independence, invariably through some combination of military force and diplomatic negotiations. The Serbs, for example, launched their "Second Insurrection" in a little more than a decade on Palm Sunday, April 23, 1815, at the Serbian Orthodox Church in Takovo, where Milosh Obrenovich announced the beginning of war

Byzantium," *St. Vladimir's Seminary Quarterly* 7:4 (1963): 190-200.

[10] George Ostrogorsky, *History of the Byzantine State* (New Brunswick: Rutgers University Press, 1957), 90. See also 320.

[11] Nicolas Zernov, *The Russians and Their Church* (London: S.P.C.K., 1968), 97-104.

[12] Harold W. V. Temperley, *History of Servia* (London: G. Bell and Sons Ltd., 1917), 125. The severe penalties imposed on the Serbs by their Turkish overlords included the desecration in AD 1595 of the relics of St. Sava, the patron saint of the Serbian people. The Turks exhumed his body, burned it to ashes at Vrachar in Belgrade, and scattered the ashes.

[13] Dimitrije Djordjevic and Stephen Fischer-Galati, *The Balkan Revolutionary Tradition* (New York: Columbia University Press, 1981), 5-9.

against the Turks with full clerical blessing.[14] Similarly, the majority of Greek revolutionaries regarded the Greek War of Independence, which commenced in 1821, "as a holy war against Islam."[15] Although successive patriarchs of Constantinople, Gregorios V and Evgenios II, disavowed the rebellion against Turkish rule and excommunicated its supporters,[16] on March 25, 1821, Bishop Germanos of Old Patras "raised the standard of revolt at the monastery of St. Lavra"[17] and later personally assisted in the military capture of his city from the Turks. Meanwhile, numerous village priests in the Peloponnesos entered the ranks of the burgeoning Greek army.[18]

These few examples are, however, the exceptions that prove the rule. As Nicholas Oikonomides concludes confidently, Byzantium "never knew a real 'holy war,'" and the Church refrained from blessing any killing as a "laudable act," from granting remission of sins to Orthodox warriors for their military service, or from recognizing fallen warriors ipso facto as martyrs – all of which were key features of the Western crusade and Islamic jihad.[19] The Emperor Nikephoros II

---

[14] Milosh also urged his compatriots to kill anyone who wore the distinctive green garb of the Turks—an example of the unrestrained crusader mentality. Leopold Ranke, *The History of Servia and the Servian Revolution*, trans. Mrs. Alexander Kerr (London: Henry G. Bohn, 1853), 199.

[15] Charles Frazee, "Church and State in Greece," in John T. A. Koumoulides (ed.), *Greece in Transition: Essays in the History of Modern Greece 1821-1974* (London: Zeno Booksellers and Publishers, 1977), 128.

[16] *Ibid.*, 129. See also Philip Sherrard, "Church, State and the Greek War of Independence," in Richard Clogg (ed.), *The Struggle for Greek Independence: Essays to Mark the 150th Anniversary of the Greek War of Independence* (Hamden, CT: Archon Books, 1973), 182f. Patriarch Polykarpos of Jerusalem also condemned the Greek rebellion.

[17] Steven Runciman, *The Great Church in Captivity: A Study of the Patriarchate of Constantinople from the Eve of the Turkish Conquest to the Greek War of Independence* (Cambridge: Cambridge University Press, 1968), 404.

[18] Frazee, "Church and State in Greece," 130.

[19] Nicholas Oikonomides, "The Concept of 'Holy War' and Two Tenth Century

Phokas (+ AD 969) did push the Church to proclaim that at least some wars could be "spiritually meritorious," but the patriarch of Constantinople and the other bishops refused to countenance this prospect.[20] An anonymous treatise on military strategy dating from the reign of St. Justinian the Great (+ AD 565) claimed that the Byzantines, unlike their enemies, "who clearly look upon the shedding of our blood as one of their basic duties and the height of virtue," resorted to war for defensive reasons alone.[21] As George T. Dennis observes, the Byzantines certainly did not view war as "a means of expansion and exploitation, a demonstration of one's superiority, or a contest which would bring the players glory and renown."[22]

Angeliki Laiou recently delivered the coup de gras to the idea of holy war in Byzantium. The key difference between holy war and justifiable war, she contends, is the legitimate authority. As the First Crusade against the Muslims in the Holy Land in AD 1095 demonstrated, holy war must be proclaimed by the Church, especially in the absence of a strong imperial presence. But in the Byzantine East, the emperor was the only legitimate authority capable of waging war; there was usually little danger of an imperial justifiable war sliding into an ecclesiastical holy war. Laiou points to a magnificent irony: in Byzantium the role of a strong emperor precluded holy war, while in the West, the absence of a legitimate emperor encouraged the papacy to fill the vacuum and even promulgate crusades![23]

Byzantine Ivories," in Timothy S. Miller and John Nesbitt (eds.), *Peace and War in Byzantium: Essays in Honor of George T. Dennis, S.J.* (Washington, D.C.: Catholic University Press, 1995), 68, 63.

[20] Mark C. Bartusius, *The Late Byzantine Army: Arms and Society, 1204-1453* (Philadelphia: University of Pennsylvania Press, 1992), 211f.

[21] English translation of text in George T. Dennis (ed.), *Three Byzantine Military Treatises* (Dumbarton Oaks Texts, no. 9; Washington, D.C.: Dumbarton Oaks, 1985), 21.

[22] *Maurice's Strategikon: Handbook of Byzantine Military Strategy.* Trans. George T. Dennis. Philadelphia: University of Pennsylvania Press, 1984), xiv.

[23] Angeliki Laiou, "On Just War in Byzantium," in John S. Langdon, et al. (eds.),

From the Byzantine era to the present, Orthodox Christian empires and peoples may have, on occasion, dabbled in holy war, but the Orthodox moral tradition – derived from the Bible, the writings of the Church fathers, the lives of the saints, canon law, liturgical and devotional texts – allows only a dual instead of tripartite social ethic of war and peace: the "justifiable war" and "pacifist" positions.

Crusades from the West

Not so the Christian West or the Islamic (farther) East.

Some scholars try to distinguish the crusade from the holy war in the West. For example, Frederick H. Russell contends that the Crusades launched in the late eleventh century represented "a peculiarly medieval hybrid" of holy war and just war traditions, the "Church's ultimate just war," while Peter Charanis views the Crusades as a subset of holy war. The key distinction of the crusade for both scholars was the unique role of the pope of Rome as the authority who summoned, organized, and guided the warriors for Christ.[24]

This may be a distinction without a difference. The Crusaders themselves did not always heed the cautions of the Roman pontiff. Raymond H. Schmandt argues persuasively that the nobles and clergy of the Fourth Crusade, who took a fateful detour and sacked Constantinople in AD 1204, flagrantly disobeyed Pope Innocent III's warning not to "seize or plunder the Greeks' land." The Crusaders also justified their behavior – in their own minds – in the classic language of justifiable war: self-defense against hostile Byzantines, redress of grievances against the new Byzantine emperor's failure to compensate them for their assistance in securing the throne, and "restoration" of

---

To Ellenikon: Studies in Honor of Speros Vryonis, Jr., vol. 1 (New Rochelle, NY: Aristide D. Caratzas, Publisher, 1993), 170.

[24] Frederick H. Russell, *The Just War in the Middle Ages* (Cambridge: Cambridge University Press, 1977), 38; Peter Charanis, "Aims of the Medieval Crusades and How They Were Viewed by Byzantium," *Church History* 21:2 (June 1952), 123f.

Roman primacy over the disobedient "Greeks."[25] But the havoc the Crusaders wrought in the Byzantine capital and primary see of Orthodox Christianity betrayed the same spirit of intemperance and fanaticism that motivated the shameless violence against the "infidel" Muslims during the first three Crusades. Donald E. Queller and Thomas F. Madden offer this harrowing description:

> In the holy sanctuaries the Latins stripped the altars of all precious furnishings, smashed icons for the sake of their silver or gems, and defied the consecrated Eucharist and Holy Blood. Patens were used as bread dishes and chalices as drinking cups. Radiant Hagia Sophia [cathedral] was stripped of everything of value. The priceless altar fashioned from precious metals, gems, and marbles was mashed into pieces and divided among the looters. So much wealth was found in the great church that mules were brought in to carry it away. Unable to keep their footing on the slick marble floor, some of the beasts fell and were split open by sharp objects they carried, thus defiling the sanctuary with their excrement and blood. A prostitute was put on the throne of the patriarch, where she provided entertainment for the looters with her bawdy songs and high kicking dances.[26]

The Crusaders, like the iconoclasts in the eighth and ninth centuries, also wantonly destroyed numerous artifacts of priceless value; they also raped women publicly in the streets, squares, and churches, and slaughtered men, women, and children with abandon. After the frenzy wound down, the Crusaders deposed the Byzantine emperor and replaced him with a pretender from their own ranks – Count Baldwin of Flanders – and did the same with the Orthodox patriarch of Constantinople.

---

[25] Raymond H. Schmandt, "The Fourth Crusade and the Just-War Theory," *Catholic Historical Review* 61:2 (April 1975), 191-221, esp. 212f, 216-18, 221.

[26] Donald E. Queller and Thomas F. Madden, *The Fourth Crusade: The Conquest of Constantinople* (2nd ed.; Philadelphia: University of Pennsylvania Press, 1997), 194.

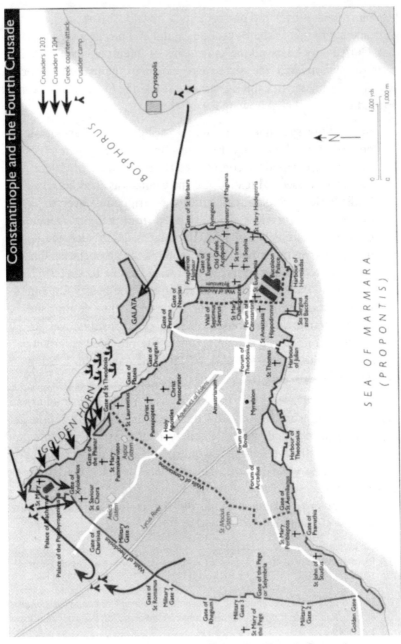

Attack on Constantinople during the Fourth Crusade

The so-called Latin Empire of Constantinople lasted little more than half a century, but the damage to Catholic-Orthodox relations was fatal. Even now in parts of Greece such as the island of Rhodes (as this writer can testify from personal experience) Western Europeans, especially those from historically Roman Catholic lands, are routinely called "Franks," after the Crusaders who inflicted "holy war" upon the Byzantines.

Still vivid in the collective memory of the Russian Orthodox faithful is the crusade launched by the Teutonic Knights early in the thirteenth century (successfully repulsed by St. Alexander Nevsky, a national hero and soldier-saint) and the complex religio-national wars of conquest by Roman Catholic Poland in the sixteenth and early seventeenth centuries. Although the Roman papacy has, together with the rest of Western Europe, disavowed its heritage of holy war, suspicions persist among the Orthodox as to Rome's imperial intentions. The modern papacy may not command any divisions, but Rome did canonize Joan of Arc, the fifteenth century holy warrior (female, no less) of France, as recently as 1920.

Crescades fom the East

Islamic teaching and practice concerning war present a more acute problem for Orthodox Christianity. Since September 11, 2001, Americans have been subjected to a barrage of assurances that Islam is a religion of "peace and tolerance." That this veritable mantra has been uttered by President Bush, Oprah Winfrey, countless scholars of religion – both Muslim and non-Muslim – and political pundits, and numerous ordinary citizens may give this claim an aura of authenticity. But Orthodox Christians know better than most the potential danger that millions of Muslim believers pose to Christians and Jews in this country and throughout the world.

It is not merely the extremists who ought to be of concern. Experts in comparative religion such as Charles A. Kimball caution us against vicious stereotypes. The vast majority of Muslims in the world were presumably outraged by the indiscriminate violence perpetrated on September 11 against New York City and the Pentagon by the al-Qaeda terrorists, who ignored the proscriptions in the Qur'an against suicide and violence upon innocent human life.[27] Islam, like other world religions, is hardly monolithic: there are "denominations" in the Western sense ranging from the mainstream Sunnis to the mystical Sufis, factions within each of those communities, and a kaleidoscopic variety of cultural manifestations, as the anthropologist Clifford Geertz has demonstrated, in such diverse ethno-political settings as Morocco and Indonesia.[28] Obviously, not all Muslims are "fundamentalists," nor are all Muslim fundamentalists extremists. The Muslim extremism expressed so brazenly by al-Qaeda's public statement on October 9 is not typical of Islam: "those youths who did what they did and destroyed America with their airplanes did a good deed. ... The Americans must know that by invading the land of Afghanistan they have opened a new page of enmity and struggle between us and the forces of the unbelievers."[29] And yet the extremists who share Osama bin Laden and al-Qaeda's twisted Islamic antipathy toward the West still form a sizable contingent. As political columnist Diana West observes sardonically, "The experts tell us militant Islamic fundamentalists, or 'Islamists,' represent a narrow, if murderous, fringe. They number no more than 10, maybe 15, percent of all Muslims. That works out to somewhere between 100 million and 150 million people. Which is a lot of murderous fringe."[30]

Although it may be politically incorrect to say so, the history of Islam since its inception in the seventh century has been one long story of conquest and reconquest. It began with the desert blitzkrieg through the Arabian peninsula led by the prophet Mohammed himself and swept through – in rapid succession – Antioch and Syria, the Holy

---

[27] Charles A. Kimball, "Roots of Rancor: Examining Islamic Militancy," *The Christian Century* 118:29 (October 24-31, 2001), 22.

[28] Clifford Geertz, *Islam Observed: Religious Development in Morocco and Indonesia* (Chicago: University of Chicago Press, 1968).

[29] "Text of Al-Qaida's Statement," Associated Press wire story (October 9, 2001).

[30] Diana West, "Islam is in the Dark Ages," *The Washington Times*, October 26, 2001, A21.

Land, Egypt, the whole of North Africa, Spain and southern France all the way to the gates of Paris, and eventually Asia Minor, Constantinople and the dwindling Byzantine Empire, the Balkans, and Eastern Europe all the way to the gates of Vienna – not to mention the eastward thrust through Persia, the Caucasus region, and the rest of Asia all the way to the Indonesian archipelago. The term "conquest" is not an exaggeration. No less reliable a classical Muslim source than Ahmad bin Yahya al-Baladhuri attests to this phenomenon in his ninth century compilation, Kitab Futuh al-Buldan ("Book of Conquests of the Lands").[31]

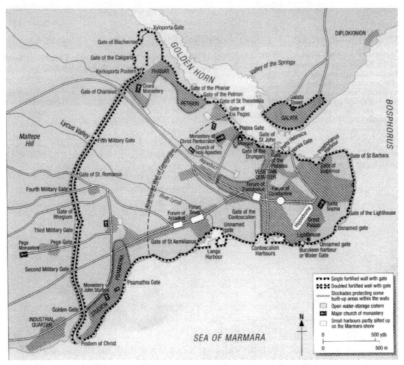

City of Constantinople when it fell in 1453

[31] Walter E. Kaegi, *Byzantium and the Early Islamic Conquests* (Cambridge: Cambridge University Press, 1995), 8, 18.

In almost every instance this new faith was spread through intimidation and coercion and usually through military means, especially holy war – a trend that continued through the last century to the present moment. Muslim scholars such as Hilmi M. Zawati may continue to insist that "Muslim jurists did not justify wars for such worldly purposes as territorial expansion, imposing their religion on unbelievers, or supporting a particular social regime."[32] But John Kelsay, a non-Muslim defender of Islam, is compelled by the evidence to concede that for "classical, especially Sunni, scholars, the norm was offensive war, at the command and by the direction of the caliph" (in Baghdad) "as a useful means of extending the territory of Islam and thus a tool in the quest for peace"[33] (albeit a Pax Islamica). In the 1996 book-length version of his essay, "Clash of Civilizations?" Samuel Huntington brings the story up to date:

> Wherever one looks along the perimeter of Islam, Muslims have problems living peaceably with their neighbors. The question naturally rises as to whether this pattern of late-twentieth-century conflict between Muslim and non-Muslim groups is equally true of relations between groups from other civilizations. In fact, it is not. Muslims make up about one-fifth of the world's population but in the 1990s they have been far more involved in intergroup violence than the people of any other civilization. The evidence is overwhelming.[34]

---

[32] Hilmi M. Zawati, *Is Jihad a Just War: War, Peace, and Human Rights Under Islamic and Public International Law* (Lewiston, NY: The Edwin Mellen Press, 2001), 107. His view reflects "the majority of contemporary Muslim jurists," according to Richard C. Martin, "The Religious Foundations of War, Peace, and Statecraft in Islam," in John Kelsay and James Turner Johnson (eds.), *Just War and Jihad: Historical and Theological Perspectives on War and Peace in Western and Islamic Traditions* (New York: Greenwood Press, 1991), 108.

[33] John Kelsay, *Islam and War: A Study in Comparative Ethics* (Louisville: Westminster/John Knox Press, 1993), 95, 35.

[34] Samuel P. Huntington, *The Clash of Civilizations and the Remaking of World Order* (New York: Simon & Schuster), 1996), 256.

Orthodox Christians are well acquainted with this legacy of religious intolerance, the popular claims to the contrary notwithstanding. One need only read The Bridge on the Drina, a gripping, historically accurate novel written in 1945 by Nobel-laureate Ivo Andric (a Bosnian Serb, no less) to learn how the Ottoman Turks stole young Orthodox boys from their mother's arms and turned them into Muslim Jannisaries to guard the Sultan, or punished rebellious Serbs and other subjugated Christians in the Balkans by sadistic impalement.[35] Or one may consider the unequivocal judgment of the great Church father, St. Gregory Palamas, who refuted the claims of his Turkish captors in fourteenth century Thessalonika that their prophet was the fulfillment of the messianic hope revealed in Matthew 24:27:

> It is true that Mohammed started from the east and came to the west, as the sun travels from the east to west. Nevertheless, he came with war, knives, pillaging, forced enslavement, murders, and acts that are not from the good God, but instigated by the chief manslayer, the devil. ... Though Mohammed may employ violence and offer pleasures, he cannot secure the approval of the world.[36]

Lest one object that even this consistent historical record fails to abide by the original teachings and intent of Islam, let us turn to the Qur'an itself. What we find in that foundational religious text is a moral code of war that echoes elements of the Old Testament ban but bears no semblance whatsoever to the New Testament. To be sure, the Qur'anic concept of jihad is not the simplistic, war-mongering militarism that has seized the popular imagination in the West. Nor is it synonymous with the indiscriminate, unlimited violence advocated by Osama bin Laden and his ilk. Literally "struggle" or "effort," the Arabic jihad refers primarily to the struggle within the heart of the Muslim

---

[35] Ivo Andric, *The Bridge on the Drina*, trans. Lovett F. Edwards (Chicago: University of Chicago Press, 1977).

[36] *The Lives of the Pillars of Orthodoxy* (Buena Vista, CO: Holy Apostles Convent and Dormition Skete, 1990), 352f.

believer to conform his will to that of Allah, and only secondarily to the use of military force "to extend the boundaries of the territory of Islam, and thus to extend the influence of Islamic values."[37] In an early sura, or chapter, however, the Qur'an itself acknowledges that military jihad may be disagreeable to Muslims: "Fighting (jihad) is obligatory for you, much as you dislike it. But you may hate a thing although it is good for you. ..." (Sura 2:216).[38] All the more, then, would Christians and Jews in America find jihad as it appears in the Qur'an quite appalling. A sampling of passages from various suras should illustrate the qualities of jihad as holy war according to Long's four criteria listed above.

First, there are verses that stress a religious motivation:

- "Fight against them [i.e., unbelievers] until idolatry is no more and God's religion reigns supreme" (Sura 2:193; cf. 8:39).

- "The true believers fight for the cause of God, but the infidels fight for the devil. Fight then against the friends of Satan" (Sura 4:76).

- "Fight against such of those to whom the Scriptures were given [i.e., Christians and Jews] as believe in neither God nor the Last Day, who do not forbid what God and His apostle have forbidden, and do not embrace the true Faith, until they pay tribute out of hand and are utterly subdued" (Sura 9:29).

Second, there are verses that promise religious rewards:

- "God has purchased from the faithful their lives and worldly goods, and in return has promised them the Garden [i.e., Paradise]. They will fight for the cause of God, they will slay and be slain" (Sura 9:111).

---

[37] See, for example, the succinct explanation in Kelsay, *Islam and War*, 34.

[38] All quotations from the Qur'an are taken from *The Koran*, trans. N. J. Dawood (9th rev. ed.; New York: Penguin Books, 1997).

- "Prophet, We have made lawful for you the wives to whom you have granted dowries and the slave-girls whom God has given you as booty" [i.e., spoils of war] (Sura 35.50).

- "As for those who are slain in the cause of God, He will not allow their works to perish. He will vouchsafe them guidance and ennoble their state; He will admit them to the Paradise He has made known to them" (Sura 47:6).

Third, there are verses that speak of Islam's enemies with unrestrained hostility:

- "Those that make war against God and His apostle and spread disorder in the land shall be slain or crucified or have their hands and feet cut off on alternate sides, or be banished from the land. They shall be held up to shame in this world and sternly punished in the hereafter. . . "(Sura 5:34).

- Prophet, make war on the unbelievers and the hypocrites and deal rigorously with them. Hell shall be their home: an evil fate" (Sura 9:73).

- We have indulged them [unbelievers] and their fathers, so that they have lived too long. Can they not see how We invade their land and diminish its borders?" (Sura 21:44).

Finally, there are verses that exhort Mohammed and Muslims to employ all expedient means:

- "Muster against them [i.e., unbelievers] all the men and cavalry at your command, so that you may strike terror into the enemy of God and your enemy ... All that you give in the cause of God shall be repaid to you" (Sura 8:60, 61).

- "When the sacred months are over slay the idolaters wherever you find them. Arrest them, besiege them, and lie in ambush everywhere you find them. If they repent and take to prayer and render the alms levy, allow them to go their way" (Sura 9:5).

- "When you meet the unbelievers in the battlefield strike off their heads and, when you have laid them low, bind your captives firmly. Then grant them their freedom or take a ransom from them, until War shall lay down her burdens" (Sura 47:4).

Although these Qur'anic verses are offered without full and proper consideration of their contexts or chronological sequence, their moral significance is quite clear. Devout Muslims claim, rather boldly, that the Qur'an contains, in the original Arabic, the literal, hence infallible, words of Allah as revealed to Mohammed by the Archangel Gabriel. Thus the full, brutal impact of this direct revelation (even in the supposedly unworthy, corrupting language of English) can be neither denied nor deconstructed. In the aggregate, the selected verses provide sufficient evidence to conclude that Islam is a religion that was conceived and born in violence. Even the Muslim scholar Majid Khadduri would agree with the thesis of this essay that jihad is equivalent to the Western concept of the crusade.[39]

Western Christianity abandoned long ago its religiously moti- vated holy wars and crusades, but the entire history of Islam has been one long crescade against unbelievers, Christians as well as pagans. Orthodox Christians and the Western world in general remain in a state of perpetual peril in their encounter with Islam. It would be in their best interests to maintain a constant vigilance.

---

[39] Majid Khadduri, *The Islamic Law of Nations: Shaybani's Siyar* (Baltimore: The Johns Hopkins University Press, 1966), 15.

Mary and the Qu'ran

Father Raymond F. Collins, STD

More than forty years ago, I spent the leisure hours of my first vacation as a newly ordained priest reading the Qu'ran. Globalization had not yet set in, yet the world was becoming smaller and smaller before my very eyes. Thus it became ever important to me who was studying the Jewish and Christian scriptures that I should become familiar with the scriptures of yet another people of the book, Islam. Thus, the leisure hours of my first priestly vacation were devoted to that project. In retrospect, the decision was a wise one as the world has become smaller yet, a single village in which more than twenty-five percent of the population embraces Islam.

A lasting memory that I took with me from my first reading of the Qu'ran was the way that Islam's sacred text speaks about Mary, the mother of Jesus. She is the *theotokos* of Eastern Christians, the Blessed Virgin Mary of Roman Catholics, and "Our Lady" of the churches of the Anglican communion. Recent events have prompted me to return to the Qu'ran in order to revisit the Islamic tradition about Mary, to whom the entire nineteenth sura is devoted. This sura is one of the oldest and most extensive gospel histories in the Qu'ran but it is not the only reference to Mary in the scriptures of Islam.

Mary, the Mother

Sura 19 is a kind of midrash on Luke's gospel narrative. Tradition has it that it was recited to the king of Ethiopia in the presence of the ambassadors of the court. The sura presents Mohammed as directed by God to include the story of Mary in the Book (19:16). The first part of Mary's story, paired with the story of the annunciation to Zechariah (Sura 19:1-15; see Luke 1:5-20), is the prophet's version of the Lukan tale of the Annunciation (Luke 1:26-35). The scene is set not in Nazareth but in some place to the east, a place apart. The messenger of the Lord, God's spirit, appeared to Mary in the form of a perfect man and announced to her that she was to have a son. The dialogue focuses on Mary's not having touched a man. The messenger of the Lord reassures her and tells her that the child will be a sign to mankind of

God's great mercy. The idea that Mary's child is to be a sign is apparently a reprise of the words spoken by Simeon in regard to the infant Jesus: "This child is destined to be the downfall and the rise of many in Israel, a sign that will be opposed..." (Luke 2:34). Thus reassured by the angel, Mary conceives and retires still further apart.

Icon of the Annunciation

The second scene (Sura 19:22-28) is apparently set in Egypt, but there is no reference whatsoever to Joseph. Mary continues to vow abstinence to the God of mercy. A miraculous provision of water and the provision of food in the form of fresh dates from a date palm tree evoke the Egyptian setting. These motifs loosely recall the marvelous gift of food and water to Israel at the time of the Exodus. As such, they imaginatively evoke the sojourn of Mary and her child in Egypt. The tradition of the presence of the infant Jesus in Egypt is developed in the Gospel of Matthew. Matthew's description of the flight into Egypt (Matt 2:13-23) is an imaginative midrash on the Exodus motif. His use of this biblical motif is most apparent in the citation of Hos 2:11 in Matt 2:15, "Out of Egypt I have called my son." In its allusion to the sojourn of Mary and her child in Egypt the Qu'ran gives no indication of any direct dependence on the Matthean narrative. That both texts evoke the idea of time spent in Egypt by Mary and her child is, nonetheless, quite striking.

The third scene (Sura 19:28-34) has no parallel in the New Testament Infancy narratives. In this third scene Mary brings the new born child to her people. They chastise her because she has "done a strange thing." Her "strange thing" is all the more unseemly in that she was the daughter of parents with unblemished reputations. In defense of Mary, the Infant himself speaks out[1] and proclaims that he is a servant of God, a prophet to whom the Book has been given. He has been charged by God to be "duteous to her that bare me" (Sura 19:33).

The Qu'ran provides no setting for this scene. The narrative loosely recalls the defense of Mary by means of a revelation from God in Matt 1:20-23 where the evangelist describes a revelatory dream in which Joseph's resolve to dismiss Mary quietly is dispelled by the angelic announcement that the child which she is carrying had been conceived from the Holy Spirit.

---

[1] Sura 3:41 says of "Messiah Jesus the son of Mary" that "He shall speak to men alike when in the cradle and when grown up."

The Qu'ran scene also appears to evoke two of the temple scenes in the Lukan Infancy narrative, the "presentation in the temple" (Luke 2:22-38) and "the finding of the boy Jesus in the temple" (Luke 2:41-52). In the first of these Lukan scenes a prophetic figure, Simeon, acknowledges that he is God's servant (Luke 2:29) and announces the prophetic vocation of Jesus with an allusion to Isa 42:6, "a light for revelation to the Gentiles" (Luke 2:32). The Qu'ran places the identification oracle on the lips of the Infant, "I am the servant of God; He hath given me the Book, and He had made me a prophet" (Sura 19:31). The text seems to have transferred the identification oracle from the lips of Simeon to the lips of the Infant. The Qu'ran's reference to the servant of God (Sura 19:31) and to the peace of God (Sura 19:34) surely recalls the opening words of Simeon's prophetic utterance, "now you are dismissing your servant in peace" (Luke 2:29). This transference of the proclamation of Jesus' prophetic vocation from the lips of the old man Simeon to the lips of the Infant Jesus himself enhances, almost fancifully, the prophetic role of Jesus.

The third Qu'ranic scene also evokes some traits associated with the Lukan account of Jesus' visit to the temple at the age of twelve (Luke 2:41-51). The occasion evoked by Luke was one of the great pilgrimage festivals. Jesus' age identifies a point in his life when as a young Jewish male he would have taken upon himself the yoke of the Law and become a "bar mitzvah," a son of the commandment. Luke's narrative features Jesus "sitting among the teachers, listening to them and asking them questions" (Luke 2:46). This was presumably a discussion about the Torah, anticipating the role of the Lukan Jesus as the interpreter of the scriptures (Luke 4:14-21; 24:25-27, 32).

Jesus' expertise with regard to the Torah, evidence in these several Lukan narratives, is evoked by the Qu'ran which simply affirms that he had been given the Book. The Qu'ran also alludes to Jesus' return from Jerusalem at the age of twelve. The prophetic utterance placed on the lips of the Infant Jesus (Sura 19:33) speaks of Jesus' obedience to Mary, an idea that appears in Luke's summarizing conclusion to the scene of Jesus in the temple (Luke 2:51).

Taken together the three scenes in Sura 19 highlight the miraculous nature of Jesus' conception and birth[2] and the prophetic vocation of Jesus, affirmed from his infancy. Mary is the only person whose name occurs in the narrative (Sura 19:16, 22). The angel, identified as a messenger of the Lord, is not further identified. Joseph does not appear in the narrative nor does Simeon. Even the child to whom Mary gives birth is not named within the scenes.

The Qu'ran brings the three scenes to closure with a summary presentation statement: "This is Jesus, the son of Mary" (Sura 19:35). Thereafter the Qu'ran describes the divisions "among the sects" with regard to Jesus and the offenders who are "in manifest error." With its diptychs the Qu'ran contrasts the role of Mary as God's instrument in the conception, birth, and presentation of the prophet with what Mohammed held to be human error with regard to Jesus.

Mary, the Virgin

The figure of Mary appears again in the Qu'ran in Sura 21, "The Prophets." The sura concludes its rehearsal of various biblical traditions about Moses and Aaron, Abraham, Isaac, and Jacob, Noah and Lot, David and Solomon with a "fast-forward" movement to the New Testament tandem of John and Jesus. Each of the canonical evangelists presents the two prophetic figures in tandem. Luke alone highlights the role of Zechariah with regard to John and the role of Mary with regard to Jesus. Zechariah and Mary are spotlighted in Sura 19; they return in Sura 21. This sura manifests the same hesitancy with regard to the name of Jesus that was evident in the three scenes from Sura 19. Sura 21 speaks of Mary and her son, without naming either: "And her who kept her maidenhood and into whom we breathed of our spirit, and made her and her son a sign to all creatures" (Sura 21:91).

This verse proclaims the virginity of Mary and the miraculous conception of Jesus. Mohammed seems to have firmly believed in this

---

[2] The conception and birth of Mary's son occur in a setting removed from human observation. God's creative activity (see Sura 3:42) is not perceptible to the human eye. Gen 2:21 similarly describes God as having caused Adam to fall into a deep sleep when woman was created.

pair of related truths. The Qu'ran reiterates his belief in Sura 66:12, "And Mary, the daughter of Imran, *who kept her maidenhood and into whom we breathed of our spirit*, and who believed in the words of her Lord and his Scriptures, and was one of the devout." With an affirmation of Mary's virginity and the spirit-produced conception of Jesus, the emphasized words repeat verbatim the words of Sura 21:91.

Sura 21:91 adds to its affirmation of the two interrelated truths the observation that God "has made her [Mary] and her son a sign to all creatures." This verse echoes Simeon's prophecy that Jesus will be a sign (Luke 2:34). Simeon proclaims that Jesus will be "a sign that will be opposed," adding a further observation about Mary's own suffering: "a sword will pierce your own soul too" (Luke 2:35). Under the rubric of a sign to all creatures (see Luke 2:31) the Qu'ran subsumes both the mother and her son. Their relationship is such that they cannot be separated one from the other.

Contemporary New Testament scholarship has repeatedly stated that one of the most important aspects of the New Testament portrayal of Mary is that she is a woman of faith. The single verse most often cited in this regard is Luke 2:18, "let it be with me according to your word." Mary's fiat bears upon her acceptance of the word of the Lord (see Sura 3:39).

An independent beatitude in the Third Gospel Luke proclaims as blessed "those who hear the word of God and obey it" (Luke 11:28). This beatitude is Jesus' rejoinder to words spoken by a woman in the crowd, "Blessed is the womb that bore you and the breasts that nursed you!" (Luke 11:27). Insofar as the beatitude pronounced by Jesus constitutes a reflection on Mary's maternal role, it proclaims her obedient faith in the word of God, thus confirming her fiat. The Qu'ran's portrayal of Mary moves from her acceptance of the specific word of the angel's announcement to a general acceptance of the words of the Lord as these are contained in the Scriptures. The New Testament makes no mention of Mary's belief in the Scriptures, not even in the Gospel according to Luke which presents Jesus as the interpreter *par excellence* of the Scriptures.

As a woman of faith who believes in the word of God and the scriptures, Mary is a member of the community of faith. She was, in the words of Sura 66:12, "one of the devout." Mary's faith is not separable from the community of believers to which she belongs. A similar point was made by the Fathers of the Second Vatican Council who appended to the Dogmatic Constitution on the Church, *Lumen Gentium*, an eighth chapter, "The Role of the Blessed Virgin Mary, Mother of God, in the Mystery of Christ and the Church." Many of the Council Fathers had wanted to devote an independent document to Mary. The majority voted to include consideration of Mary within the constitution on the church thereby emphasizing Mary's close connection with the church and all the redeemed. The Qu'ran had said virtually as much in portraying Mary as "one of the devout."

Mary, Dedicated to God

A description of Mary's youth is also found in the Qu'ran. It is more soberly narrated than are the tales found in the third-century *Protoevangelium of James* which shaped a good part of later Marian piety. Sura 3:31-42 describes the dedication of Mary to God as well as the annunciation of her conception. Between these two Marian segments of the Sura is the announcement to Zechariah of the birth of John.

Sura 3 describes the wife of Imran vowing the infant in the womb [Mary] to the Lord for special service. Both her mother and God specifically recognize that she is a female not a male. Having given her baby the name of Mary, Imran's wife prays "I take refuge with thee for her and for her offspring, from Satan the stoned" (Sura 3:31). With this prayer the Qu'ran proclaims that Mary is without sin.

The Lord accepted the mother's dedication of Mary. She was brought to the sanctuary where she was reared by Zechariah. According to the tradition Zechariah was chosen for this task by the casting of lots (see Sura 3:39). Reeds containing various passages of the Torah were thrown into the River Jordan. Zechariah's reed was the only reed that floated. The phenomenon was considered to be a sign from God that he was to have the responsibility to rear Mary in the sanctuary. In raising Mary, Zechariah, however, did not need to feed Mary. As often as Zechariah went to visit Mary in the sanctuary he found that she had enough food. It was God's gift to her. Assuming a prophetic role, Mary tells Zechariah that the food is "from God; for God supplies whom He wills, without reckoning" (Sura 3:32).[3] This miraculous provision of food is a sign of God's acceptance of Mary and his protection of her. It anticipates God's similar provision of food and drink to Mary at the time when she gave birth to her child.

Sura 3 describes the scene of the annunciation to Mary in a diptych of remembrances. The Qu'ran's use of the remembrance motif with regard to the annunciation once again underscores the belief that a spirit-induced conception is beyond human observation. The Qu'ran explicitly notes, in revelatory words addressed to Mohammed, "this is one of the announcement of things unseen by thee" (Sura 3:39).

Zechariah is told "Remember when the angels said, 'O Mary, verily hath God chosen thee, and purified thee, and chosen thee above the women of the worlds. O Mary, be devout towards the Lord, and prostrate thyself and bow down with those who bow.'" Zechariah was to remember God's choice of Mary as his chosen one and Mary's being one of the devout. Mohammed was to remember the Annunciation itself including the dialogue between Mary and the angel bearing on the fact that she was a virgin (see Luke 1:34; Sura 19:20):

> Remember when the angel said, "O Mary, verily God announces to you the word from Him: His name shall be Messiah Jesus the son of Mary, illustrious in this world and in the next, and one of those who have near access to God;
>
> And he shall speak to men alike when in the cradle and when grown up; And he shall be one of the just."
>
> She said, "How, O my Lord, shall I have a son when man has not touched me?" He said, "Thus: God will create what he will; When He decrees a thing, He only says "be" and it is."

According to this passage of the Qu'ran, it was revealed to Mohammed that an angel had announced to Mary that she was to be the mother of Messiah, Jesus. She counterposes her virginity. The angel

---

[3] See *Protoevangelium of James* 8.

responds with an affirmation about the creative will of God who has only to say "let it be!" and it is. Two other verses in the Qu'ran attribute the conception of Jesus to the spirit that God breathed into Mary (Sura 21:91; see Sura 19:17). The two motifs, God's creative word and the power of His life-giving Spirit recall the creation motifs of Genesis 1-2.

Sura 4:169 contains Mohammed's polemical argument against "people of the book," Jews and Christians. The verse specifically rejects the divinity of Jesus and belief in the Triune God, stating that "the Messiah, Jesus, Son of Mary, is only an apostle of God, and his Word which he conveyed into Mary and a spirit proceeding from himself." Clearly argumentative and denigrating Christian belief in Jesus, this Qu'ranic verse nonetheless portrays Jesus as both Messiah and son of Mary. It attributes the conception of Jesus to the word and the Spirit, the common teaching of Suras 3, 19, and 21.

Another argumentative verse, Sura 5:79 proclaims "The Messiah, Son of Mary, is but an apostle ... and his mother was a just person, they both ate food." This mention of food proclaims the humanity of both Jesus and his mother. She is described as a just person insofar as she eschews any role other than that determined by her relationship to God. Jesus is acknowledged as the Messiah and, as so often in the Qu'ran, identified as the Son of Mary.

A Reflection

The Christian reader of the Qu'ran cannot help but be impressed by its pervasive characterization of Jesus as the Son of Mary. More often than does the New Testament the Qu'ran identifies Jesus as the Son of Mary. This profile has two sides. One side is the polemic that speaks of Jesus as only an apostle, a mere human. The other side is the extolling of Mary's virginity and Jesus' miraculous conception. In filling out this other side, the Qu'ran rehearses early Christian traditions which focus on Mary's election by God, her dedication and devotion to God, God's miraculous care for her, and her faith in God's word. Were it not for the polemical purpose intermingled with the Qu'ran's portrayal of Mary, Christians could readily agree with Muslims on the picture of Mary as a just person and one of the devout, specially chosen by God to be the mother of the Messiah.

According to Luke, Mary's fiat (Luke 1:38) issued forth in paean of praise to God that proclaimed not only her own blessedness but also the hope that God in fulfillment of the promise made to Abraham and his descendants forever would bring to a final end every kind of exploitative injustice (Luke 1:46-55). In these critical times, the dawn of a new millennium and the birth of a new world order, we can all hope that Christians and Muslims, together with all people of good will, might pledge themselves to the promise of Mary's Magnificat.

The Plight of Eastern Christianity Under Islam

Rev. Bassam M. Madany

I - The Early Church: Western & Eastern

The Christianity that is most familiar to us in North America is Western Christianity. By this term I mean that the vast majority of Christians in this continent, can trace their background to either the Roman Catholic Church, or to the various Protestant Churches that came out of Rome early in the 16th Century.

In 312 AD, the Roman Emperor Constantine embraced the Christian religion. In 313, he published the Edict of Milan, that ended the persecution of Christians in the Empire. He chose Byzantium as his capital in 323, and renamed it, Constantinople (the city of Constantine.)

In 325, he called the Great Council of Nicea which defined the orthodox faith of the Church in a document known as the Nicene Creed.

Eventually, the Roman Empire was divided between the Western Empire, with Rome as its capital, and the Eastern Empire, with Constantinople as its capital. The language used in the Eastern Empire (known also as the Byzantine Empire) was Greek, while the language of the Western Empire continued to be Latin.

In the fifth century AD, the barbarians sacked Rome. That event marked the beginning of the end of the Western Roman Empire. However, the Western Church survived. It was this Church that experienced the event known as the Reformation (1517.) Thus, both Roman Catholics and Protestants trace their history back to the Western Church. But this is not the whole story about the Universal Christian Church.

The Eastern Roman Empire lasted another one thousand years after the fall of Rome. In 1453, the Ottoman Turks conquered Constantinople, and renamed it, Istanbul. It remained the capital of the Ottoman Empire until the 1920s.

The story of the Church in the East is quite complicated. During the First Century AD, it was understood among Christians that the rank or position of an apostle was unique, and that it ceased to exist after the death of the apostle John. Most of the apostles were not only leaders of the church, but served as channels of God's revelation. Their writings are preserved in theNew Testament.

Quite early in the subsequent centuries, the First Century form of church government composed of Elders and Deacons (with some Elders serving as teaching or preaching Elders) gradually gave way to episcopalianism. The Greek word "episcopus" literally means, supervisor, and is transliterated, bishop. It was practically synonymous with the Hebrew word, elder. Christian church leaders in large metropolitan centers, began to assume the title of Patriarch or Archbishop. There were five important centers in the early church: Jerusalem, Antioch, Alexandria, Rome, and Constantinople. The bishops in these cities were known as Patriarchs, and their specific ecclesiastical territory, as a patriarchate.

Eventually, the attempt of one patriarch (the Bishop of Rome) to assume the position of Head (or Pope) of the Universal Church, gave rise to the great division or schism of the Church. The Western Church recognized the sole leadership of the Pope in Rome; the Eastern Churches continued to recognize the historic leadership of their particular patriarchs in the East. This schism became final very early in the Second Millennium (1054).

The story of the Church in the East is even more complicated!

Let us go back to the Council of Nicea (325 AD). The great controversy that occasioned the convening of the first General or Ecumenical Council of the Christian Church was centered around the true doctrine of the Person of Jesus Christ. Arius, a presbyter in the church at Alexandria, propounded the theory that our Lord was a created being. He denied the clear teachings of the Bible such as in Psalm 2, Psalm 110, John 1, Hebrews 1, Ephesians 1, Colossians 1, and Revelation 1. Another Alexandrian presbyter, Athanasius (293-373) defended the Biblical teaching about the Messiah, by stressing both the deity and humanity of Jesus Christ. His position was accepted by the Council, and the Creed that was issued at Nicea, is known as the Nicene Creed. Since that time, it became the standard of Orthodoxy in Christianity.

The teachings of Arius became known as Arianism, and his followers were called, Arians. They were considered as heretics. Arianism spread among the Barbarians who later on invaded Rome, Spain, and North Africa.

It must be noted that delegates from of both the Western and Eastern parts of the Universal Church were at Nicea. The Council of Nicea dealt primarily with the deity of the Lord Jesus Christ. The discussions within the Church relevant to the relationship between the human and divine natures of Jesus Christ, led to further divisions. These occurred within the Byzantine Empire and the Eastern Orthodox Church.

Several Ecumenical Councils took place after Nicea, Council of Constantinople (381), Council of Ephesus (431), and Council of Chalcedon (451). At this third meeting, Christian Orthodoxy was further defined as to declare that, since his incarnation, the Lord Jesus Christ possessed two natures, divine and human. That also meant that our Lord had two wills, divine and human, but he remained one Person. Later on, this belief was set forth in a creed known as the Athanasian Creed. This creedal document is recognized only in the West, and is also known by its Latin name, *Symbol Quicunque*; (its opening words are: "Whosoever will be saved"). Rather than consolidating the unity of the Church, Chalcedon became the occasion for new divisions. Some church leaders, while strongly adhering to the deity of Jesus Christ, nevertheless defended the thesis that he possessed only a divine nature. They were known as the Monophysites. They were very prominent in Egypt and in Syria. Other church leaders, endeavoring to take full account of the Biblical teachings about Jesus Christ, went to the other extreme. They so described the two natures and wills of the Messiah as to make him almost two persons. They were called the Nestorians, i.e., followers of Bishop Nestorius of Constantinople, who was the champion of this teaching.

The Monophysite and Nestorian Churches were declared heretical by the Eastern Orthodox Churches. It is very unfortunate that the Orthodox party used also the arm of the Byzantine Empire to persecute those Christians who had not accepted the Chalcedonian formulation of the doctrine of the Lord Jesus Christ.

The Eastern Churches fall into two major categories:

The Chalcedonian Branch. It comprises the Orthodox Church, which was the State Church of the Byzantine Empire. Its territory included many parts of the Middle East, the Balkans, and Russia.

The Non-Chalcedonian Churches, having the following distinctive names within well-recognized geographical regions of Africa and Asia:

- The Coptic Church: Egypt, Sudan, and Ethiopia.
- The Jacobite Church: Syria.
- The Nestorian Church: Mesopotamia (Iraq).
- The Armenian Church: Armenia, Middle East, and the Diaspora.
- The Saint Thomas Church: India.
- The Maronite Church: Lebanon.

II - The Middle East: At the Rise of Islam

In our previous lecture, we covered the history of the early Church highlighting the development of episcopacy, and the eventual division of the Church between East and West. We alluded to the further divisions that occurred in the East, as the Church grappled with the subject of the natures and wills of Jesus Christ. As a result, more schisms took place. The Orthodox Church used the arm of the Byzantine Empire to persecute those who refused to accept orthodoxy as defined by the Council of Chalcedon in 451 AD.

The non-Chalcedonian Churches were regional, and were located in such geographical areas as Egypt, Syria, and Mesopotamia. Since Byzantium held political power over Egypt and Syria, it persecuted these independent Churches with the blessing of the Orthodox Church. This forms a sad chapter in the history of the Church, especially as these churches had already suffered during the first three centuries of the Christian era, prior to the conversion of Constantine. Beginning with 451, the persecutors were fellow Christians!

South of the Byzantine Empire lay the vast Arabian Peninsula. Most of it consisted of barren desert regions. They were inhabited by warring tribes, with a few urban centers such as Mecca and Medina. In the southern part of Arabia lay the rich land of Yemen, the home of the Queen of Sheba of Old Testament times.

In order to keep the Arabian tribes from invading the southern areas of the Empire, the Byzantines encouraged some semi-nomadic tribes to be their clients, and to act as defenders of the southern borders of the Empire. Most of these tribes had accepted the Christian faith, and for a good deal of time, they kept their agreement with Byzantium.

The great threat to the Eastern Empire lay further in the East. For centuries, Persia had been a rival of Byzantium. In fact, during most of the 6th Century, the two empires fought each other over areas known nowadays as the Middle East. Persia considered Mesopotamia (Iraq) as within its sphere of influence and had some native client tribes that kept peace on the borders of Arabia. All seemed quiet on these two fronts until the sudden rise of Islam early in the 7th century. Persia and Byzantium faced the challenge of a new faith that had a very active political component.

At this point, it must be noted that by the time Muhammad was born in Mecca (570 AD), Persia and Byzantium had exhausted their resources, having fought each other for an entire century. The subsidies promised to their client 'states' were rapidly diminishing. So, when the Arabs, after the death of Muhammad in 632 AD, burst out of Arabia and began the conquest of the Middle East, those Christianized tribes were not eager to fight them on behalf of either Persia or Byzantium. Some, joined the invading Arab tribes, while others offered hardly any resistance to their military incursions. By the middle of the 7th century, the Persian Empire fell, and the Byzantines lost Syria (including Palestine) and Egypt. By 732 AD, the Arab/Islamic armies had con- quered parts of Asia, Africa, and Spain, calling the latter, Andalusia.

As mentioned before, most of the population of Syria and Egypt were Monophysite Christians. Since they were considered heretical, they were persecuted by the Byzantines. At first, these Christians welcomed the advancing Arab armies imagining they were their libera- tors! Ironically, to the East, i.e., in Mesopotamia (present-day Iraq) the

Nestorians had enjoyed more freedom than their fellow-Christians to the West, since they lived within the Persian Empire. At that time, Persia professed Zoroastrianism, a dualistic faith that taught the existence of two equally powerful and antagonistic principles: good and evil. But Persia did not withstand the advancing Arab armies, and quickly collapsed, thus allowing the invaders to proceed further East to the borders of India.

At this point, I would like to advance the thesis that the Arabs, having adopted Islam, were no longer to continue in the age-long custom of raiding one another. Muhammad had convinced them that they had become one nation (Umma). As their local resources were scarce, they looked northward and eastward for a new source of booty. In their first incursions beyond Arabia, they were surprised by their rapid success within the Byzantine and Persian Empires. Here we must remember the historical fact that their conquests preceded their reflecting on the meaning of their spectacular successes in building a world empire. In the early history of Islam, practice came first, theorizing followed conquest. Eventually, they developed a strong belief that it was the will of Allah for Muslims to conquer the world. Thus they divided the world into two areas: Dar al-Islam (the Household of Islam), those areas conquered by Muslims, and Dar al-Harb (the Household of war), those areas yet to be conquered through warfare!

During the lifetime of Muhammad, and especially after his migration to Medina in 622, he dealt with Jewish and Christian tribes of Arabia. He had hoped that these followers of 'heavenly' (theistic) faiths who had received God's Revelations through Moses, David, and Jesus, would now welcome him as the final Messenger of God. That did not happen however. Soon after he conquered Mecca in 630, he persecuted the Jews, slew some of their men, and enslaved their women and children. After his death, his successors (the Caliphs) decreed that no Jew or Christian may continue to live within Arabia. This prohibition is still maintained today. Exception is made for non-Muslim technicians to live temporarily in Saudi Arabia, but none may hold any worship services even within the sanctity of their homes. This prohibition was illustrated by the fact that when President Bush visited Saudi Arabia in November 1990 during Operation Desert Shield, he had to leave the

Saudi territory in order to attend a Thanksgiving Day service on board of a U.S. aircraft carrier stationed in the Persian Gulf!

What about the conquered lands? The invading Arab/Islamic armies expected all pagan subjects to Islamize; but they did allow Jews and Christians to remain within their faith according to specific restrictions. The Arabs granted them the status of 'Dhimmis,' an Arabic word that literally means 'under the protection' of the new masters. The terms of this 'protection' were defined by the 'protectors.' Religious traffic flowed one way: from Judaism or Christianity, to Islam, and never vice-versa. Once a Muslim, always a Muslim. The Law of Apostasy was imbedded in the Quran, and an apostate could expect no mercy; death was the penalty for leaving Islam. Christians were restricted to worshipping within their churches, but were not allowed to evangelize. No new church buildings could be built. Christians were expected to pay a poll tax for the 'protection' they received from their new masters.

Since both the Persian and Greek administration of the conquered areas had collapsed, the Arabs allowed the Christians (natives) of Egypt, Syria, and Mesopotamia, to continue in their governmental work, and to use the local languages. But slowly, while Islamization slowed down, Arabization of the culture proceeded without delay. Within about 200 years after the arrival of the Muslims, Egypt, Syria, and Mesopotamia were Arabized. This can been seen by the fact that the first known translation of the Bible into Arabic by national Christians took place near Damascus, in the middle of the 9th century!

III - The Middle East After the Islamic Conquest

Having covered the historical background of Eastern Christianity, and the impact of the Islamic conquests, we shall now proceed to the study of the decline of Eastern Christianity in the Middle East. Our primary source is, *The Decline of Eastern Christianity, From Jihad to Dhimmitude*, by Bat Ye'or, published in 1996 by Associated University Presses, in Cranbury, NJ, 08512. The author was born in Egypt, and was a member of a sizable Jewish community that had lived in that country for centuries before Christ. The Jewish population of Egypt dwindled rapidly after the birth of Israel in 1948. Bat Ye'or (a Hebrew name that means Daughter of the Nile) migrated to France and contributed several works on the topic of "Dhimmis" (Jews and Christian) under Islam. In 1991, this book was first published in French, and five years later, the English translation appeared.

Most of what follows are quotations that illustrate the plight of Eastern Christianity since the Islamic conquests of the Eastern and Southern parts of the Mediterranean world. Professor Jacques Ellul, a well-known French Protestant scholar of the University of Bordeaux, wrote the Foreword to the book. Ellul reminds us that an intrinsic part of the Islamic faith is jihad. While modern Islamic scholars have endeavored to re-define jihad, claiming that it is primarily a "struggle with self," Jacques Ellul points out that history proves otherwise.

"But a major, twofold fact transforms the jihad into something quite different from traditional wars, waged for ambition and self-interest, with limited objectives, where the 'normal' situation is peace between peoples; war in itself, constitutes a dramatic event which must end in a return to peace. The twofold factor is first the religious nature, then the fact that war has become an institution (and no longer an 'event'). Jihad is generally translated as 'holy war' (this term is not satisfactory): this suggests both that this war is provoked by strong religious feeling, and then that its first object is not so much to conquer land as to Islamize the populations. This war is a religious duty" (p. 18).

"In Islam, however, jihad is a religious obligation. It forms part of the duties that the believer must fulfill. It is Islam's normal path to expansion" (p. 18-19).

"Hence, the second important specific characteristic is that the jihad is an institution, and not an event, that is to say it is part of the normal functioning of the Muslim world. The conquered populations change status (they become dhimmis), and the shari'a tends to be put into effect integrally, overthrowing the former law of the country. The conquered territories do not simply change 'owners.' Rather they are brought into a binding collective (religious) ideology – with the exception of the dhimmi condition – and are controlled by a highly perfected administrative machinery" (p. 19).

Coming now to our author's text, we are impressed by the thorough research and analysis of the sources that prove the thesis of Bat Ye'or, namely that the Islamic conquests had given birth for all time (within the Muslim world) of an institution that places the native populations into a permanently handicapped status. Writing about The Origin of Jihad, Bat Ye'or put it in these words:

> "The Jihad 'linked the mores of great warlike nomadism with the conditions of existence of Muhammad in' Medina where he emigrated in 622, fleeing the persecutions of the pagans of Mecca. Lacking means of subsistence, the small emigrant Muslim community lived at the expense of the new converts in Medina. As this situation could not last, the Prophet organized armed incursions to intercept the caravans which traded with Mecca. Interpreter of the will of Allah, Muhammad combined the political power of a military leader, the religious power and the functions of a judge: 'Whosoever obeys the Messenger, thereby obeys God' (Koran 4:82)" P. 37

> "In 640 the second caliph, Umar Ibn.al-Khattab, drove the Jewish and Christian tributaries out of Hijaz [he] invoked the desire expressed by the Prophet on his deathbed: 'Two religions should not co-exist within the Arabian peninsula'" (p. 39).

To go over the details that Bat Ye'or mentions in her book may sound totally out of tune with the spirit of our times when a globalized and shrinking world requires all of us to live in harmony and in peace and to forget the past. But what if in the past some civilizations were based on continual warfare, and if their histories have become normative for the present? And what if, as we notice today, Islamic radicalism is impacting our world from Indonesia, passing through Pakistan, and into the Middle East? Are we supposed to engage in self-censorship and suppress facts that are based on ancient dogmas and which still impact the present?

I have really been puzzled by the little reference made to this great work of historical research. It has been accomplished meticulously by an immigrant author who found in France a welcoming home and a proper atmosphere for the publication of her works on the plight of the Dhimmis across fourteen hundred years.

Here are a few more quotes.

"The religious obligation to fight the Christians required a permanent state of war which justified the organization of seasonal raids (ghazwa). They sometimes consisted of short pillaging incursions to collect booty, steal livestock, and enslave the villagers. Other campaigns, led by the caliph in person, called for considerable military preparations. Provinces were ravaged and burned down, towns pillaged and destroyed, inhabitants massacred or deported" (p. 48).

"For centuries after its conquest in 712, Spain became the terrain par excellence for the jihad in the West of the dar el-Islam" (p. 49).

"Under the Umayyads, the Peoples of the Book, particularly the Christians, represented the large majority of the Islamic states's subjects and – with the Zoroastrians – its principal taxpayers. This economic strength also constituted a political power that had to be controlled, since revolts would have paralyzed the Arab army, which was accumulating booty and slaves for the caliph in the dar al-harb" (p. 69).

"The two pillars of the nascent Islamic state in the conquered lands were the army – formed by Arab tribes and the slaves taken as spoils of war – and the conquered masses: tributaries, slaves, freed men, and converts, a workforce which fed the economic sector. The third pillar – juridical power – was being elaborated. It would undertake to balance and rectify the enormous demographic disparity between the conquered Peoples of the Book and the Muslims. The legal institution would formulate a collection of laws which gradually whittled down the rights of the dhimmis and confined them to a cramped condition, by transferring to the umma all the key positions that the dhimmis had formerly held" (p. 69,70).

"From the beginning of the conquests – in Syria and Spain, as well as in other conquered provinces – the Christians had ceded to the Muslims half of their churches which became mosques as a result of the Muslim influx" (p. 83,84).

"In the Maghreb, where endemic anarchy prevailed, sources mention the massacre in 1033 of five to six thousand Jews in Fez. The Almohad persecutions in the Maghreb and Muslim Spain (1130-1212) eliminated Christianity there" (p. 89).

Chapter 10 is titled: Conclusion. Bat Ye'or endeavors to bring together for the contemporary reader, a meaningful result of her research. Her goal is not merely to supply us with facts relating to the past fourteen centuries, but to enable us to understand the challenges that we faced at the end of the twentieth century, and that continue to be with us throughout the twenty-first century.

"Does the expression ' protected religious minorities' or 'tolerated religious minorities' adequately describe the dhimmi peoples?"

"In the lands conquered by jihad the Peoples of the Book formed majorities, among whom the Arabs of the first wave of Islamization and the Turks of the second wave were in the minority. Presumably the complex and little-known processes that transformed those majorities into minorities covered some three or four centuries for each wave of Islamization. By contracting it, the expression 'religious minorities' reverses a chronological process that had spread over centuries, whose result – the minority condition – is taken as its starting point."

"This interpretation, which omits the essential phase when irreversible changes occurred, conceals the political aspect of dhimmitude and reduces it exclusively to a religious minority status. In addition, the formula becomes inadequate for certain regions, such as the Balkans, where non-Muslims were in the majority until the nineteenth century" (p. 243).

"Today, it would seem absurd to describe the Rumanian, Serbian, Bulgarian, Greek and Israeli nations as former 'tolerated religious minorities.' Similarly, the common cliché 'second-class citizens' has no meaning, because the dhimmis were not citizens and the term 'second-class' is devoid of the dhimma's historical and juridical substrata" (p. 243,244).

"dhimmitude reveals another reality. Here are peoples who, spread the Judeo-Christian civilization as far as Europe and Russia. Jews, Christians, and Zoroastrians, conquered by no-madic bands, taught their oppressors, with the patience of centuries, the subtle skills of governing empires, the need for law and order, the management of finances, the administration of town and countryside, the rules of taxation rather than those of pillage, the sciences, philosophy, literature, and the arts, the organization and transmission of knowledge – in short, the rudiments and foundations of civilization" (p. 264).

"Decimated by razzias in the countryside, they sought refuge in the towns which they developed and embellished. Branded with opprobrium, the conquerors still chose to drag them from region to region in order to revive ravaged lands and restore ruined towns. Once again they built, again they worked. Once again they were driven out, again pillaged and ransomed. And as they dwindled, drained of their blood and spirit, civilization itself disappeared, decadence stagnated, barbarism reigned over lands which, previously, when they were theirs, were lands of civilization, of crops and of plenty" (p. 265).

"The elites who fled to Europe took their cultural baggage with them, their scholarship, and their knowledge of the classics of antiquity. Therefore, in the Christian lands of refuge – Spain, Provence, Sicily, Italy – cultural centers developed where Christians and Jews from Islamized lands taught to the young Europe the knowledge of the old pre-Islamic Orient, formerly translated into Arabic by their ancestors" (p. 265).

"And so this study would prefer to end with the a tribute. Indeed, as the centuries shed their leaves, these rejects of history disclose the infinite variety of the human character. Servile, corrupt, cowardly, pusillanimous, and presumptuous, but also learned, industrious, and heroic; all aspects blended and intermingled; faces of blood and tears, faces of wisdom and enquiry, molded in a thousand-year-old human magma which the historian only approaches with respect and without judgment" (p. 265).

IV - The Western Church and Its Response

Having covered briefly the history of Eastern Christianity before and since the rise of Islam, we face an important question. What is our responsibility, as Christians of the Western tradition, to our brothers and sisters still living under Islam? I trust that our survey, in the last three lectures, was not a purely academic exercise. Our concern was not prompted simply by a desire to learn more about the history of the early Church. After all, don't we confess in the words of the Apostles' Creed that we believe in one holy universal church? And how often have we sung the hymn, 'The Church's One Foundation Is Jesus Christ Her Lord,' where we also affirm the oneness of all believers?

Our study of The Plight of Eastern Christianity Under Islam should lead us to some serious reflection regarding our response. What are certain concrete things we must do so that our concern may prove genuine? I would like to make the following suggestions:

- First, Western Christians need to develop a keen interest in the history of Eastern Christianity. Many of our fellow-Christians in North America have roots in the various Eastern Christian communions of the Old World. Unfortunately, most of the churches in the West are not equipped to adequately inform their people about the plight of Eastern Christianity under Islam. I may sound rather critical of our theological institutions, but I personally experienced this deficiency in my training at two different theological seminaries. I don't mean to imply that we did not cover the doctrinal differences between East and West, or the deeper controversies that raged within the Eastern Churches leading to serious divisions. But all these matters were dealt with in a purely formal manner, i.e., within the study of specific doctrinal subjects such as the natures and wills of Christ, and the unity of the human and divine in his person. What was lacking was the story of our brothers and sisters in the East who succumbed to an invader that gradually destroyed their vibrant Christian lives, reducing them to a despised dhimmi status.

- Second, Western Christians must translate their knowledge of Eastern Christianity into a ministry of intercession. Many Eastern Christians still live under Islam, especially in the Middle East. They are facing tremendous difficulties due to the rise of radical Islam, and the continual conflicts that have beset the area since 1948. Our kinsmen in the East are greatly strengthened in their faith when they realize that their Western brothers and sisters have not forgotten them, but intercede for them in their homes and their churches.

- Third, Western Christians must act. What do I mean by this call to action? We are accustomed to all kinds of advocacy groups that seek to enlighten the public about various causes that need help or redress. So, why not speak out on behalf of suffering Christians under Islam? Did we not work hard to bring to the world attention the cause of Christians suffering under various Marxist regimes? Is it wrong to call attention to a situation that has lasted more than 70 years, yes to fourteen hundred years? Does the duration of this intolerable situation make it normal, or has it acquired a finality of an irreversible condition?

This call to action is not easy for several reasons. Most Western institutions, whether governmental, business, or educational, are not concerned about suffering Christians under Islam. As the West becomes more secularized, it manifests hardly any allegiance to a specific faith tradition. Our leaders are primarily concerned about national interest, which is nothing more than a euphemistic word for our continued economic well-being. Specifically, since Muslim nations control most of the oil reserves of the world, we are very careful not to offend them by mentioning anything about dhimmis and dhimmitude. Here are some anecdotal instances that illustrate my point.

In February 2001, the news media reported that Turkey had canceled a hefty military hardware contract from France as a protest for the French Parliament declaring that genocide did occur in Turkey against the Armenians during World War I. This sad event in the twentieth century that took the lives of over one million Eastern

Christians, both Armenian and Assyrian, has never been acknowledged by successive Turkish governments which are heir to the old Ottoman Turkish Empire. Even though France is far more secularized than the United States, it had the courage to adopt an official statement about this genocide. On the other hand, various attempts by the U. S. Congress to adopt similar statements have been discouraged by the Executive branch! What a sad commentary on our genuine interest in the plight of persecuted and martyred communities. For more than half a century we regarded Turkish sensitivities of paramount importance since they provided an Eastern bulwark against the Soviet Union. And nowadays, Turkey still supplies us with air bases that come in handy in our flights over the no-fly zone in northern Iraq!

Regardless of the callous attitude of our various cultural institutions vis-à-vis Eastern Christianity, we members of the Universal Church of our Lord should not hesitate but bear witness, individually, and corporately, to the continual plight of Eastern Christians under Islam.

Throughout my study of this subject, I have been rather puzzled, chagrined, and grateful at the same time. Puzzled and grateful because it took members of the Jewish faith to champion the plight of Eastern Christians by making a thorough study of the history of dhimmitude over fourteen hundred years of Islamic domination. It was not so much Christian scholarship that has brought this almost irreversible consequence of Islamic conquests to the world's attention. Furthermore, I have been saddened, because on the same topic, it was another Jewish scholar, the Britisher, Bernard Lewis, of the University of London, and later on, of Princeton University, who contributed numerous books on this subject. Likewise, V. S. Naipaul, also a British scholar of Indian Hindu background, undertook the task of describing the impact of Islam on other cultures! What a challenge to Christians of the new Millennium to take up the cause of their brothers and sisters who still live in Islamic countries and who have suffered silently for so many, many years!

V - The Christian in a Muslim Society

The subject of human rights has dominated the news media during the second half of the twentieth century. In the West many people were deeply concerned about the fate of Soviet citizens who had dared to challenge the authorities and who suffered the consequences in internal exile in a gulag. In the Free World, our attention was riveted on South Africa where tensions rose to a high level between the blacks and the whites due to the racial policies of the white dominated authorities. Pressures were brought upon the government of South Africa, through economic sanctions, in order to liberalize its policies vis-à-vis the non-whites.

While interest in human rights is still a live issue at the beginning of the twenty first century, we seem to be oblivious of those situations that come under the same classification of human rights violations, but which existed for centuries, specifically, if these infractions occur in the Muslim world. I am referring specifically to the plight of national Christians within Muslim societies. Early in the previous century, these large minorities had hoped to see better days under the banner of nationalism. But these hopes were dashed by the rise of radical Islamic movements in the aftermath of the Arab-Israeli war of June 1967.

At the beginning of this new century, the subject of The Christian in a Muslim Society should be of concern to all Western peoples, and more specifically to Western Christians. On the one hand, we witness the rising presence of millions of Muslims living in Europe and in North America. They enjoy equal rights with the citizens of their host countries. They build mosques, cultural centers, and schools, publish newspapers, magazines, and broadcast in Arabic on local radio stations. On the other hand, the situation is quite the opposite, when it comes to the national Christians living under Muslim rule. Throughout history, they have seldom enjoyed the rights that should be theirs; since they are the original inhabitants of their lands. They were conquered by the Arab/Islamic forces that invaded their homelands in the seventh century.

To speak about the predicament of Christians living in Muslim lands is very difficult. For the problem does not exist – as far as Muslims are concerned. Rarely does one notice any mention of the subject of the human rights of minorities in Arabic publications. For decades during the previous century, Western nations were exclusively preoccupied with the global challenge of Marxism, so they did not focus their attention on the infractions of human rights that were occurring for centuries in Muslim lands. To criticize Islamic governments would bring instant retaliation. Arab oil has been very essential for the health of Western economies. Thus, silence became the best policy vis-à-vis the Islamic countries. Some Americans may still remember the big fracas that took place when the docudrama, *The Death of a Princess*, was shown on television in the U.K. and the USA around twenty-five years ago. Saudi Arabia did its utmost to stop the telecasting of this show fearing that it would give it a bad image in the English-speaking world. And when it was shown in certain parts of America, care was taken to invite Muslim commentators who did their best to "salvage" the reputation of the strict Saudi regime.

Engraving of Rumelihisari

This is why Christians living in the free world ought to be very concerned about the status of Christians in the Muslim world. They must do their utmost to help these brothers and sisters who have almost been completely forgotten. The concerns of Western Christians should not be limited to those subjects that are on the agenda of the secular news media. We shall proceed to treat the subject of The Christian in a Muslim Society under five headings.

1. An examination of certain passages of the Quran that deal with the status of Christians

The Quranic teachings about pagans, Jews and Christians have had a tremendous influence on the Muslim attitude towards the minorities living within the household of Islam. The Quran teaches that Islam is the final revelation of God to mankind. Paganism is utterly wrong, and must not be tolerated in the lands conquered by Islam. Witness the Taliban regime in Afghanistan and their attempts to eradicate all traces of Buddhism in their land. But since Judaism and Christianity were revealed religions and thus were valid for a specific period of time, the followers of these faiths may continue to practice their religions within certain limits. Muhammad's views on the "heavenly religions" (theistic faiths) may be summed up in these words: Moses received God's revelation, the Torah, as guidance for the people of Israel. Jesus received another revelation, the Gospel or Injeel, as guidance for his contemporaries. But Muhammad received God's final and complete revelation, the Quran, intended for all mankind and for all time. The continued allegiance of Jews and Christians to their older faiths demonstrates their unwillingness to submit to the authority of God's final revelation, Islam.

Upon examining the texts of the Quran, one finds certain ambivalence about our subject.

> "Lo! those who believe (in that which is revealed unto thee, Muhammad), and those who are Jews, and Christians, and Sabaeans – whoever believeth in Allah and the Last Day and doeth right – surely their reward is with the Lord, and there shall no fear come upon them neither shall they grieve" (Surah 2: 62).

> "There is no compulsion in religion..." (Surah 2: 256a).

"And unto thee have We revealed the Scriptures with the truth, confirming whatever Scripture was before it. So judge between them by that which Allah hath revealed, and follow not their desires away from the truth which hath come unto thee. For each We have appointed a divine law and a traced-out way. Had Allah willed He would have made you one community..." (Surah 5: 48a).

The reason I quote these verses is that they have often been used as a proof for the tolerance of Islam. And indeed, taken by themselves, in isolation from other Quranic texts, and from Islamic tradition and history, one may think that they do teach tolerance of people who espouse theistic religions. The Quran declares that Jews, Christians and Sabaeans believe in one God, the Last Day, and in doing that which is right. And since God has declared "there is no compulsion in religion," one may presume that followers of these heavenly or theistic religions may continue to practice their faith without fear of persecution or discrimination.

In the last quotation mentioned above, Allah says to Muhammad (according to the Quran) that the revelation he was receiving was in harmony with the previous revelations. In other words, the Torah of Moses and the Injeel of Jesus are held in high esteem by Allah. Unfortunately, while Muhammad seemed to believe strongly that there was no conflict between the message he was receiving (the Quran) and the previous revelations, yet he realized that both Jews and Christians did not welcome his teachings. They based their lack of enthusiasm for his message on the teachings of their own scriptures. This led Muhammad, and later on Muslim theologians, to claim that the Scriptures of the Jews and the Christians had been corrupted. And yet even in this text which alludes to a conflict with Jews and Christians, the Quran teaches that the sovereign God had permitted the rise of many theistic religions: "Had Allah willed He would have made you one community."

Muhammad's intolerance of the Jews and the Christians appears clearly in various parts of the Quran. Here are some examples:

"Because of the wrongdoing of the Jews We forbade them good things which were (before) made lawful unto them and because of their much hindering from Allah's way" (Surah 4: 160).

"O people of the Scripture! Do not exaggerate in your religion nor utter aught concerning Allah save the truth. The Messiah, Jesus son of Mary, was only a messenger of Allah, and His word which He conveyed unto Mary, and a spirit from Him. So believe in Allah and His messengers, and say not 'Three' – Cease! (it is) better for you! Allah is only One God. Far it is removed from His transcendent majesty that he should have a son. His is all that is in the heavens and all that is in the earth. And Allah is sufficient as Defender" (Surah 4: 171).

While the Jews are more criticized in the Quran than the Christians, the latter are often charged with grievous doctrinal sins such as ascribing deity to the Messiah as well as teaching the doctrine of the Trinity. The Quran does not admit that these are revealed teachings. Rather, they are innovations made by Christians in the days which preceded Islam. Such Quranic texts have left a strong impression upon the Muslim mind. Christians are judged to be guilty of gross doctrinal errors; and they continue to cling to them in spite of the clear revelations of the Quran! We must remember that the Quran does not claim to bring any new teachings about God and his will, neither does it claim to contradict the previous scriptures. If the current books of the Jews and the Christians do not harmonize with the Quran, it follows that they have been altered. And this is exactly what is affirmed in Islam: the followers of the heavenly religions of Moses and Jesus have actually corrupted the books of Allah.

"And when Allah saith: O Jesus, son of Mary! Didst thou say unto mankind: Take me and my mother for two gods beside Allah? he saith: Be glorified! It was not mine to utter that to which I had no right. If I used to say it, then Thou knewest it. Thou knowest what is in my mind, and I know not what is in Thy mind. Lo! Thou, only Thou, art the Knower of Things Hidden" (Surah 5:116)

"Such was Jesus, son of Mary: (this is) a statement of the truth concerning which they doubt. It befitteth not (the Majesty of) Allah that He should take unto Himself a son. Glory be to Him! When He decreeth a thing, He saith unto it only: Be! and it is" (Surah 19: 34,35).

"And they say: The Beneficent hath taken unto Himself a son. Assuredly ye utter a disastrous thing. Whereby almost the heavens are torn, and the earth is split asunder and the mountains fall in ruins, that ye ascribe unto the Beneficent a son, when it is not meet for (the Majesty of) the Beneficent that He should choose a son" (Surah 19: 88-92).

Perhaps no other passage of the Quran has exerted as much influence upon the Muslim mind as the following. It has sanctioned, for as long as Islam dominates a community, the inferior of all non-Muslims.

"Fight against such of those who have been given the Scripture as believe not in Allah nor the Last Day, and forbid not that which Allah hath forbidden by His messenger, and follow not the religion of truth, until they pay the tribute readily, being brought low... And the Jews say: Ezra is the son of Allah, and the Christians say: The Messiah is the son of Allah, that is their saying with their mouths. They imitate the saying of those who disbelieved of old. Allah (Himself) fighteth against them. How perverse are they! They have taken as lords beside Allah their rabbis and their monks and the Messiah son of Mary, when they were bidden to worship only one God. There is no God save Him. Be He glorified from all that they ascribe as partner (unto Him)! (Surah 9: 29,31).

It is quite clear from these vehement words of the Chapter of Repentance that those who persist in their corrupt beliefs about the Messiah and their religious leaders, may only be tolerated, and must pay the special tax that marks them as inferior subjects within the Muslim society.

2. A brief overview of the history of the Christian minorities living under Islam

Most of the early conquests of Islam took place at the expense of Christian lands. When the Arab armies burst out of Arabia, soon after the death of Muhammad, they conquered Syria, Mesopotamia, Egypt, North Africa and Spain. Their conquests in the East took place in Zoroastrian and pagan lands such as Persia, Central Asia and India. When we follow the spread of Islam in its early days, we learn about the formula they used vis-à-vis the conquered peoples: aslem, taslam! Convert (to Islam) in order to have peace. However, Jews and Christians were allowed to retain their old faiths as long as they surrendered and paid the poll tax. They were regarded as dhimmis, i.e., the protected ones. Practically, this "protected" status, marginalized their existence, and imposed severe hardships that became part and parcel of the their dhimmitude.

Prior to the rise of Islam, the Orthodox Church persecuted the non-Chalcedonian churches using the arm of the Byzantine Empire to suppress their "heresies." This explains why many members of these communities welcomed at first the Arab armies, not being fully aware of the true nature of Islamic teachings. The first Arab/Islamic Empire under the Umayyads had its capital in Damascus, Syria. Since the Arabs were not capable of running the affairs of the state, they needed the fullest cooperation of the Aramaic speaking people of Syria. Thus they were inclined to be more tolerant to the native population of the Middle East than the Muslims of later times. But even in those early days of Islam, there were so many inducements to attract Christians to the religion of their conquerors. The number of converts to Islam grew steadily, and Christians ceased to be a majority in their homelands, and became a "lonely minority."

In the middle of the eighth century, after a violent and bloody destruction of the Umayyads by their distant cousins, the Abbasids, the capital of the Arab/Muslim Empire moved to Baghdad, Iraq. The largest Christian community there was the Nestorian Church. The caliphs in Baghdad employed many of these Christians in the civil service and entrusted them with important positions such as the court physicians. But often, the well being of the Christian community was totally dependent on the good will of the ruling caliph. Should the supreme head of the Islamic "church-state" decide that Christians must be persecuted, it was very easy for the populace to follow his instructions. On the whole, however, Christian minorities fared better during the ascendancy of the Arabs within the Muslim empire than later on when the power shifted to the newly converted Turks of Central Asia who had been slowly moving in the direction of the Middle East.

Even before the fall of the Abbasid Empire in the middle of the13th century, the Muslim world had become very fragmented. Early in the 16th century, the Ottoman Turks conquered the lands of the Middle East. The plight of the minorities became worse. Christians suffered many persecutions and were reduced to small groups of illiterate people and their churches were weakened. The accounts of the pioneer missionaries who went to Egypt, Syria, Mesopotamia, and Persia early in the 19th century document the tragic plight of the Christian minorities living under the rule of Islam.

The Christians of the Middle East welcomed the fall of the Ottoman Empire in 1918 and benefited from a relatively long breathing spell during the period of Western influence and colonialism. Already during the nineteenth century, many Christians were among the pioneers in the cause of Arab nationalism and the renewal of the Arabic language and culture. One example of the special role played by Middle East Christians in the literary movement could still be noticed in Egypt as late as the middle of the twentieth century. Most of the newspapers and magazines in Egypt revealed their Syrian and Lebanese Christian background through the names of their publishers!

Middle East Christians benefited a great deal from the presence of France and Britain in the aftermath World War I. That gave them an opportunity to be themselves and to enjoy freedoms denied them for centuries. This does not mean that they became stooges of the colonial powers. An impartial study of the role they played in the rise of nationalism points to the fact that they worked diligently for the realization of an impossible dream: the laicization of politics, i.e., the separation of church and state. Many of the leaders of the political parties in the Middle East were Christians, i.e., ethnic Christians. (The word Christian in the Middle East does not necessarily imply that such individual is a practicing Christian). But soon after independence,

Christians became very disappointed. For notwithstanding all their struggles for the revival of the Arabic culture and for independence, they discovered that they were being treated as second-class citizens.

3. The plight of the largest native Christian minority in the Muslim World: the Copts of Egypt

The Copts are the native Christians of Egypt. They are the descendants of the peoples who had lived in that land prior to the Arab conquest in the 7th century. Since they form the largest Christian minority within the Muslim World, it is very instructive to pay a special attention to their status within Egypt. In many ways they typify the plight of most Christian communities living under Islam. My sources are threefold, 1: Private communications received from Egyptian Christians. All such documents were unsolicited, and came to me as responses to my daily ministry of the Word of God over international radio stations that beamed their programs in the direction of the Middle East. 2. References made to the status of Egyptian Christians in the international press; and 3: A scholarly research published in 1963: *A Lonely Minority: The Modern Story af Egypt's Copts*. The author, Edward Wakin, was a journalist who showed unusual sympathy to the Copts. Even though more than three decades have passed since the appearance of the book, yet its findings are just as accurate at the beginning of the twenty first century as when they were first appeared in the early 1960s.

While Copts have always had their difficult times under the various regimes that ruled Egypt since the Arab conquest, yet the advent of the republican regime in 1952 marked the beginning of a new phase of subtle and unrelenting persecution. Even though Naser was perceived by many Arabs as a great nationalistic hero, yet he was at heart a strong Pan-Islamist leader and did very little to make the Christians of Egypt feel at ease.

One must look hard in Arabic newspapers and magazines to find a reference to the national Christians be they Copts or otherwise. Recently, I was surprised by the frank discussion of the problem in an international weekly magazine published in Paris, Al-Mostakbal (The Future). The writer was commenting on the dilemma that faces Middle East Christians who, no matter how hard they try, are not fully accepted by the Muslim majority. As an example, he cited the case of Dr. Butros

Butros Ghali. At the time, he was the only Copt with an important position in the Egyptian government. He was serving as under-secretary in the Ministry for Foreign Affairs of Egypt. After the late President Sadat's visit to Jerusalem and the accord of Camp David, both the prime minister and the foreign minister of Egypt resigned. President Sadat appointed Dr. Ghali as acting foreign minister. The writer asked the rhetorical question why not a full foreign minister? Well, Dr. Ghali was a Copt. How could he be fully entrusted with the foreign affairs of Egypt? Later on, during the 1990s, he did serve as Secretary General of the Security Council of the United Nations!

The columnist remembered a similar incident that had taken place during the Naser regime. Between 1958 and 1961, Syria and Egypt merged to form the United Arab Republic. During one of Naser's visits to the northern province of the UAR (Syria), he attended the maneuvers of some Syrian army units. He noticed that several officers had names like Michael, George and John. He asked: "How come you have so many Copts holding key positions in the army?" "Your excellency," replied a local senior army officer, "we have no Copts in Syria. These men are native Syrian Christians."

Such references to discrimination that Christians suffer in the Middle East are important and they remind us that the problem is not simply a thing of the past. It is a bitter present reality. According to Edward Wakin, the study of the status of the Copts today is extremely important, for as he puts it:

Viewed today from the West, the Copts are a major test of modern coexistence between a large Christian minority and a Moslem majority. In the Middle East, the Copts constitute the largest body of Christians in that part of the world where Christianity was born. For Egypt which is trying to mobilize all its human resources into a modern state, the test may be decisive. For a mosaic of minorities in the Middle Eastern countries of Syria, Jordan, Iraq, and Turkey, the Coptic story can be read as handwriting on the wall. For the Christians of Lebanon, who are maintaining an uneasy dominance in a country evenly divided between Christians and Moslems, their prospects in Moslem Arab hegemony can be deciphered from the Coptic situation in Egypt. It is a problem echoed nearby in the tenuous Greek-Turkish partnership of Christian and Moslem in the island republic of Cyprus. Involved, besides the Western values for which the Copts stand, is the fate of tolerance and respect for the individual in the vast self-centered world community of 400 million Moslems. On an even larger stage, the Copts share the dream of the world's minorities, ranging from the recent sufferings of Jews and Armenians to such current problems as Jews in Russia, Protestants in Spain (p. 4).

How prophetic these words have become. July 1974 witnessed the invasion of Cyprus by the Turkish army using NATO supplied arms paid for by the American taxpayer! Two hundred thousand Greek Cypriots were made homeless overnight. No one seemed to care for the human rights of these natives of Cyprus. They had been living in their island for more than two millennia. Turkey must be appeased at any cost, since it occupied such a strategic position near the borders of the USSR! It is a very sad fact that in the analysis of the problems of the Christian in a Muslim society today, no emphasis is placed on the religious nature of his plight. Christians are described in ethnic or hard to recognize terms such as: Armenians, Assyrians, Copts, Maronites, etc. While this classification is valid up to a certain extent, the true nature of the problems that these ethnic groups face is not due to their ethnicity but to the faith of their community. This is why Wakin's book is so important. Coming from a secularized culture in the USA, yet he did not allow that factor to forget or minimize the religious nature of the plight of minorities living under Islam. In the final analysis, Middle East Christians are considered as second-class citizens, and sometimes persecuted, because they belong to a community that in Arabic is known as the Messianic minority.

Many things have happened in Egypt since the death of president Naser in the early seventies. Under president Sadat, socialism was completely discarded; a new policy was adopted allowing many international companies to compete openly in bidding for projects related to the renewal of the economy of Egypt. The terrible defeat in the war of 1967 was avenged by the partial victory of the October 1973 (Yom

Kippur) war that resulted in the eventual withdrawal of Israel from Sinai. But one thing has not changed: the Muslim's attitude to the Copt. The latter is still despised, persecuted, and at times brutally murdered by radical Islamists. Whether the Copt is an ordinary layman or Pope Shenodah, the head of the Orthodox Coptic Church, Muslims look upon him with derision or suspicion. This is why the Copt has identified with the cross, a symbol of suffering more than any other Christian community. Edward Wakin described this facet of the Copt's life in a chapter entitled: *The People's Church.*

> The cross suits this cruel culture of poverty and persecution, both as identification and an outlet for the Copts. It is their brand and their balm; it gives a meaning to life when there are only blind nature and inexplicable misfortune. If Western Christianity gives prime glory to Easter, the day of Resurrection, deliverance and confirmation of Christ's divinity – Good Friday is more appropriate psychologically to the Copts. On this day when the cross was born as a universal Christian symbol, modern Copts say "Kyrie elesison" (Lord, have mercy upon us) 400 times at home, 100 times in each direction, and flock to their churches (p. 136).

> While the Copts share the cross with the rest of Christianity, with no other group is its presence so obsessive. This ranges from the Patriarch, who holds the cross in front of himself as though it were both a shield and a weapon, to the ragged village children who run after strangers, with crude blue tattoos of the cross on the inside of their right wrists and crosses around their necks. Whenever the Patriarch appears, Copts rush forward to kiss his cross. The fixation is symbolized at baptism when the infant is anointed 36 times all over his body (p. 137).

> Crosses are painted over the doors of Coptic houses in towns and villages or formed in bas- relief in mud over the openings of mud homes. Sometimes the house and cross are brick. The Copts, who are fond of reading the family Bible at home, are aware of Exodus 12:13 and the significance of a sign in order to escape the wrath of the Lord: "And the blood shall be to you for a token upon the houses and the plague shall not be upon you to destroy you, when I smite the land of Egypt (p.138).

The saddest thing about the lack of tolerance which the Copts of Egypt experience, generation after generation, is that their own homeland is robbing itself of one of its greatest resources: a purposeful and energetic community of nationals. We must keep reminding ourselves of this often forgotten fact: the Copts have been in Egypt long before the Arabs. Unfortunately, while it can be said that in the past the Copts' attachment to Egypt was so great that it kept them from leaving it, today it is no longer so. Thousands of Copts are to be found in Canada, the United States, Australia and several other areas of the Western world. Usually, they are highly educated people whose skills Egypt has lost forever. Before this migration wave became as strong as it is today, Edward Wakin wrote these moving words at the end of his book:

> Both Egypt and Islam, like all other countries and ways of life in the modern world, must meet the test of toleration. For Islam it is a moral challenge spread over its proverbial range from the Atlantic to the Indian Oceans. Citing its theoretical toleration does not silence the cry of its minorities. For a Moslem nation, it is the practical problem of using human resources. The Copts themselves, within the microcosm of their history and its manifestations in church, community, nation and minority, present everyman's tale of dream and nightmare, fulfillment and frustration in a world not of their making. Insofar as the Copts have received their due -- without ignoring their blemishes -- this modern story of Egypt's Copts is an account of the human condition.

At the end of this intimate rendezvous with the Copts, a concluding moral note is unavoidable: the obligation to oppose tyranny wherever it stands, even when the tyranny is elusive and unannounced, even unintended. It begins with labeling injustice long before shop windows are smashed, icons broken, and families torn apart. This labeling is an antidote to the danger of dulled sensibilities in our time and while the Copts can be accused of hypersensitivity, their problem is by no means imaginary. They are feeling pressures that inflict suffering without mutilating, that intimidate relentlessly without exploding sporadically that wound without bloodshed.

The Copts are numbed and helpless as well as anxious as their historic cycles of acceptance and rejection, their recurring stages of toleration, discrimination, and persecution move inexorably in the direction of rejection. Persecution is still the nightmare, discrimination the reality in the latest chapter of a long story of a people. They are there in Egypt and there they remain, the "true Egyptians," the "original Christians," the four million Copts of the Nile Valley, that troubled, enduring, lonely minority (p. 175 and 176).

4. The Tragedy of Modern Lebanon

We have dwelt at length with the story of the Christian community in Egypt. The Copts typify one way in which an Eastern Christian community chose to live within a land dominated by Islam. The Lebanese Christians chose, at least since 1918, a different way of coexistence with their Muslim neighbors. Aided by the French presence in Lebanon between 1918 and 1946, the Lebanese Christians sought to create a Western type democratic society in an arrangement of power sharing between the various Christian and Muslim groups. For example, an unwritten agreement between the various groups called for the president to be a Maronite Christian, the prime minister a Sunni Muslim, and the speaker of the parliament, a Shiite Muslim. In a house that numbered 99 deputies, 55% of the seats were allocated to the various Christian communions, while 45% went to the Muslims consisting mainly of Sunnis, Shiites and Druze.

The last census was held in Lebanon in 1932 and it reflected the above-mentioned percentage of Christians and Muslims. However, due to various factors, both internal and external, the number of Muslims living in Lebanon since the end of World War II increased rapidly. They began to ask for a bigger share in the government and wanted an end to the pro-Western policies of the Christian-led regime. The first violent explosion took place in 1958 and pointed to the growing cleavage between the two communities in Lebanon. The situation became more critical in the early seventies. After the suppression of the PLO in Jordan, thousands of Palestinian fighters moved to southern Lebanon and to camps around Beirut and sought to continue their struggle against Israel. Some parts of Lebanon were no longer under the control of the central government in Beirut. Several areas of South Lebanon were referred to as Fatahland, Fatah being the largest of the Palestinian movements under the leadership of Yasser Arafat. This situation could not continue unchallenged. The Phalange, the largest militia group of the Maronite Christian community, got involved in a violent clash with the Palestinian fighters on Easter Monday, 1975. That marked the beginning of the civil-international war that raged in Lebanon for over seventeen years, leading to the destruction of most parts of Beirut, and the Syrian occupation of Lebanon has not ended to this very day.

It is not my intention to give a catalog of the sad events that have resulted in the destruction of what used to be called the Switzerland of the Middle East. I will attempt to explain some reasons that caused a sizable section of the Christian population of Lebanon to refuse the demands of the Muslims for a greater share in the running of the affairs of the state. They knew quite well that to give more power to Muslims would have inevitably led to the eventual disappearance of the democratic country they have struggled so hard to build. Lebanon had become, and that especially since 1918, a haven for persecuted minorities and a refuge for political dissidents coming from every part of the Middle East, both Christian and Muslim. It may not be possible for Western people to appreciate the different logic of the Lebanese Christians. For their assessment of their particular situation was not made in the comfort of Western academic institutions, but from the bitter memories of persecutions and massacres that they had suffered in the 1860s, and during the horrible famine caused by the Ottoman Turks during the 1914-1918 war.

Most of all, the refusal of the Lebanese Christians to share more power with the Muslims was due to the fact that almost every Arab country that had achieved independence from colonial powers, had succumbed to totalitarian regimes, some lasting even to the dawn of the twenty first century! Sufficient to say that the Christians of Lebanon were convinced, rightly or wrongly, that Lebanon's fate would be the same, should they yield more power to the Muslims. Throughout 1400 years of history, Islam has never practiced anything that might be called democratic, its very worldview being authoritarian. All the signals received from the contemporary history of Arab countries pointed to the loss of freedom – should Muslims take over the government of the land. Consciously and unconsciously, the Christians of Lebanon opted for the defense of their way of life through an armed response to the forces that threatened them. Since no major world power was interested or willing to come to their aid, the destruction of modern Lebanon was assured.

5. How can Western Christians help their brothers and sisters living under Muslim rule?

As we reflect on the plight of the Christian minorities within the household of Islam, we face a very old and complex problem. Thus, we must not offer any simplistic answer. To begin with, we must not ignore the existence of the problem. Politically, Western governments have been very reluctant to deal with this sad lack of human rights within the Muslim world. Witness the great involvement of the USA and Western European countries in the affairs of Yugoslavia, where Muslim minorities in Bosnia and Kosovo were threatened by the Serbs. At the same time, for almost two decades, millions of Sudanese Christians and animists have been killed by the radical Islamic government in Khartoum. And yet, nothing but silence has met this ongoing tragedy.

Let me offer these points that might be of help as we further reflect on the plight of the Christian minorities living under Islam:

- The Bible has no direct teaching or reference to Islam. This is obvious since this religion is post-Biblical. The Bible does prepare us to deal with Islam by stressing the uniqueness, finality, and superiority of the Lord Jesus Christ.

- The great emphasis that the Bible places on the redemptive character of the Christian faith and the deity of Jesus Christ must be upheld at any cost as we face the challenge of Islam, not only in far away lands, but right here in the Western world. Most of our Christian brothers and sisters in the East have not enjoyed, on the whole, the benefits of the Reformation. Their churches need to rediscover the fundamental evangelical teachings of the Bible concerning our salvation. But it is to their credit that for centuries and under the most difficult circumstances, they have borne testimony, to the deity of our Lord Jesus Christ.

- By helping the Eastern Churches within the lands of Islam to rediscover the totality of the Biblical faith, we enable them to see their unique place in the evangelization of the Muslims of their homelands.

The Christian mission to Muslims will go on until the end of time. No power can stop it, since it is undertaken under the sovereignty of the Lord Jesus Christ, the Head of his Church. Christians living in the Muslim world and Western missionaries hold the key to the conversion of Muslims. As Raymond Lull, the first Western missionary to Islam, put it long ago:

"I see many knights going to the Holy Land and to other lands of the Infidel, seeking to acquire them by force of arms. But they never attain that. As for me, the only way of conquest is the old, old apostolic way, namely by love and prayer and the pouring out tears and blood."

The quotations are from:

The Meaning of the Glorious Koran, An Explanatory Translation by Mohammed Marmaduke Pickthall, A Mentor Religious Classic.

A Lonely Minority: The Modern Story of Egypt's Copts by Edward Wakin, William Morrow & Company, New York, 1963.

The Many Faces of Islam and Christianity

Father Jonathan Morse, PhD

In light of the events of September 11, 2001, many Americans are now trying to get to know Muslims and Islam. The reason for the search is to come to grasp on how some people could hate Americans as much as they do. Always someone will come up with easy answers. They hate us because of our freedom. Yes, there is some truth to that because some in the Islamic world fear "westernization" and its apparent lack of morality spreading into their families. They hate us because we are rich. Yes, there is truth to that when people are starving for a lack of food because of policies rightly or wrongly blamed on the United States foreign policy. They hate us because we are so strong. Yes, there is truth to that because we are the last of the superpowers. They hate us because we feel that we have to reform them and make them like us. Yes, we felt the same resentment towards England prior to the Revolutionary War.

These are the easy answers. These are the superficial answers that come in easy sound bites for the media. For the opposite of these answers should also be true. They love us because of our freedom, after all Islam is one of the growing religions in America because of our freedom of religion. They love us because of our wealth because even in war we send food to those in need throughout the world. They love us because of our strength because the world is farther from mass destruction than it was during the Cold War. They love us because we want to reform them and raise the standard of living for all persons. The answer is closer to the fact that we have not been talking and listening to each other for at least the past thirty years.

Centuries ago, Christendom was of one Church. The Churches of East and West were not just in communion with each other, they saw themselves as one Church. While there were disagreements within the Church, such as the early *filioque* disputes, the dispute over leaven and unleavened bread, they were disagreements within the family. Many scholars see the separation between East and West as arising from the lack of communication between the Churches. The East spoke Greek and the West spoke Latin. Neither side made any serious attempt at communicating a Christian voice; there is not one Muslim voice. Christianity was divided into East and West, the East preferring the apophatic (less defined and more mystical) approach to theology and the West preferring the cataphatic (systematic) approach. Both approaches are equally valid, while they are not exclusive of each other.

The Eastern Churches further divided themselves by jurisdiction, the different Byzantine patriarchates, or by theology, Syriac and Byzantine for example. The Western Church divided itself over approaches to Scripture, the *scola scriptura* of the Protestants and the interpretation of the *magisterium* by the Catholics. Today, as can be seen in the Catholic-Lutheran dialogue, the original points of divergence were not that far apart, and since Vatican II many of the points of the early reformers have found there way into Catholicism. Yet, there are some things that all Christians hold to be true. One cannot push any of these statements too far without getting into a point of disagreement. All Christians hold that there was a person by the name of Jesus who was crucified and died for the salvation of others. All Christians hold some understanding of a concept of Trinity.

Islam has also known theological divisions that have given rise to different communities. They all see themselves as Muslims, yet respect the diversity of belief.

Sunni is the largest division of Islam. Sunni Islam is the heir to the early central Islamic state, in its acknowledgment of the legitimacy of the order of succession of the first four caliphs, in contrast to the Shiite rejection of the first three as usurpers. This is similar to the Catholic claim of apostolic succession as the basis for its legitimacy for the Sunni as compared to the Protestant claims that the papacy lost its legitimacy through papal corruption.

The Shiites (a name derived from the Arabic shiat Ali, "the party of Ali") constitute the other major branch of Islam. Following the death of Mohammad, disagreement arose as to the necessary qualifications and exact function of his successors as leaders (Imams) of the Muslim community. The Shiites are those who insisted that only members of the Prophet's clan, specifically, the descendants of Mohammad's daughter Fatima and her husband Ali, could qualify. Although Ali became (655) the fourth caliph, he was murdered in 661, and the majority recognized the Umayyad Muawiya I as caliph. The Shiites, however, supported the claims of Ali's sons: Hasan, who died mysteriously c. 669, and Husayn, who was killed by Umayyad troops in 680 (Kerbala, in Iraq, became the major pilgrimage center for the Shiites).

Just as Western Christianity continued to break into more groups in terms of the different Protestant denominations, so too did Shiite. Shiism has three major subdivisions as well as numerous offshoots. The majority are called Twelvers (Ithna Ashariyya), because they recognize 12 imams, beginning with Ali and the twelfth disappeared in 873 but is believed to return as the Mahdi (messiah). Twelver Shiism became the state religion of Persia (Iran) under the Safavid dynasty in the 16th century; it retains that position in the present - day Islamic republic of Iran. The other two major subdivisions are the Seveners (Ismailis) and the Fivers (Zaydites).

Sunni can also be seen as the gathering of the adherents to the four extant schools of religious law (fiqh), the Hanafi, Maliki, Shafii, and Hanbali schools. With no centralized clerical institution, Sunni Islam should be understood as an umbrella identity, grouping close to 90% of the approximately one billion Muslims, stretching geographically from the Indonesian islands to the African steppes, through the Indian subcontinent, central Asia, and the Arab world. This can be seen as similar to the Catholic Church with the particular churches that make up its membership, i.e., Roman, Byzantine, etc.

As in Catholicism there is a considerable divergence of spiritual practices from the contemplatives of the Byzantine Church to the fundamentalists found in the Tridentine Catholics, there is a divergence within Islam from the ecstatic Sufism to the puritanic literalism of the Wahhabis and Salafias, through scholasticism and secularism. The scholastic formulation is the most constant expression of Sunni Islam. This could be seen as similar to the Western Christian intense interest in systematic studies of theology and scripture.

Theologically, Sunni teaches the relation of the human being with the Divine as essentially individual, with no intermediaries. In actual practice, however, religious scholars (ulama), together with mystic shaykhs, pious persons, and popular saints (awliya), are often recognized as enjoying a religious authority of varying degrees. This is similar to the Protestant expression of Christ as the only mediator, yet even some of the most fundamentalist Protestants will hold up some authorities as higher than others.

The religious authority of the Shiite clerics is derived from their role as deputies of the absent twelfth Imam. They are as such the recipients of the khums, religious tax. Shiite clerics are often referred to as mullahs and mujtahids. The Shiite clergy does not have a formal hierarchy other than the honorific ayat Allah or ayatollah. We can see a similar structure in non-mainline Protestant denominations.

Even though the Shiite Muslims are a minority, their fervor has been an inspiration to larger groups of Muslims. This is especially true because of the tragedies they have suffered. According to John Esposito, the memory of these and following tragedies and martyrdoms "provided the paradigm of suffering and protest that has guided and inspired Shii Islam." [1] This martyrdom theme has been prevalent in the most recent tragedy in the West.

Sunnis and Shiites share some areas in common and in others they disagree. A simple illustration would be:

Both

Koran could not contain errors because Allah had dictated it directly to Mohammad

Sunnis

Claimed the only intercessor between believers and Allah was the Koran

Shiites

Believed that a person rather that the Koran itself was the proper intermediary between Allah and believers

---

[1] John L. Esposito, *Islam - The Straight Path* (New York: Oxford University Press, 1991), 45.

Both

in order to establish authority needed for the particular community, a decision had to be made concerning which verses or ideas took precedence over others

Sunnis

governed by a Shah or monarch

Religious leaders separate from government

Shiites

Imam governs and has both spiritual and secular authority.

Just as there are ongoing attempts to bring unity between Catholics and Protestants or Catholics and Orthodox, there are attempts to bring unity between Sunni and Shiite Muslims. One such source, though unpublished but known widely through the Internet is William VanDoodewaard, "Islam United? A Comparison of Shi'ite and Sunni Belief and Practice", unpublished article, The University of Western Ontario, London, Canada: 1995.

Just as there are Muslims who work for unity, there are those who are extremists and find that other Muslims are not living up to the true tenets of Islam. The simplest example of this is the variety of religious communities found within Catholicism. A new group is founded when the original group is not seen as living the ideal, for example, the Cistercians and the Cistercians of the Strict Observance.

Even among extremists there are those who take extremism for religious purity and attempt through the use of force to impose their extremism on a larger society. This can be seen from the Protestant experience in England under Queen "Bloody" Mary as recorded in Fox's Book of Martyrs or the following persecution of Catholics under Queen Elizabeth I. Both scenarios involved the considerable loss of life under the guise of the defense of religious principles. In these situations there are always those who have admiration and willingness to support extremists, even if it is not politically correct. This can be seen in the support of American Roman Catholics for the Irish Republican Army and its terrorist campaign to create one Ireland. The Arab press does show some subtle support for bin Laden and the Pakistani newspaper The Nation came right out and said, "September 11 was not the mindless terrorism for terrorism sake. It was reaction and revenge and even retribution."

When dealing with extremism whether Christian or Islamic it is not possible to dialogue out of the context of "pure Islam" or "pure Christianity." As Christians cannot agree on the living out of Christian principles, for example the whole context of life issues, Muslims cannot agree on the living out of principles of the Qur'an. Each side of the question can refer to the source text.

In Christianity, there are those who support the death penalty and point to the text in the Book of Genesis, "For your own lifeblood, too, I will demand an accounting: from every animal I will demand it, and from man in regard to his fellow man, I will demand an accounting for human life. If anyone sheds the blood of man, by man shall his blood be shed; for in the image of God has man been made. (9:5-6)." Those who are against the capital punishment point not only to the commandment, "You shall not kill (Deuteronomy 5:17)" but Jesus' expansion in Matthew 5:21-22, "You have heard that it was said to your ancestors, 'You shall not kill; and whoever kills will be liable to judgment.' But I say to you, whoever is angry with his brother will be liable to judgment."

On conscience issues we can see the poles with each side quoting the Qur'an. Those who hold religious tolerance quoting the Qur'an, would say, "There is no compulsion in religion. Truth stands out clearly from falsehood; whoever rejects evil and believes in God has grasped the most trustworthy hand-hold that never breaks. And God is All-Hearing and All-Knowing." (Qur'an 2:256) Protection of the rights of non-Muslims to worship is an intrinsic part of Islamic law. It is also stated in the Qur'an: "God does not forbid you, with regard to those who do not fight you for (your) faith nor drive you out of your homes, from dealing kindly and justly with them; for God loves those who are just." (Qur'an 60:8) Islamic law also permits non-Muslims to set up their own courts and implement family and personal laws administered by their chosen religious authorities. While those who hold that Christians and Jews must "accept the truth of Islam or be fought to the death" will quote Abu Hurayrah. The reason for this intolerance is based in the Qur'an (4:156-159) which states

"And for their disbelief and their having uttered against Mary a great calumny, and their saying 'We have killed the Messiah, Jesus the son of Mary, the Messenger of Allah', whereas they neither killed him nor crucified him, but it appeared so to them. And those who differ therein are only in doubt about it; they have no knowledge about it, only following conjecture, and in truth they killed him not. On the contrary, Allah raised him up to him, and Allah is the Might, the Wise. And there is none of the People of the Book [Jews and Christians] but will surely believe in him before his death [Jesus has not died], and on the Day of the Resurrection, he will be a witness against them."

The only way of seeing the question of religious tolerance between Muslims and Christians is historically, summarizing the historical reality[2] By the end of the seventh century, as the Islamic armies advanced beyond the Arab homelands, Islamic doctrine had grown to maturity and now posed a major challenge to Christianity by its claim to be, at one and the same time, the more ancient faith from which Judaism and Christianity had developed, and God's final revelation to humanity. Similarly, Islam's total rejection of fundamental Christian doctrines, like the resurrection of Christ and the Trinity, became the "doctrinal battleground". Christians were urged to convert to Islam, and suffered varying fiscal and social penalties for not doing so; there was no general attempt to force Christians to convert

In certain areas and at certain times, Christians under Muslim rule were forced to engage in doctrinal debate because of the pressure maintained by Islam. Syrian Christians in the early ninth century were greeted by Muslims by the Islamic profession of faith - "There is no God but the One God, and Mohammad is the messenger of God" - a

---

[2] *The Oxford Illustrated History of Christianity*, edited by John McManners, Oxford University Press, 1992 pp. 174-195.

statement which attacked the doctrine of the Trinity, and which seemed to challenge the status of Jesus.

In the East, some Christian communities immediately reacted, and the earliest Christian apologetics and anti-Islamic polemics came from the seventh century by John of Damascus (ca.675-ca.750), who challenged the Muslim claim to Abrahamic ancestry, by explaining that the Arabs were called "Saracens" because they were "empty of Sarah". He asserted that Islamic doctrine was put together from the Old and New Testaments by the "pseudo-prophet" Mohammed, with assistance from an Arian monk.

There were jokes by Muslims concerning Christian beliefs: Christians were innumerate - "with them, one is three and three is one". Likewise, the Christians' reverence for the Cross exposed them to the accusation of idolatry: writing in c.725, Germanus of Constantinople instructed his readers to counter such charges by replying that the Muslims worshipped a stone called Chobar in the desert (i.e. the Ka'ba).

Church of Saint Eirene near Hagia Sophia within the walls of the Topkapi Palace complex

In contrast to this militant tradition, some Christian communities were carried along by a strong ecumenical current. The Parable of the Pearl by the Nestorian patriarch Timothy (c.728 - 823) is the earliest Christian work to acknowledge a truth common to both Christianity and Islam. Early in the next century, the patriarch Nicolas wrote to the caliph that "we have obtained the gift of our authorities [i.e. the Qur'an and the Gospels] from the same Source". It may have been as early as 717 that mosques were permitted within the walls of Constantinople for the use of Muslim visitors and prisoners of war. In the Christian West, this view is less well known, but, in 1076, Pope Gregory VII wrote to the Hammadid ruler al-Nasir that "we believe in and confess one God, admittedly in a different way", and stressed the Abrahamic roots of the two religions. This idea never seems to have taken root in Western Europe, and had disappeared completely by the First Crusade.

While it is true that the Christian communities which lived in closest proximity to the Muslims led the counter-offensive against the doctrinal challenge posed by Islam, it is also true that Islam's nearest Christian neighbors were best able to appreciate the common ground shared by the two faiths.

The attitude of Byzantium to its Muslim subjects was different. The principle of autonomous organization for minority communities was enshrined in Byzantine law and thence had been adopted by Islam. The long experience of Byzantium in dealing with its Arab neighbors determined the nature of the relationship between Greek Christianity and Islam. In the lands won back from the Arabs during the tenth century, Byzantium induced Muslims to settle and successfully encouraged many to convert to Christianity. While the Greek church had a specific ritual which enabled Muslims to reject Islam and embrace Christianity, no similar rite is known from the West. Muslims or Muslim converts were fully integrated into Byzantine society.

It is in the political arena that Christians, especially the Eastern Churches, could have meaningful discussions based upon a tradition of religion being a part of the state. Islam makes no distinction between religion and life; Islamic law covers not only ritual but every aspect of life. How can a Muslim live in a society that is not aware of their existence?

Many Muslims have lost the security of living within an Islamic state and emigrated to Western countries where not only are they minorities but live in a place where the practice of their religion is considered something private and not practiced in public.

Muslims can look to the first thirteen years of Mohammed's mission. There are passages in the Qur'an where Allah says that Mohammed's sole responsibility is to preach the message. It was not until after the Hijrah (Mohammed's flight from Mecca to Medina in 622) that Islam became political. Like Mohammed in those early pre-Hijrah days Muslims are called to live and coexist with those of other religions. This carries with it a psychological uncertainty of being a minority. Both Eastern Catholics and Orthodox are aware of the benefits and pitfalls of being a minority religion in the Western world through their diaspora communities. These diaspora communities of Eastern Christians and Muslims can discuss together the tools necessary to adjust to the real life situation without losing their identity and their membership. The dialogue is not faith but faithfulness to a misunderstood and little appreciated religious tradition.

Another common area of dialogue is the area of what happens when the state and religion are entwined. The positive and negative elements of this relationship can be seen in Islamic states of which there are many varieties of relations to the relationship of Orthodox churches in the Byzantine Empire and later in the relationship between the Russian Orthodox Church and the Russian state both with the Tsars and the Soviets. The Orthodox experience of successes and failures can be a source of practical examples for the formation of new Islamic states.

Even though Islam has laid claim to being the oldest in relation to Christians and Jews it is relatively new in dealing with the concept of pluralism. Eastern Christians have had a hundred years just in the American experience. Christianity has had a longer history in dealing with the questions of secularism in the modern world. Christians in dialogue seem to feel the need is to adjust to pluralism. Muslims seem to come to the dialogue with an evaluative judgment of what is wrong with pluralism and have less of a cause to dialogue. Some may feel that Christians should be patient and wait for the Muslims to be ready to dialogue the situation of their faithful in non-Islamic states. At the same time, it would be good for Christians to "sit at the feet" of the Muslims and listen. It would be a reminder of what Christians have given up in order to live in a pluralistic society. Orthodox Christians will be encouraged to examine what they have done in order to be socially acceptable in countries like the United States and Eastern Catholics will be encouraged to examine what they have given up to be part of the Catholic milieu. Christians need to have some outside criticism.

Muslims in many countries have shut themselves off from dialogue with the West, which includes Eastern Christians. They find the standard of living especially health care desirable, but it seems to come at too great of a price. Do they have to give up religious principles to have quality medical care? This is not just a Muslim question. The same question comes from Catholics when dealing with the questions of cloning and embryonic stem cell research. Medical questions, like environmental issues where there are common concerns is an area for dialogue. Christians need to look at whether they have sold out Christianity to the social sciences. What is the proper relationship between the teachings of Christ and His Church with that of modern "objective" science, especially the social sciences?

There are Muslims addressing the same issue. Ismail al-Faruqi has called for the "Islamization of all knowledge." He writes that western science has had a harmful influence on the young. Sociology and psychology put a question mark around the areas of faith and are taken to be of greater importance than religious teaching. Is this not the same issue that is debated within Catholicism when dealing with the issue of masturbation. Some claim that it is normal because of biology and psychology while others say from a religious perspective that it is disordered and sinful.

The influence of science has been felt in the study of Scripture. When Pope Paul VI and Patriarch Athenagoras lifted the bans of excommunication between the pope and the patriarch, it showed that it was not a major theological dispute or even so much as a territorial disagreement, even though both were involved. It was a lack of communication which was the basis for a lack of trust. There may have been one Christendom today, if communication continued. Instead each side withdrew to itself and only fringe elements carried on discussions between the Churches.

This breakdown of unity has lasted close to a thousand years and may have been avoidable. To prevent a breakdown in world peace and harmony, it is time to communicate. The question from the Christian perspective is how do we communicate with Muslims. Communication begins when one side makes an attempt to come to an understanding of the other side. In order to assist Christians in this endeavor, this essay offers an understanding of the different faces of Islam using Christian analogies.

Muslims find the Christian approach to sacred texts offensive. For the Muslim, Allah dictated the text of the Qur'an to Mohammed, who served as a scribe. This was done over a long period of time. This is reminiscent for Christians, who at one time held, for example, that Moses wrote the first five books of the Old Testament in almost the same manner. If there is no human element in the creation of the text, then there is no need for human analysis of sacred texts. This shows that the media's use of the term fundamentalists for some Muslims is inaccurate. Fundamentalists in the religious use of the term hold that the sacred writings are divine texts and are meant to be taken literally as given. All Muslims are fundamentalists in this religious sense.

The purpose of this essay was to show that it is not possible to find one representative viewpoint for Christians, which is a reality that Christians understand and accept, and that, like Christians, Muslims have a full gamut of views and positions. Therefore, as we cannot treat all Christians as one and say that Christians universally stand for one thing, we cannot expect or treat Muslims in a stereotypic fashion. Dialogue begins when one side is open to the other, and that when one dialogues honestly, each person comes from their own perspective which is not universal.

Rome, Byzantium and Islam: Need for Dialogue

Brother David Carroll, FSC, PhD

Introduction

In the Near East, the concept of one God coming from the tradition of Abraham is unique upon the face of the earth. This concept of one God has given birth to Judaism, Christianity and Islam. The history of these religions coexisting in the same region of the world has been blessed with periods of peace and also, unfortunately, subjected to periods of conflict and violence. This article will briefly touch upon some of these episodes of history which are covered in far greater detail in this volume, but this paper will focus on the Jubilee year of 2000 and the various pilgrimages of John Paul II, Bishop of Rome and Patriarch of the West, as a part of the history of the Near East. In particular, we will examine the context of interreligious dialogue which these pilgrimages represent as the Pope endeavored to facilitate the dialogue with Islam. For both Latin Christians and Byzantine Christians these pilgrimages form a significant historical effort to recognize the necessity of Christianity's dialogue with Islam most especially since the very birthplace of Christianity is now largely occupied by the Islamic Ummah. Then too, current demographic movements are bringing many Muslims into many Christian cultures around the globe. Also, the exploitation of religion on behalf of political ideologies makes it essential to foster interreligious dialogue.

Background

God called Abram from the Ur of Chaldea in modern Iraq to be His witness to humanity and to proclaim the uniqueness of the One True God in a world in which many gods were worshipped. Later known as Abraham, his belief in the One True God became the faith of Jews, Christians and Muslims. In our concern to examine the dialogue of Christianity with Islam, one must note some of the events of history which have given rise to the need for Christianity's dialogue with Islam. The preaching of Mohammed began in 610 A.D. and led to the Muslim understanding that Islam constitutes the crystallization of the one and the same religious consciousness of the monotheistic and ethical religions of pre-Islamic Arabia, Judaism and Christianity. The essence and core of this faith belief in God are one and the same, and that has been sealed by the last of the prophets Mohammed, who died in 632 A.D. In the course of subsequent Arab conquests (633-717 A.D.), this faith belief began to spread across what was then largely the Christian world of the East. Muslim scholars consistently note that the majority of the citizens of the Islamic polity were Christians and their Ummah as distinct from the Muslim Ummah enjoyed respect, liberty and a new dignity it had not enjoyed under either Christian Rome or Byzantium.

This Islamic teaching was to be borne out when the Great Schism of 1054 A.D. resulted in the separation of the Christian East and West. Around this time, Alexander Commenus appealed to Urban II, Pope of Rome for assistance against the Turks who were now confronting the Byzantine Empire (1095 A.D.). So began the history of the Crusades as the Church of the West, the Roman Church, sought to return the Holy Land to the governance of the Christian West and secure safe passage for pilgrims to the sacred sites of the Holy Land. In 1099, Godfrey of Bouillon established the Crusader Kingdom of the Holy Land. Many of the Crusaders did not take the cross in order to free the Holy Land from the control of the Muslims, both Arab and Turk. Many alliances were crafted with the Muslim leaders such as the Franco-Damascene Alliance of King Fulk of Anjou with Muin Al-Din Unur, Regent of Damascus in 1138 A.D. The Crusaders, many second and third generation children of military families in Europe were not entitled to fiefs in their homeland and thus they took advantage of the military expeditions in the Holy Land to establish fiefdoms. In so doing they crafted alliances with Muslim Arabs against Muslim Turks, and vice versa, in order to maintain control of the land and wealth. Throughout this time of the Crusader Kingdom in the Holy Land alliances were crafted with the Byzantines. Baldwin III, King of Jerusalem married Theodora Comnenus, sister of the Emperor of Byzantium, Manuel Comnenus. Alliances were crafted as well with the Muslims, e.g., the Franco-Damascene Alliance noted earlier and later in 1280 the Alliance of Franks and Mongols against Qalawun, the Mameluke Sultan.

Often such alliances worked to the detriment of the Byzantine Christians who were often misunderstood by the Latin Catholics. The ultimate misunderstanding of the Christian East occurred in 1204 A.D. when the Crusaders sacked Constantinople, capital of the Christian Empire of the East. This past 4 May, 2001 the Pope of Rome, on pilgrimage following the steps of St. Paul the Apostle, asked God's forgiveness, "For the occasions past and present, when sons and daughters of the Catholic Church have sinned in action or omission against their Orthodox brothers and sisters, may the Lord grant us forgiveness we beg of Him."

The Patriarch of the West in honest and open dialogue was seeking to establish, from the roots of the history of the region where Christianity was born, a rapprochement which would permit interreligious dialogue to grow from the seeds of turmoil sown in the region between and among the Latin Christians, the Byzantine Christians, the Oriental Christians and Islam. The most fruitful way to explore the component which focuses on the dialogue with Islam is to follow the events of the jubilee year pilgrimage of Pope John Paul II to the Holy Land.

The Pilgrim Pope and Islam

As part of the Jubilee 2000, Pope John Paul II had chosen to travel to the lands where Christianity has its roots. Initially, the Holy Father had hoped to travel to the Ur of Chaldea, in modern Iraq, to the place from whence Abram, later Abraham, came to Hebron now in disputed territory claimed by Israel and the Palestinians. It was Abraham who developed the concept of one God, a belief shared by Jews, Christians and Muslims representing some 45% of the world's population. The political situation in Iraq precluded this hoped for pilgrimage from taking place. Thus the beginning of the Jubilee 2000 pilgrimages was the Holy Father's trip to Egypt. The pilgrimage to Egypt, where the Pope visited Mt. Sinai, the sight of God's presentation of the Ten Commandments to Moses, contained a few surprises for some U.S. Catholics who are not fully aware of the traditions and history of the ancient Christian Churches of the East. First among these is the fact that the Coptic Orthodox Church is led by another Pope, His Holiness Pope Shenouda III. The very title Pope was first attributed to the Patriarch of

Alexandria and then passed on to the Bishop of Rome. Pope Shenouda III is the current Patriarch of Alexandria. A second surprise was the fact that about 10% of Egypt's population of 64 million are Christians and that these Christian communities trace their roots back to apostolic times. These Christians take great pride in the fact that the Holy Family lived in exile in Egypt for three or four years and that St. Mark, author of a synoptic gospel and secretary to St. Peter, evangelized the region. The third surprise was the greeting of the Holy Father by the Muslim leaders of Egypt.

Beyond the greeting of the political leaders of Egypt, the Holy Father met with the Grand Sheikh of Al-Azhar, Grand Sheikh Mohammed Sayyed Tantawi who heads Al-Azhar University and is seen as Sunni Islam's highest religious authority. Before discussing the statements of Pope John Paul II and Sheikh Tantawi, let us first establish the role of Al-Azhar and its importance to Sunni Islam. First, it is important to understand that just as there are many Christian churches, of which Roman Catholicism forms just one, Islam is divided into several faith communities due to various juridical differences with respect to leadership and what are considered heretical interpretations resulting in the separation of some from the mainstream. Sunni Islam constitutes the mainstream of Islam and it accounts for 85 to 90% of the followers of Islam.

Al-Azhar, founded in 973 was originally a Shiite Islamic institution of learning founded by the Fatimid dynasty. Shiites today constitute roughly some 9% to 10% of the followers of Islam. However, since political power bases in the region have shifted throughout history, Al-Azhar has become the leading institution of learning for Sunni Islam in the world. The university plays the role of arbiter of modern Islamic thought in Egypt and beyond its borders. A school of some 190,000 students in 55 colleges, it also has numerous other students enrolled in affiliated schools throughout the world. There are some 5,000 of these schools. Interestingly in a way, these schools are similar to pontifical universities and institutes spotted throughout the Catholic world. Key to understanding the relationship between Roman Catholicism and Islam is that as the pontifical universities and institutes train priests, religious and laity for evangelization, similarly Al-Azhar has a faculty to train "missionaries" and preachers to propagate Islam. In Islam this activity of propagating the faith is called "dawah" and it is estimated that the Da-wa faculty of Al-Azhar has to date prepared some 25,000 degreed missioners to act as propagators of Islam.

Grand Sheik Mohammed Sayyid Tantawi heads Al-Azhar. Pope John Paul II visited with the sheikh in his residence. Let us review the statements of these two religious leaders, one the head of the Roman Catholic Church with over one billion adherents and the other the highest religious authority for some 900,000 or more Sunni Muslims. As host, Sheikh Tantawi greeted the Holy Father as a "wise man", noting, "the Pope's efforts for peace, love and moral values and virtues are precisely the goal of all revealed religions".

Further the Sheikh explained that dialogue is a duty of Islam and authentic Shari'a law (Islamic law), " for the good of humanity and the propagation of virtues sustained by all religions Dialogue between religions allows us to listen to each other, to learn and compare ideas which commit us in love, truth and justice". However, he warned about the danger of "dogmatic dialogue" which he opined " can only widen the gap between the interlocutors. Only God can speak of dogma." It is interesting to note that Sheikh Tantawi agreed to travel to Rome in 2001 to participate in the dialogue meeting of the Standing Committee of Al-Azhar for Dialogue among Monetheistic Religions and the Pontifical Council for Interreligious Dialogue. This dialogue was established by mutual agreement in 1998.

However, this proposed meeting did not take place as planned. On the first Sunday of Lent, 12 March 2000, in a Mass at St. Peter's Basilica, Pope John Paul II pronounced a "request for pardon" for sins of the past committed by the Church's members. Since the seven specific requests did not include a direct reference to the Crusades, and the harm which these caused Islam, the Muslim participants in the dialogue requested that the proposed meeting be deferred until some further study and work could be completed which would lead to a resumption of this Dialogue, properly addressing the concerns of the Muslim participants.

Continuing our discussion of the Holy Father's visit with Sheikh Tantawi, in response to the greetings of his host, Pope John Paul II spoke as follows, "Thank you for your kind words. Permit me to continue with your ideas. God created human beings, man and woman, and gave to them the world, the earth to cultivate. There is a strict connection between religions, religious faith and culture. Islam is a religion. Christianity is a religion. Islam has become a culture. Christianity has also become a culture".

Further in his address, the Holy Father noted " I am convinced that the future of the world depends on various cultures and on interreligious dialogue".

In essence, both religious leaders have agreed on the need for interreligious dialogue. The pilgrimage of the Holy Father to Egypt and his meetings with religious leaders was in truth quite positive. A quote from the Egyptian TV correspondent, Halim Ismail, carries the tone of its success, "If the Christians are looking forward to the visit, Egyptian Muslims also think the event is important. They know the Pope is a man of peace who fully supports the peace process in the Middle East, and they are sure the event will help to further stability in the area". He was not disappointed.

When the Holy Father exited his plane in Cairo, he greeted the crowd saying, "As-salamu 'alaikum – Peace be with you". In that greeting Pope John Paul II singled out Islam stating, "The advent of Islam brought splendours of art and learning which have had a determining influence on the Arab world and on Africa".

The emphasis of Sheikh Tantawi and the Holy Father was on the shared moral values of Islam and Christianity and the need to openly discuss those areas where there is agreement and likewise to address matters where there is no agreement. Although the Second Vatican Council proclaimed its openess to dialogue with Islam in October 1965 in the document *Nostra Aetate*, it was not until 1978 that formal structures of dialogue began to fall into place. Many local (arch)diocesan dialogues were begun with local Muslim communities before the official activities with the Holy See were initiated.

Clearly the Egyptian pilgrimage of the Holy Father took place in a favorable climate of acceptance to the concepts of dialogue. However, this is not a universal phenomenon. In Egypt, itself, there exist fundamentalist groups which seek to destabilize the government and to do so engage in violence occasionally stating that "religious violence against Christians" is necessary to maintain Islamic culture. Here one must frankly ask if this is a misuse of religion for political purposes. Also, the presence of such groups in Egypt is worrisome to its government.

Again, in his Cairo airport greeting to President Hosni Mubarak, the Holy Father identified this complex issue when he stated, "The unity and harmony of the nation are a precious value which all citizens should cherish, and which political and religious leaders must continually promote in justice and respect for the rights of all. Mr. President, your own commitment to peace at home and throughout the Middle East is well known. All reasonable men and women appreciate the efforts made so far, and hope that goodwill and justice will prevail, so that all the peoples of this unique area of the world will see their rights respected and their legitimate aspirations fulfilled".

As he does in so many of his statements, the Holy Father spoke on behalf of "human rights" and "legitimate aspirations". These topics are "the stuff" of dialogue. In the real world, it is important that dialogue not be polyannish. Extremism fostered in a religious context can be a source of conflict and violence. Dialogue must be used to prevent this abuse/misuse of religion. Today in the world, there are places where conflict exists between Muslims and Christians. One only has to pick up the newspaper to read of events in the southern Sudan, Nigeria or the Molucca Islands of Indonesia. Such events, however, are not solely the province of Muslim/Christian conflicts as can be illustrated by the problems involving other religious communities in Sri Lanka, India or China where Christians endure persecution and/or endure the status of second class citizenship.

What is important is that people of faith and goodwill do not permit extremists to exploit religious fears on behalf of a political agenda. In comments to the Catholic News Service, Sheikh Tantawi responding to a question about western fears of religious extremists noted, "Fear should be far from interreligious dialogue, because it causes a gap between peoples."

On occasion, one will hear in the news that a state has opted to follow the shari'a or Islamic law. How are the rights of the minority

Christians maintained under shari'a? Does such a law place an undue burden on Christians so much so that they convert to Islam, not for religious reasons, but to maintain equal opportunity under the law for employment and social services? Here again, one must raise the question, respectfully in such a way as to foster a dialogue on issues which deeply affect the rights of human beings and which thereby can be resolved.

Key to a constructive understanding of such dialogue with Islam is that for the believing Muslim there is no separation of Church and State. For the Muslim, the good leader of state is the good leader of religion. In some Islamic republics, e.g., Iran, the religious leaders are leaders of government (See also the Taliban in Afghanistan). Often in an Islamic country, the Grand Mufti of the country (its religious leader) is appointed by its political leader. For the westerner, this integration of religious authority and political power is an alien thought and for the Founding Fathers of the U.S.A. was a most worrisome thought. However, in the west if one looks back 400 years or so at its own history, such a system of government was for the west normative.

An article of this brevity can not hope to resolve such complex matters. What is important to understand is that the success of the Holy Father's pilgrimage to Egypt provided an opening to discuss with people of goodwill those things which keep us apart, and which sad to say, in the past were often addressed through violence and warfare. The Holy Father's pilgrimage was a call to witness that true peace can transcend the impulse of original sin to resolve differences through conflict.

Quite obviously religious freedom was one of the items of dialogue, addressed in October 2000 by both Cardinal Angelo Sodano, the Holy See's Secretary of State and Cardinal Josef Tomko, head of the Congregation for the Evangelization of Peoples, each citing the Church's uncompromising support of religious freedom. On October 17, Cardinal Tomko speaking at the opening of a missionary congress in Rome spoke about the right to profession of faith, freedom of worship and freedom of propagation. He said, "This is not just the demands of one religion, but an international norm concerning human rights. So we insist on reciprocity."

Cardinal Sodano on October 18 at the inauguration of the new international center of the lay movement, "Communion and Liberation," was equally specific in his comments. He noted, "Everyone has the right to their places of worship throughout the world. For this reason, the Holy See asks Saudi Arabia to open a church or at least a chapel in a hotel." It is noted here that Saudi Arabia is home to Islam's sacred city of Mecca, birthplace of the Prophet Mohammed, founder of Islam. Only Muslims are permitted to publicly practice their faith in Saudi Arabia.

Also, it should be noted that there is a significant population of Filipino and Indian Catholics in the Saudi kingdom numbering several hundred thousand who serve as manual laborers or domestics in the Saudi economy. They can not worship in public, yet the kingdom of Saudi Arabia for reasons of its oil has received significant support from the United States of America where the right to the free exercise of religion is guaranteed by the Constitution of the United States of America. Is it proper to assume that a constitutional guarantee of religious freedom does not carry the weight or value as economic collaboration; that principle in this case can be ignored for economic gain?

In Pakistan, on May 6th, 1998, Bishop John Joseph took his life on the steps of the Sahiwal Court protesting the second class status of Catholics imposed on them by the law of shari'ah as exercised by the government of Pakistan. A Christian named Ayub Masih has been given a death sentence in Pakistan for the crime of blasphemy against Islam.

Clearly then, religious freedom is a topic for the interreligious dialogue which must be addressed since as Cardinal Tomko noted, "As we here profess religious freedom for other religions, thus we ask that in various nations, not only constitutions, but laws respect this norm and this freedom."

Pope John Paul II continued his Jubilee 2000 pilgrimage (20-26 March 2000) to the lands where Jesus Christ was born, preached, cured the sick, died and rose from the dead. Here the Holy Father continued with this theme of reconciliation and dialogue. The Holy Land, where he traveled, encompasses the political boundaries defined by Jordan, Israel, Lebanon, the Occupied Territories and the Palestinian Autonomous Territories. It was in these lands together with Egypt that in Christian belief Jesus Christ, Redeemer of the human race, lived and preached his message of salvation.

The Holy Father's pilgrimage to the Holy Land began in Jordan where King Abdullah II expressed in welcome the following: "Your Holiness, this is a unique and emotional moment that brings closer the meaning of tolerance and coexistence from a distant land of dreams. It is a moment that witnesses a pilgrimage by a holy man to a crossroads of history and geography, where religion started, and civilization first emerged." He then compared the pilgrimage of the Holy Father to that which he recently completed, with millions of other Muslims, to Mecca. Bear in mind that the Hashemite Royal Family traces its lineage to the prophet Mohammed and had been until the founding of Saudi Arabia, after World War I, the sherifs (protectors) of Mecca and Medina.

Once the Holy Father had visited the Christian holy places in largely Muslim Jordan, he went to Israel and the Palestinian Autonomous Territories where he met with the religious leaders of Christian, Muslim, Jewish, Druze and Ba'hai faith communities.

On March 23 at the Notre Dame Pilgrimage Center in Jerusalem, Pope John Paul II participated in a trialogue with Chief Ashkenazi Rabbi Israel Meir Lau and Sheikh Taysir al-Tamini each representing their respective religious communities. Alas, political acrimony overwhelmed the planned theological discussions of that event, complete with outbursts from the audience. For his part, the Holy Father in his prepared remarks stated, "Thank you for the support which your presence here this evening gives to the hope and conviction of so many people that we are indeed entering a new era of interreligious dialogue. We are conscious that closer ties among all believers are a necessary and urgent condition for securing a more just and peaceful world. Thus, concern for justice and peace does not lie outside the field of religion but is actually one of its essential elements." In his allocution to the trialogue, John Paul II continued that "when we love our neighbor we are showing love of God, and when we hurt our neighbor we offend God. This means that religion is the enemy of exclusion and discrimination, of hatred and rivalry, of violence and conflict. Religion is not, and must not become, an excuse for violence, particularly when religious identity coincides with cultural and ethnic identity. Religion and peace go together! Religious belief and practice cannot be separated from the defense of the image of God in every human being."

First, it is important to note that earlier that same day, the Holy Father met with Rabbi Lau and Chief Rabbi Eliahu Bakshi-Doron at the ceremonial offices of the chief rabbinate in Jerusalem for a private 15-minute meeting. The cordiality of that meeting which was private seemed to have been converted to use the trialogue as an opportunity to state a political platform since this event was now in the public forum of a worldwide television audience.

Secondly, the very elements of the violation of justice referred to earlier by the Holy Father in his statement to the trialogue, ignored in the debate of that day, have in truth now erupted in the political violence of the Holy Land since late September 2000. The very breakdown of political dialogue has resulted to date in the deaths of many Palestinian Arabs, Israeli Arabs and Israeli Jews.

On the last day of his pilgrimage, March 26, the Holy Father visited the Temple Mount known to the Muslims as Haram al-Sharif. There he was greeted by the Chairman of the Islamic Supreme Committee, Grand Mufti Sheikh Akram Sabri. The Holy Father expressed his gratitude to the Grand Mufti, " for receiving me within the Haram al-Sharif which is connected with the memory of Abraham, who for all believers is a model of faith and submission to Almighty God." As Catholics we must recall that this is the site of the Temple wherein Jesus was presented; where He was lost as a boy among the scholars; where He drove out the money changers; where He often engaged in discussions with the learned. During his time on Haram al-Sharif, the Holy Father visited a complex of holy buildings which includes the al-Aqsa Mosque, situated on Temple Mount just above the Western Wall, sacred to Jews.

Finally the Pope in his 23 March allocution affirmed that "The Catholic Church wishes to pursue a sincere and fruitful interreligious dialogue with the members of the Jewish faith and the followers of Islam. Such a dialogue is not an attempt to impose our views upon others. What it demands of all of us is that, holding to what we believe, we listen respectfully to one another, seek to discern all that is good and holy in each other's teachings and cooperate in supporting everything that favors mutual understanding and peace."

Pope John Paul II, the Bishop of Rome, Patriarch of the West, has opened the new millennium traveling to these same lands and where Jesus Christ was born, lived and died. The Holy Father forcefully proclaimed his message – Peace be with you. Bear in mind only three Popes have traveled in the Holy Land. The first was Peter, the second was Pope Paul VI in 1964 and in 2000 it was Pope John Paul II.

The final pilgrimage of Pope John Paul II for Jubilee 2000 was to the East of Islam where his pilgrimage to Syria followed in the steps of St. Paul. As part of this pilgrimage he visited the Omayyad Great Mosque of Damascus. Warmly greeted by the Muslim leaders in attendance, he visited the marble sarcophagus traditionally said to hold the head of St. John the Baptist. Later in his allocution to his hosts he noted, "(we are) called to acknowledge and respect the absolute priority of God in all things. Christians and Muslims agree that the encounter with God in prayer is necessary for the nourishment of our souls, without which our hearts wither and our will no longer strives for good but succumbs to evil." He indicated further,

"It is important that Muslims and Christians continue to explore philosophical and theological questions together, in order to come to a more objective and comprehensive knowledge of each others' religious beliefs. Better mutual understanding will surely lead, at the practical level, to a new way of presenting our two religions *not in opposition,* as has happened too often in the past, *but in partnership for the good of the human family*" (emphasis in the original).

Finally, he concluded, "Interreligious dialogue will lead to many forms of cooperation, especially in responding to the duty to care for the poor and the weak. These are the signs that our worship of God is genuine."

This visit to the Omayyad Great Mosque was the first time a reigning Pontiff had visited a mosque and was thus highly reminiscent of the same Pontiff's visit to the Synagogue of Rome in 1986 again a first time event.

Engraving of the Hippodrome, Sultanahmet mosque and obelisques

Conclusion

Certainly the intricate history of cultures in the birthplace of Christianity, which is now largely Muslim, indicates the importance of dialogue between and among the religions. In a frank evaluation of the time of the Crusades, it is clear that Eastern Christians and Islam still harbor significant tensions with respect to that period of history when the Christian West came to the Holy Land. During his various pilgrimages to the region, Pope John Paul II attempted to bring these issues into the realm of open discussion. His call for dialogue and that of other religious leaders focuses on the need for dialogue about substantive issues which separate the monotheistic faiths. In his encyclical, *Ut Unum Sint*, the Pope asked for assistance in helping to define the role of the Bishop of Rome in bringing peace to the relations among those who profess faith in the One God. Clearly, if substantive dialogue was in place during the time of the Crusades, perhaps the conflicts and violence which attended that period, and the consequent apologies of our time would have been unnecessary.

The efforts of the Second Vatican Council to open the channels of communications for both ecumenical and interreligious dialogue and the subsequent efforts to bring life to the theory of dialogue are extremely important in this day and age when the manipulation of religion to achieve political goals has been cast upon the modern world as the flames of religious fanaticism have now ignited the fires of war. Through dialogue the religious leaders of the world must show that religion is a cure not a cause of conflict. Unhappily today the simplicity with which the media views the complex cultural events of history often result in digesting a thousand years of interaction into a 30-second summation of what is today's problem and how steps are being implemented for the "quick fix." Such a view does not bode well for the future, for unless we can deal with our differences in a substantive way, we will be condemned to repeat the errors of the past and in some instances relive the conflicts and perhaps even the violence which resulted from the incomplete or erroneous understanding of those differences.

A Just War

Stavrophore Maximos

Around 1537, the Moldavian prince, Petru Rares, an important figure in Romanian history, commissioned the painting of holy icons on the exterior of the main church of the monastery of Moldovitsa. Among the icons he had painted, one in particular stands out: a depiction of the seige of Constantinople by the Turks in 1453. The painting retains to this day much of its vividness. Nothing of the horror is left out. Cannons boom. Missiles fly. The massed ranks of the invaders stretch into the distance, while within the city the doomed people take up their holy icons along the walls to beg for a miracle of deliverance. A miracle that never came.

Why is this picture on the wall of an Orthodox church? Surely it is there as catechesis. A common view among Orthodox monks was that Constantinople fell to the Turks because of the sins of the Orthodox people. Petru Rares was engaged in a struggle against the Ottoman Turks. His monastic painters were warning the people about the danger of sin.

The idea that sin leads to war, and even to defeat, is an important one in the tradition of Eastern Christianity. In a prayer service of the Slavonic tradition, the first troparion of the canon puts it clearly: "On account of our sins and transgressions, O Righteous Judge, You have permitted our enemies to oppress us".

It is important for us as Byzantine Christians, in this time of war, to be aware of this theme in our Tradition. But it is also important to understand the subtlety of the teaching. We cannot support the view put forth in the immediate aftermath of 11 September by some conservative Protestant figures that God had "withdrawn his hand" from America due to the specific failings of named groups. This idea sits very ill with orthodox Christianity.

"You came into the world to save sinners, *of whom I am the first*". Echoing the worlds of St. Paul (1 Tim 1:15), we remember the truth at every Divine Liturgy in the prayer before Communion. Petru

Rares did not show his people the fall of Constantinople to remind them of the sins of the Greeks a century before. He did it to remind them of their own sins in their own time.

Emperor Constantine XI at the breach in the wall of Constantinople when it fell to the Turks in 1453

There is a great mystery here. It is too simplistic to think that divine justice functions according to the laws of Newtonian physics. Every action does not have an equal and opposite reaction. The guilty are not always punished in proportion to their wrongdoing, and the innocent are certainly not spared according to the measure of their purity.

"Why do the wicked prosper?" asks the prophet Jeremiah (12:1). Our faith teaches us that all evils in the world – natural and man-made – are the result of sin. If the 11th of September teaches us anything, it is that the geometry of evil is of a kind too ghastly for comprehension. "Between the Holy Trinity and hell there is no other choice" says Father Pavel Florenksy. We can live either within the perfect order and harmony of God's life, or we can exist amid the chaos that is outside of Him. Through sin, we choose chaos. Fallen with the rest of creation, the laws of cause and effect have themselves been corrupted. A single evil can produce untold and unpredictable consequences. How apt, for once, is the jargon of military analysis, which describes terrorist attacks as "asymmetrical".

Perhaps this is why Byzantine theology has never attempted to devise a theory of "just war" as has been done in the West. The East has seen no point in trying to make a system of what is essentially the antithesis of system. You cannot herd cats, and you cannot make chaos neat. The East has not sought to open up the ethics of war to dialectical analysis. War is not an intellectual problem to be solved so much as it is an existential fact, or rather, an existential disaster. Reflecting on the asymmetry of the fallen world, war must be endured as a necessary evil – but with the emphasis on evil.

Even when we must take up arms for protection (as is surely the case in the present conflict), we must never forget that to fight a war is to participate in evil. God ordered His world out of chaos and called it "good". Wars are the eruption in creation of that same chaos. How can this ever be called "good" or "just"?

"Save your people O Lord, and bless your inheritance. Grant victory to the emperors over the barbarians..." So goes the Troparion of the Cross in its original Greek, pronouncing as best it can, a blessing on the warfare of Christians. But it immediately adds: "and protect your city by your Cross". Ultimately, it is the Cross which is our true salvation. Caesar must fight, of course, and we must support him. Our sin has made such warfare inevitable. But we must never forget that true victory is not to be found in superficial things. No "system", be it military, political, economic or even theological, can ever succeed against the chaotic asymmetry of evil that my own sin has unleashed on creation. No system can succeed, but only a Person, and a Cross.

Which brings me back to the painted siege on the wall of Moldovitsa. The ultimate collapse of the entire Byzantine political system is depicted here. A little further along the wall, the onlooker will see revealed an even more profound collapse: the end of time, and the Last Judgement. The artists' aim was to put into perspective all our attempts to improve the world by means of politics, social action and war. The catechesis is this: do not fear the dissolution of human systems. Do not fear and do not despair. Work to make these systems bear fruit by uniting them more completely with the One who alone can order eternal life beyond the collapse of earthly existence.

Looked at in the light of the end of all things, the *eschaton*, all our human activities show up their myriad imperfections and corruption. Christian life is seen in the East as an ascesis, as the process of purifying our lives and actions by careful exposure of all that we do and think to the cathartic light of Christ's judgement. War is no exception. For Eastern Christians there is something utterly stupid about debates between warmongers and peaceniks. In the light of Christ, we see that there is rarely an "either/or" when it comes to war. What matters is that the choices we make be examined constantly in that same penetrating spiritual Light. We must seek out evil wherever the Light reveals it to be: in our enemy, in our national and international policies, and above all, in our own hearts. There is no room for the sentimentality of either the jingoist or the pacifist. There is room only for the intellectual and spiritual honesty of ascesis, as individuals and as a nation,

Eastern Christians can wholeheartedly embrace the following statement of Vatican II, quoted in the section of the Catechism of the Catholic Church that deals with War. "insofar as men are sinners, the threat of war hangs over them, and will continue to do so until Christ comes again; but insofar as they can vanquish sin by coming together in charity, violence itself will be vanquished and these words shall be fulfilled: 'they shall beat their swords into plowshares, and their spears into pruning hooks; nation shall not lift up sword against nation, neither shall they learn war anymore'" (*Gaudium et Spes*, 6, quoting Isaiah 2:4).